The Edge of Friendliness

THE
LAKEVILLE
STUDIES

Under the Direction of MARSHALL SKLARE

VOLUME I   Jewish Identity on the Suburban Frontier: A Study of Group Survival in the Open Society
by Marshall Sklare *and* Joseph Greenblum

VOLUME II   The Edge of Friendliness: A Study of Jewish-Gentile Relations
by Benjamin B. Ringer

A Research Project of THE AMERICAN JEWISH COMMITTEE

*A Study of
Jewish-Gentile
Relations*

THE
EDGE OF
FRIENDLINESS

BENJAMIN B. RINGER

Basic Books, Inc., Publishers

NEW YORK LONDON

© 1967 by The American Jewish Committee
Library of Congress Catalog Card Number: 67–17393
Manufactured in the United States of America
Designed by Florence Silverman

To Rosalind, Verna, and Louise

FOREWORD

This book and its companion volume, *Jewish Identity on the Suburban Frontier: A Study of Group Survival in the Open Society,* continue a long-standing pursuit of the American Jewish Committee: the support of social-science research and its use in the practice of intergroup relations.

The origins of this pursuit go back to the 1930's. During that decade, in an unprecedented step, the Committee began to take periodic polls of public opinion concerning Jews—initially for the purpose of obtaining guidance in combating Nazi influence, which was then a serious problem in the United States. Opinion polling quickly proved useful in planning program activity of this and other kinds and has been continued since that time.

The accumulated findings were eventually compiled and reanalyzed in book form for whatever broad insights they might reveal when considered together. The first such reanalysis, *Education and Attitude Change* (1961), by Charles Herbert Stember, explored the relationship between formal education and prejudice. It was followed by a more comprehensive work, *Jews in the Mind of America* (1966). In this volume Mr. Stember reviewed virtually all public opinion data concerning Jews from 1937 to 1962, demonstrating the over-all trends of public attitudes during that quarter century; a symposium of distinguished sociologists, social psychologists, demographers, and historians interpreted the trends he found in the light of their respective disciplines.

A major scientific endeavor of another kind was launched by the American Jewish Committee in 1944. That year, a Scientific Research

Department began to operate, under the direction of Max Horkheimer, who had previously organized and headed the Institute for Social Research at Frankfurt, Germany. The new department, established in the wake of a conference of leading social scientists, embarked on a group of research projects eventually published as *Studies in Prejudice* (1949–1950). The basic volume in this series, *The Authoritarian Personality,* by T. W. Adorno and others, proved a milestone in social science and exerted an enormous influence on the entire field of the psychology of prejudice.

For more than twenty-five years, the American Jewish Committee has involved itself with questions of Jewish identity and continuity in the United States. As overt hostility against Jews declined and the society became more and more open, these issues came to loom increasingly large. Eventually, they were to stimulate important research in new directions.

When the Committee began to work on questions of Jewish identity, the chief impetus came from the agency's activities in intergroup relations. It was felt that the relations of Jews to other groups, though primarily determined by outside forces (such as the nature of the society, or the intensity of anti-Jewish feeling), depended also on the Jew's attitude toward himself. To be treated as an equal, it was reasoned, a man had to consider himself an equal, and he probably could do so more effectively if he knew his traditions and the meaning of his group identity.

As time went on, the Committee shifted to what might be termed a "personality health" viewpoint. It was now stressed that a Jew needed to be surefooted in his identity and to accept himself for what he was, not only for the sake of his relations with non-Jews, but also in order to preserve or attain an integrated personality. Knowledge and understanding of the group heritage appeared essential to achieve this goal.

During the past decade, the American Jewish Committee's work on Jewish identity has been chiefly inspired by still another line of thought: the conviction that Judaism as a way of life can be an invaluable guide to modern living and human progress. Making Jewish tradition relevant to the ethical and moral issues of the day became the paramount task.

For planning program activity along this line, information was needed on such matters as the social characteristics of Jews, their adherence to religious practices, Jewish education of the young, the Jewish home,

Jewish institutions, and Jewish-Gentile intermarriage. The Committee's Scientific Research Department accordingly expanded its program to include studies of the internal life of American Jewry. The first such inquiry focused on an East Coast city ("Riverton"); it was conducted by Marc Vosk and Marshall Sklare, who were then, respectively, Director and Associate Director of Research. The *Riverton Study* has been published in summary form (1957). It deals with a community consisting mostly of second-generation Jews, exploring their own and their children's feelings about their Jewish heritage, as well as their attitudes toward Gentiles, toward Israel, and toward various other matters of significance to American Jewry.

But, in addition, an even broader undertaking was needed: a large-scale community study that would embrace Jews of the third and fourth generations, as well as the second, thereby giving us further insights into the future and direction of Jewish life in the increasingly open society of the United States. That study, conducted in a midwestern suburb known in these pages as "Lakeville," now appears as Volume I of the present series. It is the work of Marshall Sklare, until recently Director of the American Jewish Committee's Division of Scientific Research, and Joseph Greenblum, Study Director in the Division.

The present book, Volume II of *The Lakeville Studies,* deals with a different but closely related set of factors in the life of the same Jewish community. It examines relations between Jews and Gentiles, portrays their attitudes toward each other, and scrutinizes the behavior patterns and value systems that enter into the experience of living together in the community. The author, Benjamin B. Ringer, was associated with the Committee's Scientific Research Division for many years.

These two volumes, based on field data painstakingly acquired and carefully analyzed, represent the labor of nearly a decade. We believe they will stand as a significant contribution to social science. Even more important, we hope that they will shed new light on the entire problem of Jewish integration—the question how American Jewry can achieve full participation in all areas of this nation's life while retaining its religio-cultural identity. In this sense, the studies should prove of service to Jewish educators, synagogue groups, Jewish community center workers, and communal planners. But they should also be of interest to intergroup relations practitioners, social scientists, and all who are concerned with the status of minority groups in America. It is with these hopes that the American Jewish Committee presents *The Lakeville Studies* to the Jewish and the larger American community.

New York   JOHN SLAWSON
January 1967   Executive Vice President
                                        The American Jewish Committee

PREFACE

One of the distinctive features of the unfolding relations between Jews and Gentiles in America is the fact that they no longer live so completely isolated from each other as they did in the past. As a result, a methodology which served so well when contact was minimal seems no longer adequate for the study of these relations. For example, we need to go beyond the examination of specially selected subjects in classrooms, laboratories, or clinics and beyond the querying of widely scattered individuals who are part of a nationwide or regional sample. We need, in other words, to focus on the real-life settings in which Jews and Gentiles are relevant parts of each other's environment and in which each has to come to terms with the other. The Lakeville Studies take this as a basic premise, and therefore this volume focuses on the local community as the place in which to understand more fully the dynamic and complex nature of present-day relations between Jews and Gentiles.

Through the years, the American Jewish Committee has reflected in its studies this shift in methodological emphasis and has through its cumulative efforts in supporting basic research in intergroup relations contributed to the social sciences as few other non-academic—or even academic—organizations have done. Much of the credit for the Committee's commitment to research in general and to this study in particular goes to Dr. John Slawson, Executive Vice President.

Many others have helped move this study from plan to reality, and I wish to take this opportunity to express my gratitude to them. I wish to thank, for example, the lay and religious leaders of the community that was investigated; their service on an advisory committee provided access to members of this community and reassured them that they were involved in a widely supported and worthwhile undertaking. I am also grateful to a number of other people: the several donors in Lakeville and Lake City whose financial support made it possible to augment the scope of the study; the regional staff of the American Jewish Committee for their assistance and cooperation; the many respondents, Jewish and Gentile, who made room in their busy schedules for exhaustive interviews; the interviewers, whose dedication and competence made it possible to deal with a subject matter of considerable delicacy and to obtain data rich in detail and expressiveness; the field staff of the National Opinion Research Center of the University of Chicago, which conducted a phase of the field work; past and present members of AJC's Division of Scientific Research: Sally Hoffman, Elizabeth Keller, Nancy Schmiderer, Judith Gimple, and Ruth Ballan, who skillfully carried out secretarial and statistical tasks, and my professional colleagues—Joseph Greenblum, David Ryan, and Alfred Levin—who were most helpful in frequent discussions of methodological and substantive problems; the staff of AJC's Blaustein Library who provided bibliographic assistance; SRDS Data, Inc., which gave excellent service in processing data and running tables; and Hugh Rogers, a former Vice President and General Manager of SRDS, who displayed a strong sense of identification with the study.

I feel most indebted, however, to Theodore Solotaroff and Dr. Marshall Sklare, former Director of the Division of Scientific Research. Mr. Solotaroff contributed his great editorial skills to the book. His gift for lucid expression and apt criticism proved invaluable in making this a more finished and readable volume. Dr. Sklare and I worked together from the very beginning of the project; we shaped its development and worried through its difficult phases. Throughout my work on this book Dr. Sklare provided encouragement and support; he read the various drafts of the manuscript, and his incisive comments and suggestions strengthened it.

Hunter College, New York   BENJAMIN B. RINGER
January 1967

CONTENTS

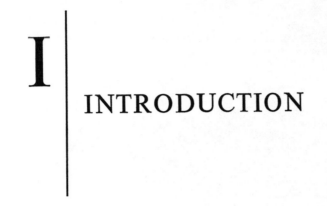

INTRODUCTION

1

THE SETTING

Some Background Considerations

American culture has inherited many of the anti-Jewish sentiments of Western Christendom. In the New World, however, these sentiments were not reinforced by basic institutional arrangements, particularly between church and state, and consequently failed to develop decisive social significance or political potency. Except for a few abortive efforts to restrict Jewish rights in the early Colonial times, American Jews have never been subjected to the persecution and alienation that was common in most European countries. Their rights as Americans were guaranteed by the law of the land; they were one of many minorities; they lived in a society dominated by secular values which stressed egalitarianism and regarded no religious or ethnic differences as immutable.

Despite this favorable political climate, relations between Jews and Gentiles have been marked not only by inherited group prejudices but also by the tensions of social conflict. The immigration of a significant number of German Jews in the 1840's and 1850's, and of several million Eastern European Jews in the period from the 1880's to World War I, produced significant patterns of hostility and discrimination. Historians differ over whether the opposition encountered by the later immigrants

3

had a particular anti-Semitic character or were merely the expression of a general antipathy to aliens that became prevalent among native Americans who feared they would be engulfed by the new minority communities. Nonetheless, the later Jewish newcomers found themselves in a society which had revived many of the canards of traditional anti-Semitism and many of its tactics of economic and social exclusion and segregation.

Though discriminated against and disapproved of, the immigrants—and more especially their children—steadily advanced into the society through a remarkably rapid process of acculturation and upward mobility that brought most Jewish families into the middle class within the span of one generation. This process has continued to the extent that today the typical American Jew resembles his Gentile neighbor or colleague more distinctly than he does his immigrant forebears. He is increasingly likely to live in a suburb rather than in the original ethnic enclaves of the major cities. He is also increasingly likely to be employed in a profession or occupation that cuts sharply across ethnic lines. Both his home and vocational environments, therefore, bring him into new and broader contacts with Gentile life, requiring accommodation and adjustments which would have been quite beyond the powers, and possibly the desires, of the immigrant generation.

At the same time, the norms of contemporary American society are markedly different from those encountered by Jews as late as thirty years ago. Survey after survey, especially those done after World War II, consistently shows that as time passes the American public tends to express fewer anti-Jewish sentiments, to minimize differences between Jews and Gentiles, and to accept Jews in most settings as a matter of course.[1]

In sum, contemporary America enables Jews and Gentiles to explore new possibilities of relating to each other. The question remains, though, whether the Jewish experience in America will be qualitatively different from that in any other country where Jewish acculturation has flourished. This question does not rest upon the growing similarity between Jews and Gentiles but rather upon their surviving differences and the dominant group's response to these differences. For if to be fully accepted the Jews must pay the price of assimilation and the abandonment of their effort to maintain a distinctive group identity and communal structure which is compatible with the larger society, then the

[1] See Charles Herbert Stember *et al., Jews in the Mind of America* (New York: Basic Books, Inc., 1966).

American experience will merely prove to be a more humane and peaceable example of a familiar historical process. Throughout most of Western history Jews have had the option of giving up their group identity, converting to the Christian religion, and thereby freeing themselves of the disabilities of their separateness.

The issue, then, is whether America can sustain an equality and comity whose basis is diversity and difference as well as similarity. The final resolution remains in the future. But the issue itself forms the major interest of this study. Accordingly, this is mainly a book about how Jews and Gentiles feel, think, and behave toward each other in a suburban community which we shall call Lakeville, located on the outskirts of a major city in the Middle West which we shall call Lake City. We have focused on the sociological, psychological, and cultural factors that bring Gentiles and Jews together in some meaningful way as well as on those that divide them.

The History of the Community

On many grounds Lakeville provides an excellent setting for studying the relations between Jews and Gentiles. Unlike other small communities it has not insulated itself from society but has, instead, been receptive to social change. It has been—and remains—more cosmopolitan than provincial in outlook, more urban than rural in its orientation, and relatively more open than closed to newcomers.

The community's location on one of the Great Lakes and its proximity to Lake City have been decisive factors in its history. The first phase of the town's development began in the 1850's, a decade or so after the area was opened for settlement. Initially, efforts were made to develop it as a port for transporting cargo to inland markets. Although the scheme collapsed after the advent of the railroad and in the face of the increasing predominance of Lake City, it gave impetus to the development of the community both as a commercial center for the immediate hinterland and as a site for some light industry.

During the 1870's business and real estate interests decided to make the most of Lakeville's secluded atmosphere, rolling hills, pleasant vistas, and lakefront by promoting the town as a recreational and residential community for wealthy families from the metropolis. The town was plotted on a park system to help preserve its natural beauty, new plank sidewalks were built for the business district, transportation facilities were improved, and various public buildings were constructed. Within two decades the scheme began to succeed, and Lakeville became a fashionable summer resort. As its appeal grew, lakefront land sold for as much as $10,000 an acre. Mansion after mansion arose along the lakefront, and more modest summer homes sprang up in the adjacent areas.

Several country clubs were organized, and they soon established Lakeville's reputation as a golfing community. In time a luxury hotel and a harbor for pleasure craft were built, and a tract of land, originally planned as a beer garden, was turned into a center for the performing arts, which attracted major musical and theatrical artists and fashionable audiences.

Lakeville was thus introduced to an elite style of life that went far beyond anything its local residents could hope to emulate. However, the summer elite, which set standards of consumption whose imprint is still felt today, had no interest in controlling the business life of the community. Their business interests, frequently of a large-scale character, were centered in Lake City. In addition, they had little to do with the year-round residents, for they played and socialized with their own kind.

Many of the local businessmen in Lakeville looked upon the summer elite with mixed feelings. On the one hand, its presence appealed to the status image which they wished to cultivate for the community, and they liked the money that was poured into the community each summer. On the other hand, they were disturbed at the sluggishness that enveloped the community and its economy with the coming of cold weather. In addition, they were worried about the influence which the summer people had over officeholders and others who were in a position to serve their special interests and needs. And finally, the local businessmen resented the facts that the style of life of the summer people was beyond their means and that the various clubs patronized by the summer residents were not inclined to offer them membership.

Under the circumstances these local businessmen, who controlled the economy of Lakeville but who could not function as a social elite, merely felt a commercial interest in the valuable lakefront property and supported a non-restrictive policy concerning its purchase and sale. In contrast, many of the other fashionable communities that developed along the lakefront but had no previous histories as commercial towns were quick to adopt discriminatory practices. Thus, despite the fact that this was an era when such practices became common among the

Protestant elite, Lakeville realtors continued to rely upon the impersonal workings of the marketplace. As a real estate circular of the time put it, Lakeville was a "democratic place, considerably more so than some of her sister towns . . . which have much the air of exclusiveness about them. Nevertheless, Lakeville numbers among its residents many of the wealthy business and professional men of [Lake City] and people who stand high on the social scale." A columnist in the local newspaper expressed the prevailing attitude more bluntly: "We hear some very fine people are a bit disturbed over the settlement among us of some excellent families of the Hebrew faith. Tastes do differ, but why object? . . . rather we commend them for they pay their bills 100 per cent on the dollar every time and that kind of thing goes a long way with us. We welcome them."

By the end of World War I, Lakeville began to develop as a suburb of Lake City. The population grew from 6,000 to 12,000 during the 1920's. While some of its new permanent residents came from the old summer elite, the majority were middle-class "white Anglo-Saxon Protestants" who preferred a house and garden among congenial neighbors in the suburbs to an apartment in the city. They brought with them the values of responsible family life and citizenship, and they promoted a major expansion and improvement of the educational, religious, philanthropic, and community institutions, so that Lakeville became one of the more attractive and progressive communities in the area. The process of suburbanization lagged during the Depression and World War II, but took on a powerful impetus in the late 1940's. Because of its excellent facilities, particularly in education, and its traditions of leisure and culture, the town was especially attractive to the younger generation of middle-class residents of Lake City, who, like their counterparts throughout the country, were intent upon leaving their urban neighborhoods and making a different life for themselves in the suburbs. A steady stream of new residents entered the community, and though a substantial number of the older residents moved away, the total population increased from 17,000 to 25,000 during the 1950's.

Jews in Lakeville

One of the salient characteristics of this influx was that many of the newcomers were Jewish. In good part, this phenomenon was due to the "democratic" tradition in Lakeville that we have already noted. There had always been Jews living in the town, and though their number was never very large, they had been part of each phase of its development. Thus among the early merchants of Lakeville was a Jewish jeweler and clothier. Lakeville's first theater had been built by a Jew who became relatively prominent in the community. Similarly, when Lakeville became a summer resort it attracted a small number of Jewish millionaires who built mansions along the lakefront or small estates in the wooded areas of the community. Members of the German-Jewish elite, they were joined by other prosperous Jewish families, and finding that they were excluded from the elite Gentile clubs and facilities, they tended to form a summer colony of their own whose center was the Jewish country club. In time many of the Jewish summer people became year-round residents.

Their number increased after World War I, but the population growth during these years was predominantly Gentile. Moreover, during this period the elite class of Gentiles who took up permanent residence in Lakeville became increasingly influential in the political and social life of the town. The effect of this development was to make the Jewish group even more isolated in the community, since the main thrust of discrimination came from the Gentile elite. Accepting their marginal position in Lakeville, the Jewish group discreetly kept their distance while making substantial contributions to the cultural, educational, and philanthropic institutions of the community.

The 1920's also saw the tentative beginnings of a Jewish communal life in Lakeville. A number of its residents joined with Jews in nearby suburbs to organize the first Jewish temple in the area. But aside from their activities in the temple and the country club, they remained unwilling to develop a strong Jewish community for fear that it would increase their conspicuousness as an out-group. They preferred to remain a relatively accepted minority of wealthy and accommodating citizens who had adapted to the norms of the community—one of which was that Jews led a separate social life and did not disturb the prevailing Gentile tone of Lakeville.

These grounds of mutual adjustment were dramatically altered after World War II with the heavy migration of Lake City Jews to Lakeville. Within a decade, the Jewish population grew from an insignificant minority to the stage where one out of every three households in Lakeville was Jewish. Though the Jewish newcomers to Lakeville were generally younger, wealthier, better educated, more urbane, and less ethnocentric than the average new Jewish suburbanite, a majority of them were of Eastern European ancestry rather than from the highly acculturated German-Jewish stock. On the whole they were much less inclined to take an inconspicuous place in the community than their Jewish predecessors in Lakeville had been. They were more willing to play an active role in community affairs, to maintain the manners and mores they had acquired in the urban Jewish neighborhoods, and to organize purely sectarian associations and institutions. They established new temples and founded chapters of several national Jewish organizations. Within a short time, a quite visible and variegated structure of Jewish communal life developed in the town.

During the same period, a significant number of the elite Gentile residents moved out of Lakeville. It is difficult to determine to what extent their departure was provoked by the influx of Jews, by the growth and alteration of the community in general, or by the attraction of a more "ex-urban" rather than suburban environment. There is no question, though, that many of the Lakeville people who remained in the community believed that this exodus was in response to the Jewish migration. Certainly it seems probable that many of the elite families who left would have been no more willing to share Lakeville with the Jewish newcomers than they had been to share their clubs with the older Jewish residents. Be that as it may, their emigration, combined with the influx of Jews, inevitably altered the social character of the town. While some wealthy and influential Jews continued to move into Lakeville, many Gentile newcomers tended to be young, middle-class families who did not replenish the ranks of the elite group. In sum, the Jewish influx meant that Lakeville had lost its social *éclat* for the Gentile.

Contemporary Lakeville

Surprisingly enough, the Jews of Lakeville correspond more uniformly today to the suburbanite image than the Gentiles do. Although the latter include a large number of middle-class business and professional men who commute to Lake City, there is also a significant proportion of Gentile working-class families who are employed in the community. Almost all the Jews of Lakeville are solidly middle or upper-middle class in both occupation and income.

The homes of the Jews and Gentiles also reflect these differences. The recent Jewish residents are likely to live in new houses of modern ranch design. Gentiles occupy a range of dwellings, ranging from inexpensive frame houses in the center of town to early American or early modern houses in the more affluent neighborhoods. The wealthy group of longtime Jewish residents occupies older, elaborate mansions or radically modern dwellings that rest on stilts in the hilly area of the town. Most of the neighborhoods, however, have developed a variety of housing designs which typifies the heterogeneous mixture of Jews and Gentiles, longtime residents and newcomers, who now make up Lakeville.

LOCAL GOVERNMENT

In the 1950's the local government structure was reformed. Under the new plan, policies are set by an elected mayor and a city council of six members and executed by a professionally trained city manager, who assumes responsibility for the day-to-day operation of the city. This change has been successful and today Lakeville is governed more efficiently than ever before. The departments of accounts, engineering, public works, fire, police, and building inspection have been reorganized; more efficient administrative procedures have been adopted, and lines of authority are clearly drawn. The board of health, the zoning committee, and the planning and traffic commissions formulate proposals for the city council and administer their respective services. There is also an efficient library board, civil service commission, and playground and recreational board. The building appeals board has played a particularly important role in regulating construction and zoning during the building boom in the 1950's. With its revamped structure and competent manager, the community has thus been able to cope with the municipal problems created by its rapid growth and to contain the social stresses bred by rapid changes in the character of the community.

Adoption of the council-manager form of government was primarily due to the spirited action of a variety of civic groups, including the Lakeville Voters' Association, the Lakeville Civic Association, and the Lakeville League of Women Voters. These groups operate a continuous program aimed at arousing public interest and action in community affairs. Perhaps the most effective of these organizations is the Lakeville League of Women Voters, which is reputed to be one of the most enlightened and active chapters in the state. The League's activities include a variety of civic projects ranging from school and health surveys to public meetings concerning political issues and candidates. The efforts of the League to register voters have enabled the town to maintain one of the highest percentages of registered voters in the nation.

In addition to the League and to other typical community-wide civic groups such as the Lions and Kiwanis clubs, Lakeville has developed a number of neighborhood improvement associations during the past two decades. While they focus on the interests of their members, they inevitably become involved in general community affairs. The associations typify the widespread desire in the community to protect it from creeping commercialism and suburban blight. All in all, Lakeville is distinguished by a strong will to maintain itself as a desirable residential area populated by public-spirited citizens.

BUSINESS AND ECONOMIC ACTIVITIES

Much of Lakeville's current economic life is devoted to serving the needs of its immediate population. There is no heavy industry in the community, and relatively little light industry. Manufacturing is confined to communication and electrical equipment and to toys and novelties. What Lakeville does possess in abundance are retail establishments; they number over 200 and cater to the full range of consumer needs.

The business district reflects both the old Lakeville and the new. While the main street is lit by modernistic fluorescent arcs, the side streets still have old-fashioned lamps. Venerable stores that evoke an atmosphere of the nineteenth century are interspersed with sleek contemporary shops that bespeak the sophistication of the modern suburb.

The Jewish influx has had some impact on the shopping district. A kosher butcher shop has been opened on a side street and a Jewish delicatessen on the main street. The appearance of Chinese restaurants is also possibly due to the Jewish influence. Moreover, long-established merchants of conservative taste have found themselves forced to adapt to the tastes of the young style-conscious and affluent Jewish customers.

THE SCHOOL SYSTEM

Lakeville's school system has long been a source of pride to its residents and is one of the main inducements for Jewish families, traditionally oriented toward education, to move there. The high rating of the system was achieved by years of painstaking effort and liberal expenditure of public funds. During the postwar boom, when other community services deteriorated, the schools were able not only to maintain their standards but even to improve them—a fact that testifies to the public investment in education.

The system is divided into districts. Each is governed by an independent board of education which consists of five elected members who serve without compensation. Candidates for the board are nominated in an open caucus formed by members who represent the PTA boards within the school district. An effort is made to coordinate the work of the various districts through periodic meetings and workshops.

The elementary school districts, only one of which lies completely within the boundaries of Lakeville, include over a dozen schools. The schools reflect the ethnic, religious, and class composition of their neighborhood. Since there are virtually no Negroes in Lakeville, and few in immediately adjacent areas, the districts have not had to face the problem of racial integration.

Lakeville High School serves some neighboring areas as well as the township, and draws its students from Catholic parochial schools as well as from the public school system. The school brings together diverse economic, religious, and ethnic groups: children of low-income Italian Catholic families from the small community to the southeast of Lakeville, native American Protestants in modest circumstances from central Lakeville, and the children of affluent Jews and Gentiles from the preferred residential areas. Despite this heterogeneity, the major emphasis of the curriculum and the teaching is preparation for college, and four out of five of its graduates attend college.

RELIGIOUS INSTITUTIONS

Protestantism was firmly established in Lakeville from its inception as a community. After the Civil War, the Lakeville Building Company sought to make the community a Baptist one, but Presbyterian, Episcopalian, Methodist, and Lutheran congregations were also established in rapid succession. Though Protestants constituted the preponderant majority in the past, they make up somewhat less than one-half the present population. Today there are seven Protestant churches in the community, the largest denominations being Presbyterian and Episcopalian.

Despite the early dominance of the Protestant faith, Catholics have resided in Lakeville for many years. The first Catholic parish was organized in the 1870's. At one time the local church supported a parochial high school, but financial difficulties caused it to close; the parish continues to operate an elementary school. Catholics comprise about one-fifth of the Lakeville population.

The Jews, the last of the three major faiths to organize a congregation in Lakeville, founded a Reform temple in the 1920's. At present there are three other Reform congregations and one Conservative synagogue in the community or in immediately adjacent areas.

Relations between the various religious groups in Lakeville are considered to be cordial. In recent years the Lakeville Ministerial Fellowship has sponsored an interdenominational Thanksgiving Eve service in which a number of Jewish and Protestant congregations have participated. Ministers and rabbis have also tried to work out a compromise on the celebration of Christmas in the public schools, which has been the major divisive issue between the two faiths.

PHILANTHROPY

Most Lakeville residents are devoted to a variety of humanitarian and philanthropic causes and institutions. The most important local philanthropy is the hospital, which now has over 150 beds and a million-dollar budget. The Women's Auxiliary of the hospital, organized in the 1920's, has become one of the most important health and welfare associations in Lakeville. It provides the hospital with many thousands of hours of volunteer service, contributes significant sums of money, and runs a profitable gift shop and snack bar at the hospital. Membership in the Auxiliary is open to all women in the area, but its officers and board members tend to be drawn from the affluent class of the community.

Many other organizations also contribute to the health and welfare needs of Lakeville. Chief among these are the Family Service, which was organized in the Depression years as the Social Service Committee, the Mental Health Association, the Golden Circle for Senior Citizens, the Visiting Nurse Association, and local chapters of the Red Cross. Another prestigious association in Lakeville is the Infant Welfare League, which raises funds for baby clinics and settlement work in Lake City. Along with these non-sectarian health and welfare associations, there is also a group of sectarian philanthropic institutions.

RECREATIONAL FACILITIES

Lakeville's past as a summer resort is still evident in its highly developed recreation facilities. The community has five private golf clubs as well as a yacht club. Its public facilities include bathing beaches, boating facilities, tennis courts, golf courses, and playgrounds.

In addition to the Park District, which manages these facilities, Lakeville also has a playground and recreation board. The site of many of the indoor activities sponsored by the board is a modern recreation building, which features a large gymnasium, a commodious community room with a stage, a game room with a soda bar, various club and conference rooms, a workshop with power and hand tools, and a well-outfitted kitchen. During the fall, winter, and spring, the gymnasium and the meeting facilities in the recreation building are used intensively. During the warm weather, the board conducts a variety of recreational programs for several different age levels at its playgrounds, parks, and swimming pools.

CULTURAL ACTIVITIES

Just as Lakeville's unusual recreational facilities can be traced to its past as a summer resort, so the extent and quality of its present-day cultural activities are an outgrowth of the cultural tradition established by the summer elite. The outstanding facility in the community is still its center for performing arts, which continues to provide first-rate musical and theatrical programs during the summer season. Lakeville also has a community concert series which is held in the high school during the winter, a music club that provides entertainment at community gatherings, and even a barbershop quartet.

Through the support of the Library Board and the Friends of the Library, the public library has become a vital cultural force in the community. It has good facilities for young people, and some 8,000 borrowers have a choice of over 140,000 volumes. The library also has an active music department—there are some 800 individual records and 250 albums available for loan and over 3,000 pieces of sheet music. Discussion groups, such as the Great Books study group, are held in the library.

Every year the community sponsors an adult education program at the high school. Courses range from sewing to municipal government, and from woodworking to foreign language and literature courses. In addition to formally organized associations such as an art league and film society, there are informal groups such as literary clubs, play-reading groups, and book clubs. In short, Lakeville's present position as a community of the educated and affluent, combined with its past as a luxurious summer resort, has made a diversified set of cultural and intellectual activities available to its residents.

The Study

SELECTION OF THE COMMUNITY

The choice of Lakeville for our study was neither accidental nor arbitrary. While the social characteristics of its Jewish population were of central concern—in order to provide material for our accompanying volume—the intergroup situation was also an important factor in our choice. Wishing to investigate the conditions which facilitate relations between Jews and Gentiles, we sought a community where such relations are relatively good. The openness of Lakeville to Jews and the absence of any significant incidents of anti-Semitism in its history help to make it a suitable laboratory for studying the development of inter-faith relations in a more or less favorable social climate.

We also wanted a community that could provide us with a glimpse into the changing nature of these relations as religious pluralism establishes itself in American society and minorities become even more acculturated and integrated into the main stream of American life. Thus we were less concerned with what is perhaps still typical today; we tried to find a more advanced state of Jewish–Gentile accommodation and adjustment to serve as a model for the future. In this respect Lakeville has much to offer. Its Jewish population is predominantly native-born and strongly acculturated, while its Gentile community is firmly established and at the same time progressive in its social attitudes.

Further, we believed that a realistic assessment of the changing character of interfaith relations could only be derived from a community that reflects the sociological position of the Jews in contemporary society. Thus we sought a town where they are a minority and have to adapt to an environment dominated by Gentiles. At the same time we wanted a town with enough Jewish residents to comprise a relevant part of the community environment—and one with which the Gentile majority was trying to come to terms.

We were also of the opinion that the unfolding relations between Jew and Gentile can best be studied in a situation where the Jews are not a new and alien force. Instead, we wanted a community where the "pioneering" phase of intergroup contact has been accomplished and where benchmarks for the integration of the Jew into the community have already been established. We felt that channels of communication and contact between the groups should have been more or less worked out, so that members of both groups would be less likely to treat each other as undifferentiated social categories. Here too we found that Lakeville—because of its longtime Jewish residents—particularly suited our requirements.

Besides these intergroup criteria, Lakeville also met several other requirements necessitated by the type of field study which we contemplated. For example, it is a medium-sized suburb small enough to be investigated with the means available to us but large enough to offer challenging variety. It also has an institutional structure autonomous enough to allow it to be treated as a distinctive community.

Like all real-life settings, however, Lakeville had its limitations for our purposes. An especially significant one is that the social characteristics of its Jewish and Gentile population differ sharply. Of course we did not want a perfect overlap, for since Jews do not constitute a mirror image of the general society, any community which would provide such an image would be an atypical—even exotic—one. Nevertheless, differences in social characteristics do complicate our analysis, for distinctions in attitude and behavior which we discover may not be a function of religio-ethnic differences but rather of age, education, income, and so forth. Accordingly, wherever possible we attempt to match Jews and Gentiles on various social characteristics in order to control for any independent effect which such characteristics may have.

SAMPLE DESIGN AND RESPONDENT INTERVIEWS

Our research design required many more Jewish interviews than Gentile ones in order to collect the data analyzed in Volume I. It was therefore necessary that we establish the religious identity of the members of any sample of Lakeville residents before we actually interviewed them. Because of the actual ratio of Gentiles to Jews in the community, to have done otherwise would have produced too many Gentile interviews.

To meet this problem we first obtained as complete a list as possible of all households in Lakeville. By spot-checking selected streets, we discovered that our listing comprised approximately 99 per cent of all Lakeville households. With an estimate of Lakeville as being one-third Jewish, and with a target of over 400 Jewish interviews and about 250 Gentile interviews, we drew a probability sample from this listing using tables of random numbers. Next, we checked the names of the heads of these households against membership listings of certain sectarian organizations. Those whose group identity could not be ascertained by this procedure were contacted by means of a telephone survey. The survey used a short questionnaire based on a theme which would not provoke anxiety and would lead naturally to a query on religious identity.

After excluding from our sample those who were married to a member of the other group, we arranged for interviews with people in the order that they were drawn for the sample. In all, we obtained 432 interviews from adults who considered themselves Jewish and 250 from those who considered themselves Gentile. (In each case the interviewer was of the same faith as the respondent.) The former figure represents 86 per cent of the Jews who were approached for interviews; an additional 10 per cent refused to cooperate, and 4 per cent had moved or were deceased. The latter figure represents 65 per cent of the Gentiles from whom interviews were sought; an additional 20 per cent refused to cooperate or were unavailable despite repeated call-backs, 2 per cent were too ill to be interviewed or had died, and 13 per cent had moved from Lakeville.

We confined our interviews to one adult in a household; among those who were married and living with their spouse, we alternated between the husband and the wife in successive households. Those interviews of married people comprised 96 per cent of the Jewish interviews and 83 per cent of the Gentile ones. The rest of the people interviewed were widowed, divorced, or unmarried heads of households. The preponderance of women in these groups produced a larger proportion of women respondents in the study (56 per cent of the Gentile group and 52 per cent of the Jewish group) than men.

This volume reports the results from both Jewish and Gentile interviews, all of which were completed by the middle of 1959. On occasion, however, we rely exclusively on data from our Jewish respondents. While similar questions on intergroup issues were asked of both groups, the questionnaire for the Jews was more detailed: each interview averaged 3½ hours in contrast to 1½ hours for the Gentile ones. As a consequence, in certain areas we do not have comparable data from Gentiles.

In addition, as we have already noted, the Gentiles are not a homogeneous group with respect to religion. However, except for Chapter 9 we do not distinguish their denominational affiliations because our analysis revealed that the attitudes of an individual Gentile toward Jews, his length of residence in the community, and other characteristics were the more relevant influences in his relations with Jews.

SOCIAL CHARACTERISTICS OF THE JEWISH AND GENTILE RESPONDENT

As we indicated earlier, Jews are the more recent arrivals in Lakeville: their median length of residence is 4.5 years in contrast to 14.4 years for the Gentiles. But they are no more likely than Gentiles are to have arrived recently in the United States: only 8 per cent are of the immigrant generation, as compared with 12 per cent of the Gentiles. Their parents, though, were more likely to have been immigrants: 39 per cent, in contrast to 17 per cent for the Gentiles. In both groups, however, a majority of the parents (53 per cent for the Jews and 71 per cent for the Gentiles) were native-born.

Jews are an average of six years younger than the Gentiles: the mean age of the Jews is forty-one and that of the Gentiles is forty-seven. Accordingly, their children are much more likely to be of elementary school age: 65 per cent of all the Jewish children, in contrast to 49 per cent of all the Gentile children, are 12 years of age or younger. Both Jewish and Gentile respondents are unlikely to have more than two children, the figures being 71 per cent for the Jews and 68 per cent for the Gentiles. The Gentiles, however, are twice as likely to have four or more children: 13 per cent, as compared with 6 per cent for the Jews.

Jews earn more than Gentiles do: their median annual income is approximately $18,000, while that of Gentiles is approximately $10,000. They are also much more likely to have attended college: 86 per cent of the Jews have done so, in contrast to 51 per cent of the Gentiles. However, the same proportion of the fathers of the respondents in both groups attended college—approximately 25 per cent of the Jewish and Gentile fathers had some higher education.

In respect to occupation, Jewish men are much more likely to be self-employed than the Gentile men (61 per cent versus 26 per cent). Sixty-five per cent of the Jewish men make their living in business, while

34 per cent practice a profession. Somewhat fewer Gentile men are engaged in a profession (30 per cent), many fewer make their living in some business activity (45 per cent), and a full 25 per cent are employed as manual or service workers.

In addition to these average differences between the Jews and Gentiles, the distribution of the various characteristics within each group also differs significantly. The range of income, education, and age, for example, is much greater among Gentiles—in large measure because they include a greater number of the less educated, low-income, and older persons. The Jews therefore are a more homogeneous group.

2

THE CLIMATE OF
INTERGROUP RELATIONS

From all outward appearances, Lakeville is an attractive place to live. Despite its rapid postwar development it has retained many of its natural advantages: a frontage on one of the Great Lakes, combined with woodlands and hills that provide distinctive settings for many of its homes and create a general atmosphere in its residential neighborhoods of pastoral spaciousness and seclusion. As one long-standing Jewish resident puts it, "We live in the country, at the seashore, and in the city at the same time."

The dominant feature of Lakeville's environment is the lake itself: the town hugs its shoreline, the streets curving back from the harbor and beaches so as to preserve as much proximity to the water as possible while following the contours of wooded hills. Along with its variety of water sports, which in the late spring and summer transform Lakeville into a resort-like community, the huge expanse of lake provides a feeling of openness and variety that is often lacking in more landlocked suburbs.

Extending east from the lakefront, the network of hills creates a variety of terrain in Lakeville and also limits the number of homesites. This area forms the older, elite residential section. Its old-fashioned street lamps and streets that wind without sidewalks through the trees, shrubs, and lawns of the neighborhood, its lively mixture of traditional and modern homes, each of them substantial and well situated, further suggest an intimate relation between the natural and social atmosphere of the community.

Farther east, the hills give way to a belt of flat, green country, along which the five golf courses of Lakeville are situated. Here and there new housing has sprung up along the fairways and connecting streets. However, the expanse of greensward to the east, like the lake to the west, still forms one of the boundaries of Lakeville and preserves its tone of suburban leisure, privacy, and tranquility.

The Benign Atmosphere

The social climate in Lakeville has much in common with its physical appearance and material well-being. For the most part it is benign, open, live-and-let-live. "Everyone in Lakeville has money and anyone can close his door if he does not want to see somebody," according to a young Jewish businessman in the course of explaining the absence of group conflict in the community. "There is still enough room to stay by yourself," asserts an elderly Gentile cabinet-maker. "No friction, no discord." However, there are also other factors, distinctive to the mores of Lakeville, that explain its favorable social climate.

As we noted in Chapter 1, the early development of Lakeville as an independent municipality has preserved it from becoming an enclave of the wealthy—as several of its sister suburbs are—and from being dominated by elitist social and ethnic restrictions. Though the town's aspirations to become a significant commercial port have long since been abandoned, the tradition of local initiative and self-sufficiency has remained part of the civic and social character of the community. The influence of its wealthy summer residents, many of whom eventually became permanent members of the community, was to refine the town's native progressive spirit and to turn it to cultural rather than commercial goals. This is reflected in Lakeville's impressive summer concert series, as well as its plethora of art exhibits, flower shows, theater groups, literary societies, chess clubs, and other long-standing cultural groups and activities. The later growth of the community as a metropolitan suburb has further strengthened these tendencies and helped to keep Lakeville abreast of the times, to diversify and stimulate community activity, and to raise its levels of urbanity and enlightenment, while maintaining its atmosphere of affluence and well-being. The public institution that is usually pointed to as most expressive of Lakeville's progressivism is its excellent school system, the product of high levels of public interest as well as expenditure.

If one looks at a typical issue of the weekly *Lakeville Bulletin,* the social character of the community emerges in small but suggestive ways. The lead story deals with spiraling population growth and taxes— matters which we shall take up in the following chapter. Other items include the construction of a combination municipal swimming pool and ice-skating shelter, the donation of a private greenhouse to the local park district by a local Jewish family, and an expansion of the public library facilities so that residents may obtain loan and research services by telephone. One news story discusses the coming school board election at length; another reports on a recent meeting of the board of education to review the various programs to improve methods of teaching mathematics and to introduce a college course in analytical geometry for advanced seniors. The League of Women Voters of Lakeville held a meeting devoted to municipal planning, and has scheduled three workshops in local school finance. Amid the usual coverage of the active social-club life of Lakeville, one also notices that news of the Sisterhood of a local temple follows an item on a local Women's Auxiliary unit of the American Legion, and that a story on the courses being offered by the Lakeville YMCA stands side by side with the announcement of a lecture by a local rabbi on the novels of Bernard Malamud. In general, the activities of the Jewish community receive a significant amount of coverage in the *Lakeville Bulletin,* roughly equivalent to the present numbers of Jews in this once predominantly Gentile community.

This comfortable, enlightened, and enterprising community spirit reflected in the *Lakeville Bulletin* is highly valued by the townspeople and provides the background for good relations among them. Seven out of ten Lakeville residents regard themselves as very satisfied with their life there. Gentile respondents tend to emphasize the attraction of Lakeville's "physical characteristics" and "facilities," while Jewish ones emphasize its "way of life" and its "beneficial effect on family living"; however, both groups agree that "its people" are among its chief assets. A typical Jewish newcomer from the city observes that "everyone seems friendlier here. For example, my wife can't stand to handle rabbits. We had several on the road near the house. She called up and someone came quickly and removed them." "Nice, friendly group of people here who mind their own business," says a Gentile resident of nine years. "They don't lock doors. They're always ready to help." A Jewish housewife who came to Lakeville from New York remains impressed by her first experience in the community:

> When we came here everybody was so wonderful. . . . We never expected such cordiality and we really felt that it was sincere and that these people wanted us for their neighbors and were glad that we moved in. I guess I feel that they made the transition from the East so easy for us that I still feel nice about it.

Another Jewish housewife analyzes group relations in somewhat more detail:

> This is a fairly comfortable community and all can afford to be friendly. People here have more poise on the outside than the average person, they're better educated and maybe more refined. What goes on inside I don't know about.

In their outward aspect, at least, relations between Jews and Gentiles conform to this general image of social amicability and placidity. Though the heavy influx of Jewish residents during the 1950's is held to be responsible for Lakeville's problems of growth and change, much the same surface composure and confidence prevail between Jews and Gentiles as in the overall life of the community. According to one inter-group agency, Lakeville enjoys a reputation for being particularly free of religious prejudice and overt group conflict. One neighboring community still maintains an elaborate system of customs and tacit agreements that makes it extremely difficult for Jews to purchase property there. Another town that admits Jews has had an intermittent history of Gentile hostility that was most dramatically expressed by painting swastikas on the windows of a temple. Such symptoms of generalized community antagonism toward Jews are virtually unknown in Lakeville. Only 17 per cent of our Jewish respondents report having had "a personal experience with anti-Semitism" in Lakeville; an additional 18 per cent report that they have heard of such an incident. This latter figure is particularly revealing: if such incidents were at all characteristic of the daily life of the town or were significant enough to have had community-wide implications, we would expect that most, if not all, of Lakeville's Jews—who remain quite sensitive about their place in the community—would have "heard" about their existence.

Most of the "anti-Semitic incidents," however, involved individual issues and interests—property rights and upkeep, disputes over the activities of dogs or children, unreciprocated favors or other overtures of friendship; in other words, the ordinary disturbances and abrasions of suburban life rather than any detectable outcropping of ethnocentric prejudice, defensiveness, and general ill-will. Nor do such disputes— three out of five of which took place in the immediate neighborhood— appear to be noticeably drawn along religious lines. Another 9 per cent report "an unpleasant experience" with a Gentile neighbor which they do not attribute to anti-Semitism. In sum, 19 per cent of the Jewish respondents have had an unpleasant incident with a Gentile neighbor, but 21 per cent have had one with a fellow Jew. Finally, our data indicate that the great majority of Gentiles as well as Jews of Lakeville detect little, if any, significant strain in the relations between the two groups (see Table 2–1).

T A B L E   2 – 1   Estimated Degree of Strain between Jews and Gentiles by Religion

Would you say that on the whole, relations between Jews and Gentiles in Lakeville are	Gentile Respondents	Jewish Respondents
Very strained?	2%	1%
Fairly strained?	23	8
Only somewhat strained?	30	34
Not at all strained?	45	57
	100%	100%
	(225)	(422)

In sum, then, three out of four Gentiles and nine out of ten Jews find that the climate of intergroup relations in Lakeville is not seriously impaired by religio-ethnic differences, and one out of two in each group believes that such differences have no detrimental effect at all. Before going into these responses in more detail, it is well to keep in mind the following points: (1) Some degree of specific interreligious tension does remain apparent to many of the inhabitants; (2) for the moment we are dealing with Jewish–Gentile relations in terms of outward behavior rather than of underlying attitudes and feelings; as one of our Jewish informants quoted earlier put it, "What goes on inside I don't know about"; (3) the relative tranquility of the atmosphere in which Jews and Gentiles meet in Lakeville is not necessarily an index of the extent and depth of mutual comity and intimacy between members of the two groups, or even an accurate reflection of their real regard—or lack of regard—for each other. Indeed, as we shall see in the following chapters, the way Jews and Gentiles *feel* about each other is often at variance with the way they *behave* toward each other. Further, as we shall have occasion to observe in this chapter, the frequent gap between personal feelings and social behavior is evident not only in the quality of Gentile–Jewish relations but also in the rather unrealistic notions that prevail in each group about the feelings of the other. All of which is not intended to minimize the existence or importance of the peaceable atmosphere in Lakeville. The absence of overt conflict with a strong ethnocentric cast is a significant feature of its daily life, both in the private and public sectors. It is also a necessary condition, if not a sufficient one, for the development of mutual understanding and friendship between Jew and Gentile.

The Bases of Tranquility

The Jewish and Gentile respondents who detect little or no strain in intergroup relations offer a variety of explanations. By far the most popular one, which slightly more than two out of five in each group mention, is the favorable "manners, morals, and character" of Lakeville's residents, with a particular emphasis upon the acceptability of the Jewish ones.

Some respondents emphasize the norms of civilized behavior that prevail in Lakeville. "This isn't a typical community," says a Jewish resident, the well-educated wife of a successful printing executive. "Most of the people out here are fairly well educated . . . and everybody is of about the same financial or social status. If there is strain, they are too well-bred to show it." Much the same response comes from a Jewish plant manager: "The Gentiles I know are upper middle class, well-to-do, well educated, worldly. If they have feelings they screen them." Gentiles who detect little or no strain between Jews and Gentiles seem more inclined to take the civility on both sides at face value and not concern themselves with the negative feelings it may mask. "I think communities with above-average intelligent people learn to live with all kinds of different faiths," says the Gentile wife of a wealthy manufacturer. "We all have to be courteous." Or, as a Gentile advertising executive puts it, "There is no strain between Jew and Gentile because the kind of people who live in Lakeville is not the kind which causes strain."

Other respondents find some degree of deliberate moral initiative in the interfaith tranquility of the community. "If people care enough, you can get along if everyone makes an effort," says a Gentile resident whose husband is president of an engineering concern. "People in this neighborhood are willing to make the effort." A Jewish banking executive associates this initiative with the changing mores of American society: "I think people are beginning to wake up to the fact that it is not a nice thing to be intolerant. It's not a credit to Americanism and not socially acceptable." Others comment on the influence of the local churches and temples, which are active in promoting interfaith values through programs such as the annual joint Thanksgiving services.

Such practices on the part of the Jewish community are indicative of its almost uniformly high level of acculturation and adaptability. Whatever effect this may have on the scope and content of Jewish identity in Lakeville (matters which are taken up in Volume I), it is viewed by Jews and Gentiles alike as one of the decisive reasons why they can get along together. Commenting on the conformity of the Jews to general community standards of behavior, a Gentile banker who has lived in Lakeville for twenty-five years expresses himself as follows:

> I presume we have a pretty good class of Jewish people; people who buy a house and live here have learned by that time how to conduct themselves. I don't think that people who live in these suburban towns would have a truck parked in the driveway and sell goods from them. Jewish people who live here don't come directly from the ghetto. They are like the rest of us.

Other Gentiles reiterate that Lakeville's Jews make up a "nice class of people"—not the "loud, outspoken variety," as a former elementary school teacher puts it, "but rather educated, hard-working, neat, clean, and not much different than we are." Such a statement—which might be taken as an impromptu definition of the Protestant ethic—typifies the direction that normative values of behavior tend to take in intergroup relations in Lakeville. In other words, the issue still seems to be the Jews' ability to adapt to Gentile standards of conduct rather than the conscious effort of the Gentile community to welcome a genuine diversity of manners and mores. Or, as an elderly Gentile woman who has lived in Lakeville for a decade phrases the matter: "Jews are trying to prove themselves and Gentiles are trying to accept them."

Much the same relation between community peaceableness and Jewish conformity can be inferred from the explanations of Jewish respondents. "Relations are not strained on the surface," says a young furniture designer who plays an active role in neighborhood affairs. I think . . . the type of Jewish person a Gentile person meets in the suburbs is more nearly acceptable by his [the Gentile's] standards." Another Jew who works as a photo-engraver amplifies the point as follows:

> Jews who have moved out here are of a higher degree of education than are those in the city where our parents were from the Old Country and still [were] used to the old customs. We don't fit old Jewish stereotypes; we are fitting into the community easily.

Other respondents, particularly among the Jews, think that a more reciprocal pattern in terms of shared interests and values exists between Jews and Gentiles. Among the 26 per cent of the Jews who offer this as a primary reason for the small degree of strain they experience in Lakeville, a poised young housewife responds as follows:

> Jew and Gentile now have more in common. Ivy league education, economic and social backgrounds help break down and cross over barriers of religion. Two fellows who went to Harvard should have a common denominator.

Another Jewish housewife who came to Lakeville seven years ago and who knows of "no strain between Jew and Gentile," points out that even Jews and Gentiles of dissimilar background may find that Lakeville itself acts as a solvent of their differences: "Community life has brought them together, and neighborly feeling." Though fewer Gentiles (10 per cent) than Jews (26 per cent) find that "shared values and interests" are a cardinal reason for the absence of noticeable strain, Gentiles who do give this reason make much the same point about the integrating effect of the suburban life style. "Though we have different religions on this block," says a young Gentile mother, "we have common interests in children, homes, yards."

Such common interests and "similar ideas about life," as a highly cultivated woman of seventy-one puts it, often lead to active cooperation between members of the two groups which, in turn, becomes another important basis for social harmony. Insofar as Lakeville itself is highly oriented toward active citizen participation in community affairs, Jews and Gentiles have ample opportunities for making social contacts through voluntary organizations such as the PTA and the

League of Women Voters, as well as the local civic and charity drives. "Relations are not at all strained," says another young Gentile house-wife, "because we are all working together to improve the community." Another Gentile woman, the wife of a lawyer, who has recently moved to Lakeville, reports that "Jew and Gentile are especially cooperative in voting bonds for schools. We work together, for all have the same desire to improve the city." Speaking of the voluntary civic organiza-tions, a Jewish woman who is also married to a lawyer testifies that "all [members] are on a friendly basis. . . . We work beautifully to-gether. During these functions we all have something in common." A highly assimilated Jewish resident feels that "there is no strain between Jew and Gentile mainly because of the school situation. In a small community the PTA is active and everyone is interested in education. They get to know Jews a little better and might get to understand them better."

Other respondents attribute Lakeville's intergroup tranquility to its long-standing tradition of admitting Jews who were able to conform to its prevailing values and social tone. As we shall see in the following chapters, there has survived in the town an older class of Jewish families, some of them going back to the German-Jewish elite that founded their own small summer colony there around the turn of the century, who have so adapted to the prevailing manners and mores of the older com-munity that they appear to have much more in common with the Lake-ville Gentiles than with the Jewish newcomers. Be that as it may, the presence of these Jewish families in the community over the years is looked upon by one out of ten respondents as a salient reason for the acceptance of the recent influx of Jewish residents. "Lakeville has had Jews for so long," remarks a Gentile executive who grew up in the town, "that we've all learned to get along together."

Along with the presence of an accepted old-guard class of Jewish families, there is also the absence, as an additional one out of ten respondents observes, of a hard core of established and influential Gentile residents who were determined to resist the postwar migration of Jews to Lakeville. In this respect, the proximity of old-line com-munities that still discriminate on religious grounds has been of benefit to Lakeville's Jews, since it provides hostile Gentiles with a relatively easy option of leaving the community. In short, the migration of accul-turated Jews into Lakeville has been accompanied by the exodus of militantly ethnocentric Gentiles. As one Jewish physician observes succinctly, "Those non-Jews who might have found reason to be unhappy have moved away. Those remaining are getting along with Jews."

Part of the "groundwork" that the Jewish "old-timers" in Lakeville laid for the acceptance of the newcomers was their practice of maintaining polite but fairly guarded relations with the Gentile community. Though most were weakly attached to Jewish life, they remained somewhat apart from the general life of the town itself, and developed a code of behavior toward their neighbors that was guided by a punctilious acquiescence to Gentile norms rather than by the give-and-take of active community interests and personal friendships. With this emphasis on acceptance rather than influence and intimacy, there grew up in Lakeville a tradition of cordial relations between Jew and Gentile that respected the privacy of both parties and made little attempt to bridge the social distance between the groups. Though the contemporary Jews of Lakeville play a much more active role in community affairs, there remains embedded in the manners and mores of the town much the same pattern of "working together" rather than of having more personal relationships—a pattern which, of course, also ties in with the high value that is placed on privacy throughout the community. As one Jewish resident of more than a decade sums up the matter: "Relationships between Jews and Gentiles are basically pleasant, but as with civic drives, they are essentially superficial in nature."

In other words, the 18 per cent of the Gentiles and the 13 per cent of the Jews who believe that friendly social contacts obviate social strain between them usually have in mind these cordial working relations rather than full or developing friendships. In the eyes of many residents, the relative absence of intimacy in Lakeville between Gentile and Jew does not prove detrimental to maintaining the peaceableness between them. On the contrary, a significant number of Jews and Gentiles (approximately one out of six) offer as a specific reason for intergroup tranquility the practice of "mutual avoidance." A Gentile salesman believes "there is only some strain because most people ignore the problem. Gentiles stick to their bunch and Jews stick to their bunch." "Relations are only somewhat strained," says the Gentile wife of a local carpenter, "because people don't know one another too well. If they did, much more strain among them might be observed." "We're not in each other's way," asserts a wealthy merchant who is very active in Jewish affairs. "We have our own temples and our own social life and they have theirs." "No mixing, so there's little chance for strain," says another respondent who also identifies strongly with Judaism. Finally, a Jewish resident who is in the fur business joins the residential to the social exclusiveness prevalent in Lakeville to explain its basis of peace-ableness:

> There is no strain because [Jew and Gentile] don't fraternize—each goes his own way. There is no neighborhood feeling. People cross and don't see each other—there is no geographical barrier in [the] entire town but there is no closeness either. That seems to be the pattern.

The Occasional Eruptions

As 19 per cent of our Jewish respondents report, there are unpleasant incidents between Jew and Gentile in Lakeville. When they occur, latent fears and anxieties may become manifest, and the incident often takes on a different significance from the one it would have if both of the parties were Jewish.[1] We have already noted there is no appreciable difference in the incidence of unpleasant experiences with Gentile or with Jewish neighbors. Nor is there any difference quantitatively in the general kinds of issues that are in dispute. Conflict is as likely to occur over a property matter as it is over a personal one.

The only significant difference to be observed in the disputes over property matters is the *occasional* presence of concern by the Jewish respondent that the behavior of a Gentile neighbor has been motivated by general ill-will toward Jews. The following is typical of such responses:

> The boy next door kept bouncing his ball off my shower window and broke it. He came in very manly and I told him I'd give him a Christmas present by fixing it myself. His parents called and they said they didn't want that. I felt they didn't want anything from Jews.

> There is this character across the street. We feel he has the old under-lying feeling about Jews. We had driveway trouble.

In disputes with Jewish neighbors, the suspicion of prejudice attached only to an incident involving the erection of barriers.

The following two incidents concerned with borrowing equipment indicate the different types of feeling that are sometimes aroused by

[1] Presumably the same reaction would be found among our Gentile respondents; however, the information on "unpleasant experiences" was limited to our Jewish respondents.

neighborhood conflicts, depending on whether both parties are Jewish or not. The first respondent is a young Jewish high school teacher:

> One of our Jewish neighbors just moved in. I was annoyed—he kept knocking on the door to borrow things—hose, wrench. He usually does it at supper time. They were overly friendly.

However, there is hardly the same potential for alienation as may develop when a similar dispute involves Jewish and Gentile neighbors. A recent Jewish resident reports:

> We had a dissension over some community property. We bought some items as a group, especially a roto-tilling machine. We had an agreement among ourselves not to loan it to anyone outside of our group. One fellow, a Jewish fellow, broke this agreement. He said: "Well, I have a brother-in-law here and he sees others using the roto-tiller and that put me on a spot. So I had to loan it to him." The Gentiles in the group got very angry at the first Jew. And the next thing you know, the Gentiles are talking among themselves and ever since then we've all been a little distant with one another. I had it out with the Jewish fellow myself. But since then the Jews on the street stick a little closer together and the Gentiles aren't quite as friendly.

It is worth noting, in passing, that in the incidents between a Gentile and a Jew which involve the maintenance of property, the complainant is almost invariably the former. However, it is only the property matters which involve erection of barriers or purchase and sale of property that appear to trouble most Jewish parties about the underlying motives of the Gentiles involved.

For example, three of the four Jewish respondents who cite unpleasant experiences concerning property transactions suspect some degree of anti-Semitic feeling, whether or not it formed an evident case of prejudice. A Jewish housewife relates these experiences:

> We first tried to buy a lot and the people wouldn't sell it to us. Let us just say I choose to believe they wanted more money than we could afford to pay. Another unpleasant experience is about a snippy little lady who is annoyed with the fact that Jews are moving in.

The suspicion is less pervasive in incidents that spring up because a Gentile neighbor is growing bushes or trees or erecting fences to separate the two properties. Still, three of the eight who mention this felt that their neighbor's desire to maintain physical privacy was related to a negative attitude toward Jews. A middle-aged lawyer reports that:

When our house was going up, they put up an arbor to give them privacy. Then we both put bushes in. Honestly, their move in the first instance was fear of Jews.

At times there is some evidence to support this view. According to the wife of another lawyer,

The non-Jewish neighbors across the way in back put up a tremendous fir tree and their maid told our maid the reason they planted trees was because they hated Jews. This shocked us, particularly since we realized to what expense they went to for their prejudice.

As with other types of neighborhood disputes, an embroilment with another Jew over the building of barriers usually is ascribed to individual conflicts rather than group prejudice. A longtime Jewish resident matter-of-factly describes one such incident:

Our wives don't get along so our next door neighbor built up a big hedge to separate our lot lines.

Much the same distinction continues to be apparent in those incidents in which the barriers erected between neighbors are not physical but social in nature—direct rejection, persistent avoidance, and the like. A Gentile's aloofness is usually attributed to his feelings toward Jews. The wife of an economics professor reports that:

My next door neighbor never spoke to me. After twelve years she's now trying to be friendly. She said: "Did you have to sell to Jews?" to the former owner when we moved here.

On the other hand, if a Jewish respondent has a similar experience with a Jewish neighbor, he is likely to attribute it to personality differences:

When we moved in here and built our house, a Jewish family didn't speak to us. We had personality difficulty. That is all ironed out now.

or to a peculiarity in the offending party's character:

When we first moved in, we had a [Jewish] neighbor who was exceedingly friendly and all of a sudden they cut us off completely. They had a big party and invited everyone, even non-Jews, but not us. Later we found out that this person does this often to people.

Two further observations can be made about the reactions of our Jewish respondents to the experience of social tension. First of all, covert rejection on the part of a Gentile neighbor, such as avoidance or ingratitude, is likely to be far more indicative to them of prejudice than are direct personal conflicts (see Table 2–2).

TABLE 2–2 ATTITUDE TOWARD JEWS AS A FACTOR IN UNPLEASANT PERSONAL RELATIONS BETWEEN NEIGHBORS

Per cent of Jewish respondents who consider an unfavorable attitude toward Jews by neighbor as having motivated the unpleasantness	*Nature of unpleasant experience*		
	Rebuff or Non-Reciprocated Behavior	Avoidance	Direct Personal Conflict
with this Gentile neighbor	50% (10)	64% (14)	27% (26)
with this Jewish neighbor	9% (11)	10% (10)	3% (34)

Secondly, the intensity of the respondent's reaction tends to vary according to whether the other party is a Jew or Gentile. If the latter, the respondent is more likely to appear depressed rather than angry, resigned rather than surprised; wounded rather than stung. The following response of a Jewish newcomer is characteristic of this prevailing tone of response:

When the A's first moved in, people came to us who said, "You'll like them." We called on them, but they never came back to see us. Also take the non-Jewish family down the way. They are very pleasant when we go around collecting money. One of their children had polio. We fed the older one, gave her supper, ice cream. We couldn't have been more neighborly so that they could stay with their sick child at the hospital till nine. They never said: "Thank you" when they picked her up and we've never seen them since. You can't have anybody less neighborly. I call that being rebuffed and unfriendly.

On the other hand, if a Jewish respondent experiences a similar rebuff from a Jewish neighbor, he is likely to exhibit a stronger and more immediate sense of personal outrage. Take the following Jewish respondent, also a newcomer, who felt that one of his neighbors had been ungrateful:

Jewish neighbors want things done for them and never reciprocate. For example, running errands, watching things, and so forth. It's hurray for me and to hell with you. They're selfish and want to keep up with the Joneses and they step on people to do it.

Still another young Jewish newcomer shows much the same unfettered intragroup indignation:

> We have an unpaved road here, and a neighbor who saw a truck come to gravel and oil another road, hired it for ours. She sent a bill to us to pay our share. She never asked us. A Jewish family believes that another Jewish family can be imposed upon and asked to do things, and I have lots of those here.

The third general type of unpleasant incident—direct personal conflict—bears out these observations about Jewish reactions to social strain in Lakeville. First of all, Jews involved in such conflicts seem as little suspicious of the underlying motivation of the Gentile parties as they are in property disputes involving damage and trespass. In other words, where the source of grievance is open and enmity is overtly expressed, the party tends to behave as an individual rather than as a member of a defensive minority group who expects to be discriminated against. Consequently, he is more free to express his hostility rather than repressing it in resignation.

In Lakeville, the primary agents of outright neighborly discord are dogs and children. Such incidents are also potentially more explosive than are adult difficulties over property rights or unreciprocated favors. The latter are more likely to result in withdrawal, whereas incidents involving children and dogs tend to arouse strong feelings of affection, protectiveness, and self-righteousness which often culminate in expressed hostility between neighbors (see Table 2–3).

TABLE 2–3 Participants in Neighborly Disputes and Unfriendly Acts

Per cent of unpleasant experiences that involved overt unfriendly acts between the Jewish respondent (and/or his family)	*Participants included*		
	Children	Dogs	Adults Only
and a Gentile neighbor (and/or his family)	79% (34)	86% (14)	52% (42)
and a Jewish neighbor (and/or his family)	90% (29)	87% (23)	52% (35)

However, once neighbors become embroiled, then disputes with Gentiles—whether or not these include dogs, children, or adults only—are more likely to generate intense feelings and anger than are those with Jews (see Table 2–4). (Of the various disputes, only those confined to Jewish adults seem to remain on the level of a relatively calm discussion of the issue.)

TABLE 2–4 EXPRESSION OF ANGER IN NEIGHBORLY DISPUTES BY PARTICIPANTS

Per cent of overtly unfriendly incidents in which intense emotion or anger was expressed between the Jewish respondent (and/or his family)	*Participants included*		
	Children	Dogs	Adults Only
and a Gentile neighbor (and/or his family)	70% (27)	67% (12)	68% (22)
and a Jewish neighbor (and/or his family)	62% (26)	60% (20)	45% (18)

What clearly distinguishes the two groups of conflicts is that those with Gentiles have a tendency to evoke prejudiced feelings on either or both sides, which in turn increase tension and anger. The following are three representative accounts of such experiences in Lakeville, all of them told by Jewish women who impressed their respective interviewers by their balanced, level-headed temperaments:

This Gentile father was a boor and he dominated the family. Two older boys in the family tormented our kids. They called my children "Kike" and bullied them. It was terrible.

We've had one incident with a non-Jewish family who used to live next door. Their child called ours a "dirty Jew." Ours called theirs a "dirty Catholic." I called the mother up. She said she would have to get her husband to stop talking like that around the house.

When we first moved in here my fifteen-year-old boy became friendly with a Gentile near us. This boy told my son that his parents did not like Jews but he did not mind that my son was Jewish. He said, "You go to your church and I'll go to mine. It does not bother me." They were quite friendly for a while and this Gentile boy was here tinkering with our car, which he liked to do, and he called our car a "Jew-boat." So the kids began to argue and he pushed my son around and called him a "dirty Jew." Now this family has let it be known in the neighborhood that they do not like Jews. And they have said that the Jews have come in here and taken over their neighborhood and that we are very low class and belong in the ghetto and we should go back there. No one in the neighborhood likes them. They have no friends even among the Gentiles.

Generally speaking, a Jew in an open dispute with a Gentile does not remain long in doubt about whether the Gentile was motivated by religious prejudice. If the Gentile uses anti-Semitic language, then there is no question in the mind of the Jew that an underlying hostility toward Jews motivated his behavior. If he does not, then the Jew is disinclined to ascribe his behavior to prejudice and attributes it instead to the issue at hand. This is especially true if the Jew feels that he too may be at fault—as, for example, if he has a dog that damages property or otherwise becomes a neighborhood nuisance. A wealthy young Jewish merchant describes the following incident:

> My dog tore up his shrubbery. He reacted strongly—but it was settled amicably. It could have happened if he was a Jewish neighbor too.

In general, open disputes with Gentiles do not require guesswork as to their underlying motives. Prejudice is either overtly shown or is not regarded as an issue. In other kinds of unpleasantness with Gentiles, especially those which manifest themselves in passive aggression such as withdrawal or rejection, the Jew as a rule does not really know what motivates this behavior, but is inclined to suspect the other person of prejudice against Jews.

Private Feelings: The Problem of Mutual Ignorance

It is clear that relations between Jews and Gentiles in Lakeville have a delicacy which is not immediately apparent on the surface of community tranquility, but can be detected from the occasional conflicts that arise between members of the two groups and from the private fears and anxieties that are frequently expressed. What also makes these relations delicate is that they are usually too superficial to orient either party to the actual content of the other's feelings toward him. Thus, along with the pervasive agreement that there is little or no strain between Lakeville's Jews and Gentiles, there is an equally pervasive uncertainty about the private feelings of Jews and Gentiles toward each other.

Among Gentiles, this uncertainty is frequently expressed by a frank admission of ignorance. When asked, "How do you think most Jews feel about Gentiles in Lakeville?" more than two out of five reply that they don't know. A typical response comes from the Gentile proprietor of a local supermarket. "I don't know how Jews feel toward Gentiles. It's hard to answer. I would never know what they think."

Most Jews, however, are willing to hazard a guess about the under-lying attitudes of Gentiles. Only one out of ten replies "I don't know" to the question, "How do you think most Gentiles feel about Jews in Lakeville?" Their uncertainty, as we have already noted, tends to be expressed in another way: they suspect that the private feelings of Gentiles may be at variance with their public behavior. Here the typical response is likely to be that of the following resident who is a practicing psychologist: "Gentiles are very careful to appear most gracious. What's behind it I don't know." In this manner, then, many Jews reveal a deeply held fear that Gentiles privately do not approve of them. This fear increases in proportion to the degree of strain the respondent believes exists between the two groups, but even those who believe no strain exists show a significant tendency to nurture the fear (see Table 2–5).

TABLE 2–5 ATTITUDES OF GENTILES AND DEGREE OF STRAIN IN INTERGROUP RELATIONS AS PERCEIVED BY JEWISH RESPONDENTS

How do you think most Gentiles feel about Jews in Lakeville?	*Jewish respondents who say that relations between Jews and Gentiles in Lakeville are*			
	Very Strained	Fairly Strained	Only Somewhat Strained	Not at All Strained
Very unfavorable	(33%)*	16%	5%	3%
Somewhat unfavorable	(67)	68	62	39
Neither favorable nor unfavorable	0	6	16	28
Somewhat favorable	0	10	14	25
Very favorable	0	0	3	5
	(100%)	100%	100%	100%
	(3)	(31)	(138)	(210)

* Percentages that are computed from five respondents or less are enclosed in parentheses.

The most common basis for this judgment is the feeling that Gentiles must resent the postwar influx of Jews into Lakeville. A Jewish lawyer who has resided in Lakeville for twenty years points to the terrific increase in numbers and surmises: "They don't want too much of what they consider an alien group—as seen in restrictions in clubs. I understand in some schools there are 95 per cent Jews there." Or again, another Jewish lawyer states: "This is my impression. Most of the non-Jews have been here longer than Jews and I feel they feel they are being invaded and overwhelmed." A third: "They must feel uncomfortable with more Jews. We'd be uncomfortable with more Gentiles."

Other respondents believe that this influx did not create prejudice toward Jews so much as trigger what was already latent in Gentile attitudes. As a young Jewish economist analyzes the problem: "Problems become more acute—they change from general to specific. In general, the born and raised Lakeviller would have a vague general animosity toward Jews whom he never really knew. Now with contact he directs it at specific Jews." Much the same "general animosity" is attributed to Lakeville's Gentiles by a longtime Jewish resident who heads an advertising agency: "The general feeling among Gentiles is not one of being in love with Jews. It's no different from any other community." A housewife who holds a college degree in philosophy believes that "they consider us different and set us apart as a different breed, and we're not different. But I can't help but feel they are always thinking that."

On the other hand, those Gentiles who are willing to hazard a guess tend to be much more optimistic about Jewish attitudes toward them. Only the few who believe that relations are "very strained" are inclined to assume that Jews don't like them (see Table 2–6).

TABLE 2–6   ATTITUDES OF JEWS AND DEGREE OF STRAIN IN INTERGROUP RELATIONS AS PERCEIVED BY GENTILE RESPONDENTS

How do you think most Jews feel about Gentiles in Lakeville?	Gentile respondents who say that relations between Jews and Gentiles in Lakeville are			
	Very Strained	Fairly Strained	Only Somewhat Strained	Not at All Strained
Very unfavorable	(50%)	10%	0%	8%
Somewhat unfavorable	(25)	28	10	5
Neither favorable nor unfavorable	0	14	8	17
Somewhat favorable	0	34	52	25
Very favorable	(25)	14	30	45
	(100%)	100%	100%	100%
	(4)	(29)	(40)	(60)

However, even the optimists express some doubt as to what Jewish attitudes really are. "I think the Jews' feelings are somewhat favorable," says a tennis instructor. "However, I never heard them say so. They seem to get along fine with everybody. I have heard it the other way around, though."

The main truth to be gathered from these answers is that even in the benign social climate of Lakeville, intergroup relations still contain a large element of fantasy. Few Jews and Gentiles appear to be in a position to gauge the feelings of the others with any accuracy, and thus they consult their own underlying anxiety or complacency, as the case may be. Were they in touch with reality, they would have to revise their opinions quite radically.

Our data show this most clearly for the Jews. We asked our Jewish respondents to estimate the percentage of Gentiles in Lakeville who would agree with the following statements used in similar studies:

ITEM 1   Persecution of Jews would be largely eliminated if the Jews would make really sincere efforts to rid themselves of harmful and offensive faults.

ITEM 2   The trouble with letting Jews into a nice neighborhood is that sooner or later they spoil it for other people.

ITEM 3   One trouble with Jewish businessmen is that they are so shrewd and tricky that other people don't have a fair chance in competition.

We then asked our Gentile respondents whether they agreed or disagreed with each statement. By totaling the responses of all Gentile respondents, we obtained the proportion who *actually* agreed with each item. These were then used as the base lines for assessing the accuracy of the estimates of Jews.

On each item the estimates of less than one out of four Jewish respondents could be considered reasonably accurate—within 10 per cent of the true Gentile proportion. A respondent could be said to qualify as a "realist" when his estimates were correct for at least two items which elicited a strikingly different proportion of Gentile agreement. Only a very small number—4 per cent—of our Jewish respondents could so qualify. (As will be seen in Table 2–7, the proportion was somewhat higher for those Jews who considered relations with Gentiles fairly strained.)

In effect, then, almost all the Jews in Lakeville are largely unaware of the prevailing attitudes of Gentiles toward them. Were they to become more aware, those who believe Gentiles to be favorably disposed toward them or who see little or no strain between Jew and Gentile would probably be more concerned than they are. As Tables 2–7 and 2–8 indicate, most Jews are in fact overly optimistic about how Gentiles feel toward them, despite the frequent suspicions of underlying prejudice. On the other hand, those who believe Gentiles are unfavorably disposed toward Jews or who see a great deal of strain in relations between the two also would probably change their minds if they were more adequately informed about the actual private feelings of Gentiles, which are much less generally hostile than they assume them to be. Table 2–7 shows that the more a Jewish respondent believes group relations to be strained, the more he overestimates the extent of Gentile prejudice.

TABLE 2–7 ESTIMATES OF GENTILE OPINION BY ASSESSMENTS OF INTERGROUP STRAIN AMONG JEWS

Estimates of Gentile response to items about Jews.	*Jewish respondents who say that relations between Jews and Gentiles in Lakeville are*			
Per cent who:	Very Strained	Fairly Strained	Only Somewhat Strained	Not at All Strained
Underestimate Gentile responses	0%	16%	45%	55%
Overestimate Gentile responses	(100)	52	37	28
Balanced estimate*	0	19	14	13
Realistic estimate	0	13	4	4
	(100%)	100%	100%	100%
	(3)	(31)	(138)	(226)

* Respondents who overestimated the response on one and underestimated the response on the other of the set of two items.

Similarly, as Table 2–8 shows, the more a Jewish respondent believes most Gentiles to be unfavorably disposed toward Jews, the more he overestimates the extent of Gentile prejudice.

To conclude, behind the public calm of intergroup relations in Lakeville is a widespread ignorance of how each group really feels about the other. Among Jews there are also a deep-seated anxiety on the one hand, and an undue optimism on the other, concerning the real state

TABLE 2–8 ESTIMATES OF GENTILE OPINION BY THEIR ATTITUDES TOWARD JEWS AS VIEWED BY JEWISH RESPONDENTS

Estimates of Gentile response to items about Jews	*Jewish respondents who say that most Gentiles feel the following toward Jews in Lakeville*				
Per cent who:	Very Un- favorable	Some- what Un- favorable	Neither Favorable nor Un- favorable	Somewhat Favorable	Very Favorable
Underestimate Gentile response	11%	38%	56%	67%	93%
Overestimate Gentile response	63	44	23	19	7
Balanced estimate*	21	13	17	7	0
Realistic estimate	5	5	4	7	0
	100%	100%	100%	100%	100%
	(19)	(184)	(83)	(70)	(14)

* Respondents who overestimated the response on one and underestimated the response on the other of the set of two items.

of affairs in the community. Thus, many of them are quite ambivalent about the question of how Lakeville's Gentiles regard Jews. It is no accident that the most realistic appraisal of the situation is to be found among the respondents who avoid the more extreme evaluations of Gentiles and describe relations between Jews and Gentiles as being fairly strained. For they will prove to be so in the following chapters that deal directly with the impact of the postwar migration of Jews to Lakeville.

II | THE JEW AS A NEWCOMER

3

COMMUNITY CHANGE AND
THE JEWISH NEWCOMER: THE
REACTIONS OF THE GENTILE

As we have already noted, the postwar migration to the suburbs did not bypass Lakeville. It started slowly in the late forties—the population had increased only 16 per cent by the end of the decade—and picked up speed in the early fifties. So rapid was the influx that by 1960 the population had increased 52 per cent, from 17,000 to 25,500. As early as 1947, town officials, expecting an increase of new residents, had developed a city plan for an expanding community. However, the size of the community projected for 1970—26,000—was reached in less than half that time, with the major increase coming within a period of five years.

As a result, by the early 1950's the town virtually lost control of its development. All its civic facilities were badly overtaxed, and its placid business district turned into a snarled web of traffic. Its financial structure foundered: under the pressure of ever-mounting costs, some necessary services such as police and fire protection became inadequate.

In its residential neighborhoods, the formerly open spaces and the staid, more or less traditional styles of architecture rapidly gave way to a building boom that reflected the confused pattern of growth in the

45

community at large. The following description of this new housing, taken from a recent history of Lakeville, also suggests its impact on the community, as viewed by a representative longtime resident:

> Ranch houses, low and boxy dwellings nestled beside two-story and attic size homes. Ranch styles were painted pink and dove-color blue; their picture windows framed the traffic on local thoroughfares. [The community] regretted the replacement of cherished treescapes by "outdoor living" scenes of families next door. Houses on the bi-level, tri-level and stilts featured transparent walls and air-conditioners. Subdividers acquired a talent for coaxing three units on two lots. Before the half-way mark of the fifties [the community] comprised more than a thousand postwar designs.

The writer goes on to indicate another aspect of these sweeping changes in describing the commercial part of town:

> The business district began to sprawl west down the C—— Avenue hill, S—— Street lured traffic with a new post office, a dial telephone building, and the city's second bank. New super stores featured grocery carts, baby carts and similar reasons for car-puffed thoroughfares. . . . The treasured rose garden was buried under the third of a trio of gas stations one block west of the tracks. Prosperity and the lifting of wartime bans checkered the city with a Recreation Center, Legion Hall, medical clinics and a reducing salon.

Not until the mid-1950's did the community begin to regain some measure of control over its development. At that time the municipal structure was overhauled in order to cope with the array of new problems. A city manager was installed: under his supervision departments were reorganized, more efficient administrative procedures were adopted, and in time the machinery of government began to function more adequately. By setting its administrative house in order, Lakeville did not solve all the difficulties that had overtaken it. But these reforms did provide the community with a more rational and flexible system for coping with them and helped to reassure some of its older residents that their once stable and distinctive community would not be swept away by the tides of change.

The Gentile Reaction to Change

A majority of our Gentile respondents have lived through these chaotic years of growth in Lakeville (57 per cent have been residents for eleven years or more), and, as might be expected, many of them express misgivings about what has happened to the community. But relatively few of these longtime residents now regard the postwar development as an unmixed curse, and by and large they tend to believe that the new residents have proved an asset to the community. Indeed, more of the longtime Gentile residents are favorably disposed to the new Lakeville than are not, though this affirmative majority is not quite as large as that in the current Gentile population as a whole (see Table 3–1).

TABLE 3–1 GENTILE EVALUATION OF COMMUNITY CHANGE BY LENGTH OF RESIDENCE

General evaluation of community change in recent years*	Gentile respondents Length of residence		
	5 Years or Less	6–10 Years	11 Years or More
Wholly good	34%	18%	27%
Mostly good	39	51	32
TOTAL	73%	69%	59%
Relatively balanced	9	21	20
Mostly bad	5	5	12
Wholly bad	13	5	9
TOTAL	18%	10%	21%
	100%	100%	100%
	(56)	(43)	(138)

* The exact wording of the question was: "In recent years Lakeville has experienced a great deal of growth and change. On the whole, do you feel that this growth and change has been good or bad for Lakeville?"

A lifetime resident, active in community affairs, speaks for this consensus of favorably disposed oldtimers as follows:

Well, the growth is good in the sense—if this can be expressed, recognizing that every city has to grow—that Lakeville has controlled it. We have an enlightened management in government from civic-minded people, a minimum of bad politics, the service of conscientious people who have the interest of their fellow citizens at heart and perform service. That is all to the good and we appreciate it.

Since Lakeville's mushrooming growth in population forms a major ground of the tensions—often covert—between Jews and Gentiles, it is well to explore community reactions to the issues of change in some detail. To do so, we asked our Gentile respondents what they liked or disliked about the growth of the community and classified their responses into four categories (see Table 3–2).

TABLE 3–2   GENTILE REACTIONS TO VARIOUS KINDS OF CHANGE BY LENGTH OF RESIDENCE

Categories of community change	Gentile respondents Length of residence		
	5 Years or Less	6–10 Years	11 Years or More
Political and Governmental Structure			
Good effect	37%	46%	39%
Bad effect	16%	31%	19%
Community Facilities and Physical Environment			
Good effect	63%	68%	72%
Bad effect	62%	71%	70%
Economic and Fiscal Matters			
Good effect	14%	24%	17%
Bad effect	38%	11%	28%
Character of the Community			
Good effect	47%	32%	30%
Bad effect	35%	37%	57%
TOTAL WHO MENTION SOME GOOD EFFECT	(49)	(41)	(126)
TOTAL WHO MENTION SOME BAD EFFECT	(37)	(35)	(101)

It is evident that the one benefit which Gentile residents—the long-timers as well as the others—agree has accrued to Lakeville is the change in city government. As one longtime resident points out, "We could not have had a city manager with a 9,000 population." The new city manager system is widely hailed, usually for reasons similar to those offered by a newcomer to the community, a young housewife, who is pleased by the professional acumen, efficiency, and disinterestedness of the new officials. "They have a better grasp of the problems and have better solutions than the mayor and councilmen did. Also the city manager does not have an axe to grind." Along with the superior leadership and competency provided by a professional administrator, the caliber of the various departments and municipal facilities is also seen to have risen as a result of the expansion and modernization of the municipal structure. A high-ranking police officer who moved to Lakeville four years ago remarks:

> The increase in population has forced changes in the local government. These things are usually indirect but can be traced to the increase in the population. The police department, for example, has higher standards than before. I think change is even going to come in the magistrate's office, because this is no longer a small town. It's a small city.

In general, then, the rapid suburbanization of the postwar years is considered to have improved the government of Lakeville. It has also tended to educate the residents in practical municipal problems and to strengthen the ties between the public and their officials. A longtime resident, active in the PTA and the local League of Women Voters, puts it this way:

> The growth has forced a citizen awareness. It has forced integration of thought and planning and an awareness of the fact that we have problems with growth and if they are allowed to run wild, we will end up with a city that we don't like.

Objections are occasionally entered against the impersonality and bureaucratization that have attended these reforms, the inadequacy of the zoning laws, the spiraling costs of administration and services. More typically, however, Gentile citizens of Lakeville appear either to accept or to welcome the forms that political change has taken, and to experience more misgivings or ambivalence over other aspects of Lakeville's transformation into a full-sized suburb. The area of greatest ambivalence is that of the "physical" growth of the community—the proliferation of new neighborhoods and styles of architecture, the advent of the supermarket, and the Saturday afternoon traffic jams, as well as the expansion of community facilities and services.

One of Lakeville's institutions that has received the direct impact of the population boom is, of course, the school system. A long-standing source of community pride and effort, the Lakeville schools are generally believed to have met the challenges of a burgeoning enrollment and profited from the new opportunities for building construction and curriculum improvements provided by the increase in school revenues. A local teacher, who believes "it is good for any town to grow," voices the positive reaction in these terms:

> The growth has been good for the schools. As a teacher, I know it's been good because we've been able to increase our tax valuation, thus giving

the schools more to operate on. Also, an increase in population ensures an adequate school population.

Other respondents also attribute the improvements that have been made in the teaching staffs and in the board of education to the dynamic of change that has been operating in the community at large. A smaller number of respondents, however, object to the overcrowding that prevails in some of the elementary schools, while others use the school situation as a focus of their general discontent. A typical reaction comes from one longtime resident who sends her own children to parochial schools:

> What's been bad about the growth is its effect on our schools. We need schools but are building to extremes. Their encouragement of foreign languages in high school is fine, but in the fourth, fifth, and sixth grades? It's going to cost us taxpayers money.

"New schools are way out of line," remarks an elderly widow, another longtime resident. "There's no point in making them so luxurious."

In general, the reaction to the school situation is characteristic of the two contrasting views of the recent growth and development of the community itself. On the one hand, there is widespread approval of the addition and modernization of facilities, which have created, in the words of one longterm resident, "a metropolitan atmosphere." Some respondents point to the upgrading and diversification of the shopping facilities, which they believe to be now on a par with those of Lake City. Others are pleased by the increase in cultural activities or by the expansion of social services that has followed in the wake of the town's growth and suburbanization. This point of view is perhaps best summed up by an enlightened and civic-minded clubwoman, who has resided in the town for thirty-six years:

> I liked Lakeville when it was small, but yet every place has to expand. The town has improved in the right direction. . . . We have better schools, hospitals; we also have a family service, which is for family problems, and a good psychiatrist for mental problems.

On the other hand, there are a large number of respondents who are more conscious of the negative aspects of the population growth and the disadvantages of expansion. They tend to believe, in the words of a housewife who is disturbed by the new subdivisions, that "the growth is too rapid. It affects roads, sewerage. If the growth weren't so rapid, we could absorb the changes more gracefully." Though the population boom had subsided by the middle 1950's, the feeling persists that the town is still holding a tiger by the tail, that "it can't keep up with the growth at its present rate." A lifetime resident who is married to a successful commercial artist declares that:

> The community was more country style when it was small. Now it's a monster. They put curbing in and caused the town to become ugly. Gas lines are put in without proper refurnishings of sidewalks. The town is overcrowded. There is no good planning. They are insensitive to beauty.

Such critics of the new Lakeville are likely to feel surrounded and impinged upon by the increased numbers of residents. Habituated as many of them are to the leisurely ways of the former community, they are particularly sensitive to the new traffic problems and to congestion in the stores. In tone as well as content, the following response from an elderly resident living in one of the newly built-up neighborhoods is typical of this form of reaction:

> It's changed so much with all these people moving in. They drive down the street and it's as if you don't even exist. It's the same way in the stores. You get pushed around. You're not used to it. You feel you can't take it. You try to be polite and considerate but they aren't.

As with the pressure on facilities, so is it with the pressure on Lakeville's real estate. In fact, the threat of a polyglot, crowded mass community, foreshadowed by the new housing in the eastern section, is the leading source of apprehension about the evolving physical character of the town. The Gentile newcomers to Lakeville appear to be as concerned about this phase of growth as the longtime residents. A homeowner in a newly developed area remarks: "It's bad that poorer land areas are being developed. It means more homes on a small lot." "I don't like built-up suburbs," says the wife of a federal government official. A third newcomer, a middle-aged businesswoman, sums up this type of reaction with the terse statement: "I wish they hadn't sold those lots around me and put up such strange architecture."

There is little contrast or ambivalence among the recent and longtime Gentile respondents in assessing the economics of Lakeville's growth. Many of them are troubled by its costs and are particularly concerned about the steadily rising tax rate. Some attribute the strain on their budgets to the objective requirements of community expansion. A salesman in the lower-income bracket observes that "for the city, growth could be good; for me, personally, it is not so good. Taxes are rising for schools, sewers, bridges. The city is growing too fast." Others attribute the high taxes to the special demands and tastes of the newcomers in educational and other community services. Though a relative newcomer herself, the wife of a wealthy executive bitterly complains, "Taxes have probably doubled with the influence of people from [Lake City]. They vote for everything that's presented to them." Here and there one finds a respondent such as the police official previously quoted, who speaks of the rise in taxes in more disinterested and favorable terms:

> The increase in population has resulted in an increase of income. It has increased the economic activities in the city and the valuation of the city's property, thereby permitting an increased tax revenue which has made possible increased and improved public works.

However, more respondents are inclined to consult their tax bills than to take the long view.

On the whole, the reactions to these three types of change do not vary appreciably between the short- and the long-term residents. Both groups tend to favor the administrative reforms, to have mixed feelings about the physical, commercial, and cultural development of the community, and to dislike the high costs and taxes. There is a sharp difference of opinion, however, between these two groups concerning the changing social composition and character of Lakeville.

Not surprisingly, the newcomers tend to believe that the town has benefited from the recent growth. They see themselves as part of a new wave of residents who have stirred the town from its complacency and lethargy and injected fresh energy, consciousness, and purpose into its community life. They point chiefly to their youth and competence as the qualities that have rejuvenated and strengthened civic interest. A successful young executive remarks: "For one thing the growth has brought in young people. As a result you have more political activity. It has made the old Lakevillers more aware of their town." "We have new blood in Lakeville," says a housewife who had just finished disapproving of the physical changes in the town. "Energetic young people. They are more willing to partake in more functions. . . . Older people tend to take things for granted."

Along with the energy of youth, the newcomers also possess the incentive of being the parents of young children, a stimulus which quickly transforms itself into public interest and service. This is particularly true of Lakeville's new generation of citizens, who see themselves—with considerable justification—as an unusually solid and enlightened group. A housewife of twenty-five, married to a civil engineer, develops this point:

> Because of the growth in population there have been new ideas. The city has grown along with the population. It is a generally accepted fact that people of higher income brackets can contribute more to a community. There are more college-educated people, people who aren't afraid to do something new. I'm comparing Lakeville to the place where I grew up. Here new things are being tried in the nursery school; new courses in the high schools. I am most interested in the schools because my children are the most important thing to me right now.

While some of the native residents are quick to acknowledge that the newcomers have "new ideas and work for improvements," in the words of another young housewife, and that they are "forcing issues out into the open that have been ignored," in the words of a telephone company executive, the large majority of this group regret the passing of the sheltered and neighborly community they have lived in and the advent of the new suburbanite whom they hold responsible. "The growth has torn the hell out of the town," reports an outspoken resident devoted to civic works. "It used to be a friendly town. Now people hurry alone. . . . Merchants are eager to take advantage, to commercialize the town. . . . The greedy, grabby people are chasing thinking people out of the community." As a class the new residents, like the merchants, are considered to be out of step with the traditional pace of life in Lakeville, indifferent to its established manners and values, and insensitive to its beauty. Thus, it is not only the number of new residents that has altered the social character of Lakeville but also the alien behavior and values that they have introduced into the community.

Community Change and the Jewish Newcomer

The new residents that most of these critics have in mind are Jews. According to our estimates, some 60 to 70 per cent of the newcomers to Lakeville are Jewish—a powerful new fact in town life that is quickly sensed in the schools, streets, and shops and that is much on the mind of its older inhabitants. Gentile responses to this development were elicited by two sets of questions: (1) "Many of these newcomers have been Jewish. Insofar as you have seen or heard, what are these Jewish newcomers like?" and the probe "Is there anything (else) you particularly like or dislike about them?" and (2) "In what respects are the old Jewish settlers like or different from the [Jewish] newcomers?" A well-educated career woman, active in liberal causes, replies:

> Too many Jews are moving in. It's a social problem. We are getting a flavor of Jews and the flavor of any one group is not good for intellectual and social growth. It leads to in-breeding. It's not truly representative of the American way of life. It's not that they are Jews. I wouldn't care to live in any community where there is a predominant race or religion.

Such responses are fairly common, often couched in a disclaimer of prejudice and a concern with maintaining a balanced religious and ethnic population. Be that as it may, 54 per cent of the longtime Gentile residents, as contrasted with 18 per cent of the more recent ones, are unfavorably disposed to the influx of Jews. Moreover, the longtimer's attitude toward Jews is closely related to the view he takes about the other changes in Lakeville (see Table 3–3).

Not surprisingly, the longtime residents who disapprove of all the changes in the community are the most likely to disapprove of the

TABLE 3–3 GENTILE ATTITUDES TOWARD THE JEWISH NEWCOMER BY ATTITUDES TOWARD COMMUNITY CHANGE

Attitudes of Gentiles toward Jewish newcomer	*General evaluation of community change in recent years*		
	Good Only	Mostly Good or Both Equally	Mostly Bad or Bad Only
Gentiles with 1–10 Years of Residence			
Favorable	68%	51%	54%
Balanced	32	20	15
Unfavorable	0	29	31
	100%	100%	100%
	(22)	(55)	(13)
Gentiles with 11 Years or More of Residence			
Favorable	53%	25%	10%
Balanced	12	20	17
Unfavorable	35	55	73
	100%	100%	100%
	(34)	(67)	(29)

Jewish newcomer. But even those who endorse most of the changes, while retaining some doubts about others, are still inclined to disapprove of him. The only group of longtime residents that contains a majority who are favorably disposed to the Jewish newcomer is the group whose members have no misgivings at all about what has been happening to Lakeville. However, even this majority is small—only slightly over half the members.

Gentile newcomers, on the other hand, are much less inclined to object to the Jewish newcomer. In many cases this is true whether their reaction to community change is favorable or not. Even those who have considerable misgivings about the new Lakeville show a fairly high level of tolerance of the Jewish newcomer—at least as high as that found among the longtimers who accept the community changes. The major shift in attitude occurs among Gentile newcomers who are ambivalent about their Jewish counterparts: those whose feeling about the new community is negative tend to resolve their ambivalence about the Jew in the direction of hostility.

Also, as Table 3–4 indicates, Gentile attitudes toward the different categories of change have quite different correlations with attitudes toward the Jew.

TABLE 3–4 GENTILE REACTIONS TO JEWISH NEWCOMERS AND CHANGE

Per cent who express an unfavorable attitude toward Jewish newcomer among those who assess changes in	Gentile respondents who consider effect on community of specific change as being			
	Good Only		Mixed or Bad	
Physical structure	43%	(80)	42%	(113)
School situation	32%	(54)	43%	(21)
Economic situation	45%	(33)	48%	(44)
Governmental structure	34%	(65)	64%	(36)
Character of community	29%	(42)	62%	(83)

Whether a Gentile likes or dislikes the economic or physical changes in the community does not seem to have much bearing on whether he approves or disapproves of the Jewish newcomer. The reactions toward the school situation show some correlation: those who disapprove of the new building and curricula programs are also more inclined to disapprove of the Jewish newcomer.

Even more striking are the attitudes of those who are concerned with the changes in the governmental structure or in the social character of the community. The Gentiles who are disturbed by these developments are the most disturbed by the presence of the Jewish newcomer, while those who approve of the modernized city government and the more lively and urbanized Lakeville are among the most favorably disposed toward him. This is true for both recent and longtime Gentile residents, though the quantitative level of disapproval of the new Jewish population still remains much lower among the former.

Thus, Gentile reactions to changes in government and community life emerge as the most sensitive barometers of opinion toward the Jewish newcomer. Evidently the respondents who back these changes view him as an important ally and asset. In their individual responses they tend to place him in the vanguard of the newcomers who have brought fresh awareness and energy into the community. A sophisticated young housewife, married to a college teacher, comments as follows:

> Because of the high percentage of Jews in the population, the intellectual level of the community is higher. I think that they are interested in many more cultural things and activities than the average Protestant family. They also promote interest in concert-going. I find that I have a great deal in common intellectually with many Jewish families. They are stimulating; they read a great deal. They feel that it is an important part of their lives; for example, I regularly discuss records, politics, and other intellectual matters with my Jewish neighbor.

The prevailing positive image of the Jewish newcomer is of an intellectually alert and active member of the community. "Most of the Jewish newcomers are young," says a young editor in trade publishing. "Most of them are executives. Many are in advertising. When you get people like this, they are vitally alive." The particular virtues that the Jews are seen to have brought into the community can be inferred from this image. According to a Gentile housewife who grew up in a Jewish neighborhood and is active in PTA work:

> I would say the Jewish newcomers are the ones who come here for the excellent schools. They have the background to want this cultural aspect. . . . They take part in all the recreational plans for children. Jewish people are especially attracted to these things. The rest of us should but don't always. This makes for a good community when people are so interested. They [Jews] help put things through.

Or again, an Army dentist who recently moved to Lakeville remarks, "They hold top executive jobs in the city. They have a tendency to lend weight to the jobs they take on in the community. They have the knowledge and ability to lead. They take a situation and follow it through."

Such are the repeated themes of Gentile approbation, whether the respondent is a longtime resident or a newcomer himself. Otherwise, approval of the new Jew is likely to be a matter of vague generalities to the effect that Jewish neighbors are friendly and well behaved. "If you didn't know that they were Jewish, you would never have guessed it," says a typical respondent. "You know, they are not loud and that sort of thing." That is to say, when Gentile approval is strong and specific, it is likely to be concentrated upon the qualities of the new Jews as a progressive element in the community. On the level of personal intercourse and behavior, Gentile approbation tends to be fairly superficial, vague, and banal—mainly that their Jewish contacts are "nicer" than they expected.

The Unfavorable Image of the Jewish Newcomer

The negative responses to our questions about what the Jewish newcomers are like and what the respondents particularly liked or disliked about them tend to be more frequent, varied, and lengthy than the positive ones. They rarely consist of vague generalities. Rather than being confined mainly to the influence of the new Jewish population on civic life, they cover a range of contexts: community, status, interpersonal, and family. In other words, respondents who don't like the Jewish newcomers tend to disapprove of them for a variety of fairly specific reasons.

In analyzing these responses we found that four "themes" of negative opinion about the new Jews could be classified in one or more of the four contexts of relations—interpersonal, status, community, and family. The themes of Gentile discontent have to do with Jewish behavior in terms of power, manners, money, and group orientation. As Table 3–5 illustrates, the weight of each theme tends to vary with the context; in other words, Jewish power, or aggression, is the most frequent complaint in the areas of interpersonal and community relations; the impropriety of manners is the most frequent complaint about Jewish family life; and the excessive materialism (money) and cliquishness (group orientation) are the most popular objections to the status be-

TABLE 3–5 THEMES AND CONTEXTS OF UNFAVORABLE REFERENCES TO JEWISH NEWCOMER

Theme	Social contexts				
	Interpersonal relations	Status relations	Community	Family	Total who mention theme
Power	*Too aggressive* 40%	Status striving; arrogant 10%	*Dominate the community* 35%	—	64%
Manners	Inconsiderate 25%	Lack of social refinement 15%	Lack respect for tradition 11%	Unmannerly children 15%	50%
Money	Materialistic 7%	*Nouveau riche—Conspicuous consumption* 23%	Support lavish community expenditures 6%	Overindulge children 1%	34%
Group orientation	Unfriendly and prejudiced toward Gentile 22%	*Social cliquishness* 24%	Not integrated into community 4%	—	39%
Total who mention context	63%	57%	46%	15%	100% (137)

havior of the Jews. These contexts and themes provide a relatively clear picture of the range and emphasis of Gentile disapproval as it arises in the various walks of life in Lakeville where the Jewish new-comers are encountered.

Moreover, by connecting the modal themes to their variants in each of the four contexts, we are able to reconstruct the images of the Jewish newcomer as viewed through the eyes of his Gentile critics. First of all, he is an aggressive man who pushes people around; he thinks himself superior, strives constantly for status, and seeks to gain control of the community. "The Jewish newcomers are the same as the rest of the Jews," exclaims an otherwise affable dowager. "Pushers who want to be waited on first and want to be first in everything." An elderly school-teacher who describes a traffic and parking incident with a Jewish woman—a frequent source of tension and hostility among our respond-ents—concludes, "They are very aggressive. That's natural, that's the way they are and nobody can do anything about it. . . . There are some very fine old Jewish people. It's these kikes I don't like." The wife of a local carpenter remarks, "Many Jewish newcomers make you feel that they are better than you and have more than you. They have less some-times but they still like to pretend they do. There is an air about them that gives you this feeling." Overbearing and arrogant, the new breed of Jews in Lakeville "always seem to want to keep up with or surpass the Joneses," says an electrical contractor who claims that most of his customers are Jewish. Moreover, according to the wife of a cement finisher, they appear to want to dominate the Joneses. "They tell you what to do. I lived here all my life and they come and tell me how to run my yard and house. In the city elections four out of five who are running are Jews. They are just trying to run everything." That is to say, Jews in Lakeville's politics correspond to the imperious driver or shopper or property owner. Another contractor, active in the PTA and the Boy Scouts, offers a detailed critique of their quest for and tactics of power:

> Some [Jewish newcomers] have the attitude of pushing themselves to the fore in any situation. They'll express their opinions and use Lake City political tactics in trying to put their ideas across at the village meeting. For example, we had an open council meeting in connection with dedicat-ing the railroad right-of-way for a road. A strong committee formed against it. Lots of the Jews on the committee spoke against it. One man in particular threatened the mayor. He said that if the mayor didn't go along with him there would be an election coming along and the mayor

had better think about that. Although I don't think they are necessarily the only ones who use similar tactics, lots of them got up and ridiculed the way things were said. They didn't state facts or argue the facts; they just ridiculed. We didn't use to have such wild meetings in the town.

Secondly, the Jewish newcomer is seen as crude and inconsiderate in his personal life and relationships. He lacks social grace and tact and, moreover, is indifferent to those community customs and norms that would provide him and his children with more acceptable models of behavior. "The Jewish newcomers are immigrant types," remarks a young housewife who has lived in Lakeville all her life. "I have no prejudice against the old settlers. The newcomers are low-class and they are here for the address and prestige of the town." "I don't like some of the women," complains an elderly bachelor. "Too much make-up and loud talk." "I'm anti-Semitic I guess," declares the wife of a municipal employee whose daughter's boyfriend is Jewish. "Jewish newcomers are a low grade of Jews, the kind that dresses in brief sum-mer dresses." "I think they are rude," observes the wife of a chauffeur. "I think I really notice it in the grocery stores. They bump and push and never apologize." "Jewish newcomers lack good manners and thoughtfulness for others," adds an articulate elderly resident who is active in the League of Women Voters. "Women park over at school two deep and wait and wait until Johnny comes out."

Thirdly, the Jewish newcomer derives his values from a blatant materialism. Having recently acquired his money, he is eager to display it in building and furnishing his home, in spoiling his children, and in promoting lavish and unnecessary expenditures in the community. One housewife who speaks of her "moderately friendly contacts with Jewish newcomers through PTA work" goes on to say that "many of them are of a get-rich-quick type. They don't have the manners of the [Jewish] old-timers and they lack the culture." "Many of the Jewish newcomers have a lot of money," reports a wealthy commercial artist who has lived in Lakeville for five years. "They buy property, build ugly houses. They have no taste and culture and ruin the country by making it look like a city." A working-class woman of fifty-five echoes a popular complaint against the new Jews: "I have heard it said that a lot of them have children and they are the ones raising the taxes for the schools." Or, as a piano teacher who is the wife of a civil engineer puts it: "Jews demand luxuries that we feel are unnecessary for edu-cational purposes. The influx of the wealthy Jew causes schools to become like country clubs. . . . You don't need extra side rooms for children to paste and paint in or for teachers to have as offices."

Finally, the Jewish newcomer is characteristically viewed as defensive and hostile toward Gentiles, clannish and ethnocentric. A widow who baby-sits for Jewish families remarks, "Jewish people have a chip on their shoulder because they feel they have been picked on." "Jews have more prejudice than Gentiles," observes a salesman who reports that many of his business contacts are Jewish. Another longtime resident explains why she knows no Jews socially, though one out of two of the families in her immediate neighborhood is Jewish: "Jewish newcomers don't want to be absorbed. They want to be distinct . . . and people who isolate themselves have different customs and aren't as congenial." Still another critic of Jewish separatism puts the matter as follows: "Some of these newcomers, such as the Old-World Orthodox Jews, maintain their customs and do not assimilate into other groups. I feel they are always Israeli and not American."[1]

The Anxieties of the Gentile Community

However much or little these images of the Jewish newcomer may correspond to reality, they are threatening to many of Lakeville's Gentiles, particularly those who feel that they are being swamped by an unabating tide of Jewish migration. Thus, they fear that their way of life is in danger of being swept away by these aggressive, materialistic, and vulgar newcomers, and they experience great anxiety over what they take to be their declining position of leadership and influence in the community.

THE MINORITY COMPLEX

At present Gentiles still comprise a fairly large majority—approximately 65 per cent—of Lakeville's population. However, the high proportion of Jews among the newcomers has evidently led most of our Gentile respondents to exaggerate the numerical importance of the Jews. As a result, the average Gentile newcomer and oldtimer believe

[1] It is noteworthy that the complaint about the Jew's cliquishness does not usually imply that he withdraws from community affairs. Evidently Gentiles in Lakeville are concerned that there is too much rather than too little involvement of the Jewish newcomer in the community.

that the community has already become more than half Jewish and that the percentage will continue to rise until it is somewhat over 60 per cent by the end of the next decade.

It is also evident that a small number of Lakeville's Gentiles are already developing the psychology of a minority group. First of all, they tend to be worried about being excluded from community activities and personal contacts. For example, a well-educated young woman who has recently moved to Lakeville observes that "most of the Jewish women in this area belong to ORT. I am envious that the Jews get out and meet people right away and I have nothing comparable." Further, they worry that Jewish power and influence will operate against them. An insurance broker who lives in one of the new neighborhoods believes that "there's a problem with a Jewish majority. Jewish people, by and large, look to their own kind in giving jobs, for instance. It's a true class situation. Jewish people are better than others in looking out for their own welfare and that of their own friends." A few respondents are concerned that their children are facing or will have to face problems of exclusion. A junior high school teacher (a Methodist) complains, "My children are excluded from social activity in school and also on the outside. This is because they are in a school where there are mostly Jews."

Others are concerned that their children may be disoriented by Jewish religious and ethnic customs. A young Protestant mother, who is married to a Catholic and is living among Jews for the first time in her life, believes that:

> Problems might arise with religion when you have children going to school. Conflicting ideas in religion might confuse them. It is also easier for them socially if they are all of one kind of religion.

Another frequent complaint is made by the wife of a municipal worker who dropped out of the PTA because "the Jews took over":

> Jews don't celebrate Christmas and my younger daughter is influenced because she is so young. They get off vacations when our kids don't. They are the only religious group that has holidays. That makes a big difference in school.

A newcomer who lives in a predominantly Jewish neighborhood complains that:

> Christmas is not Christmas. There are no wreaths on the doors or [Christmas] trees in our neighborhood. The Jews are so unlike us. Their children

don't believe in Santa Claus or the Easter Bunny, and I have a hard time keeping those things with our children.

Other parents anticipate that problems will increase as their children begin dating classmates, and a few express some anxiety about the threat of intermarriage.

In general, however, the fears of becoming a cultural minority are fairly nebulous, and only one out of ten Gentile respondents holds them.

THE DECLINE OF TRADITIONS

Many more of our Gentile respondents are disturbed by the undue influence of Jews on the traditional character of the community. This fear is most frequently voiced by the longtime Gentile residents; almost two out of three of them express the opinion that Jewish newcomers have shown a greater desire to change the customs and practices of the community rather than to accept them. The Gentile newcomers, on the other hand, tend to be less apprehensive. Approximately three out of five believe that the Jewish newcomers are more inclined to accept than to reject Lakeville's traditions.

The critics of the Jewish influence are particularly disturbed about its impact on the town's religious and political customs. They associate the rise in Jewish population with the declining role of the Christian religion in the schools and in the community. In response to our question, approximately two out of five of our Gentile respondents say that the observance of Christmas and/or Hanukkah in their neighborhood schools has created a problem. For like a number of communities in recent years, Lakeville has been revising the practices of celebrating this holiday in public schools which are attended by a significant number of Jewish children. In the past, carols were sung, Christmas trees were decorated with religious symbols, and *crèches* were built and displayed. Today, Christmas observances in several schools have become less devotional, occasioning a marked amount of bitterness and apprehension. According to a native resident who teaches in a Sunday school:

> If they have a Christmas play having to do with the birth of Jesus, they can't show it or use it. Christmas is now just a tree celebration. They can't have any religious idea. They don't even want Christmas cards. That's happened since my son's been in grade school.

Those who disapprove of the curtailment of devotional observances attribute it to the influx of Jews into the community, and more specifically to the pressure exerted by Jewish parents. An elderly member of the Lutheran church who has lived in Lakeville for three decades comments:

> There are no Christmas plays on the school stage or assembly. Jewish people on the school board put up a motion that all religious significance be cut out of the program.

Conversely, some Gentile respondents are disturbed by the attempt to introduce observances in the schools of the seasonal Jewish holiday Hanukkah. One critic, a well-informed clubwoman active in the League of Women Voters, bases her objections on the separation of church and state:

> At Christmastime there is a group who will not participate in Christmas celebrations but who insist upon their own Orthodox forms of celebration being observed. I think it's wrong to have a division of anything in the public schools. The less religious practices are observed in them the better, as far as I'm concerned.

More commonly, however, Hanukkah observances are objected to as a violation of community custom. A longtime resident married to a deacon of the Presbyterian church believes that

> The Jews have insisted on Hanukkah being celebrated, almost to the exclusion of the Christmas pageant. There was a commotion over that. I feel that since Christmas was the original celebration in Lakeville schools it should not be pushed into the background.

Or in the words of another longtime resident who belongs to the DAR and whose four closest neighbors are now Jews:

> I feel old traditions should be continued. I feel that they [Jews] should fall into our ways instead of us yielding everything to them.

The intrusion of Jewish traditions and holidays into the public schools has raised issues that go beyond the Christmas–Hanukkah dispute. Gentile respondents complain that their children are being overexposed to Judaism. One long-standing resident who teaches at Lakeville High claims that:

> My grandson learns more about Jewish holidays than he does about Christmas. Maybe he gets it on the school grounds or in the classroom. It seems peculiar that teachers should mention specific Jewish holidays in class. I don't think it's right. I don't feel schools should give in to Jews.

More generally, there is a good deal of grumbling about Jewish holiday absences which their own children envy, or about the practice of closing schools on certain holidays. Some of our respondents regard such matters as an inconvenience, but others see a more ominous meaning in them. As one worried resident married to a municipal official reports: "Jews are taking over the stores, businesses. In some ways they have changed the schools. They close down schools during Jewish holidays." Or, as it is explained by a longtime resident who is a lay leader of his Evangelical church: "The Jews want to bombard us with their culture while rejecting ours."

As we have already indicated, the threat to Lakeville's traditional Christmas culture in the public schools is of greater concern to its older than to its newer Gentile residents. Whereas three out of five of the former would retain these customary observances, approximately the same number of the latter would modify them. These more recent Gentile residents, being less steeped in the town's traditions, and perhaps being somewhat better adjusted to the egalitarian and pluralistic spirit that has come into American life in the past decade, are accordingly more likely to suggest a compromise solution to the Christmas–Hanukkah problem: that of celebrating both holidays in the schools.

Opinions among the newcomers who favor this compromise range from relative indifference to an active interest in general religious education. "I don't think that it's a great problem to get excited about," remarks one mother of four school-age children who teaches in a Presbyterian Sunday school. "If I were in a school where a problem came up whether to celebrate Christmas and/or Hanukkah, I'd go along with what everyone had decided. There is a church if you want to sing Christmas songs." Or again, "Christmas is a national holiday in a Christian country, not a religious celebration," declares a Baptist woman, married to a high school administrator. Most of the newcomers who see a problem here, however, believe that plans should be made to celebrate both holidays as religious ones. Some base this compromise on practical considerations. A Catholic salesman who sends his children to parochial school reports he heard that in one public school a Jewish teacher hung a "Happy Hanukkah" sign beneath one that said "Merry Christmas." "Perhaps some people resent this but I didn't," remarks this respondent. "After all, the school itself is 25 per cent Jewish." Others believe that the compromise helps to promote democratic values. "In a new school there are decorations put up in each classroom for the holiday," says a young mother of four children. "The class votes on

which to celebrate. . . . It's very good and educational for the child."
And virtually all this group of newcomers would agree that observing
both holidays promotes religious understanding and tolerance. Speaking
for the compromise, a career woman who has no children candidly
concludes:

> I am not a good person to discuss this problem of Christmas or Hanuk-
> kah with. I'm too liberal. It can be good or bad. It can educate children
> that there are other beliefs than their own. I don't know if it affects the
> children greatly. It might be good for children. Also it might help our
> international relations. There is educational value in learning about people
> other than ourselves.

The other pillar of Lakeville's heritage that is felt to be shaking under
the impact of the Jewish influx is its political traditions. Lakeville has
always been a Republican town—a fact reflected by the political preference of seven out of ten longtime residents. A majority of the Gentile
newcomers are also Republicans. Three out of five Jewish newcomers,
on the other hand, are Democrats.

The fact that Lakeville's days as a solid Republican stronghold appear
to have ended is less disturbing to our Gentile respondents than the
fact that the Jewish newcomers are having a large impact on local
politics. That is to say, control of city affairs is currently passing out
of the hands of the Protestant conservatives. The wife of a landscape
gardener who has lived in Lakeville for almost half a century remarks:

> Jews are councilmen in the city. Whenever they want certain things
> pushed, they are there to fight for them. They wanted to get S——
> property for one massive park. Between Jews and Catholics, Protestants
> don't have a chance.

It is clear, though, that Jewish aggressiveness is felt to be the main
lever of change in Lakeville. A school supervisor makes a typical
complaint:

> I feel the Jews are running for office. They want changes. Jews like to do
> things. They are pushing themselves forward. They have a lot of time
> and have maids.

The most apprehensive of the longtime residents are those of low
and moderate income. Some 36 per cent of the group that earns less
than $10,000 annually and 43 per cent of middle-income earners
($10,000 to $19,999) regard the Jew's political aggressiveness as their
reason for disliking him. In contrast, only 17 per cent of the high-income

longtime residents give this reason. It is clear from their responses that the long-standing residents with modest incomes feel less able than those with high incomes to cope politically with the innovations they associate with Jewish pressure. At the same time, these low- and middle-income citizens feel the pinch of increased taxes and do not believe that they are getting a fair share of the town improvements. A widow who lives on less than $5,000 a year remarks:

> Jewish newcomers have tried to change many traditions in the government and city hall. There is nothing we can do about it. It doesn't do us little people any good to try to change things.

The political resentment of the native is expressed by an elderly woman who reports that most of her friends have moved away:

> They [the Jews] want everything their way about schools. They even have their maids and nurses vote. They raise taxes. They are all running for politics here in Lakeville. I don't like it. I think that when you've lived here a long time you feel like you're being pushed out of things.

"Jews seem to get improvements they want but we don't," says the widow quoted above. "Maybe they are more aggressive. Jews have mail service. We still have rural delivery."

If the high-income Gentile, on the other hand, shows less concern about the political motives and power of the Jewish newcomer, the main reason seems to be that he still finds himself close enough to the center of political power in the community to believe that his interests and values will continue to be represented. "I feel it's up to the Gentile to speak up when the Jew steps on his toes," says a longtime resident whose husband owns a thriving supermarket. Their security also enables this group to be somewhat more objective and circumspect about the Jewish role in the community. In quantitative terms, 46 per cent of the high-income longtime residents tend to discount the claim that the Jewish newcomers are actively working to transform Lakeville, while 66 per cent of their low- and middle-income counterparts tend to endorse it. A more or less typical response of the former group is that of a successful salesman active in local politics.

> I don't think they have sought to make changes. The changes have been brought about merely because of the influx of the Jews into Lakeville. It is inevitable. If it becomes unacceptable to me, I'll just move.

It is worth noting that among the Gentile newcomers, 56 per cent of those who earn $20,000 or more annually are apprehensive about

Jewish influence in the changing community, while only 45 per cent of those who earn less than this figure evidence similar concern. The probable reason for this difference is that the members of the latter group tend to be younger, more sympathetic to programs of social growth, reform, and community readjustment, and more inclined to identify the goals and influence of the Jewish newcomer with their own.

THE JEWISH NEWCOMER AND CLASS TRADITIONS

If Lakeville has been traditionally Protestant and Republican, it has also been a community whose social manners and standards of prestige have been set by an affluent class. Since many of the Jewish newcomers aspire to belong to this class and have enough money to do so, their social behavior enters significantly into the Gentile appraisal of their effect on the community. Indeed, the focal point of Gentile distress appears to be the image of the Jewish newcomers as a group of vulgar, *nouveau riche* social climbers, and hence a threat to community conventions of taste, decorum, and propriety, rather than as an anti-Christian bloc or as an aggressive faction of liberal reformers. In fact, once we control for income and length of residence, no other Jewish mode of behavior comes in for more criticism generally than does the pursuit of upper-class status.

As might be expected, the longtime wealthy residents are the most observant and disapproving of the status claims of the Jewish newcomers. At the same time, however, they and the wealthy newcomers are the least threatened by such claims. In order to analyze the Gentile image of the *nouveau riche* Jew, we isolated the three leading themes of criticism—status striving and claims, lack of refinement, and conspicuous consumption—and then computed the percentage of the respondents who mention one or more of these themes in their criticism (see Table 3–6).

Since none of the members of the wealthy Gentile elite of the community mentions the Jewish newcomer's pursuit of status, we can presume that however much they object to his lack of refinement and his display of wealth, they are not concerned that he may undermine the established social manners and hierarchy in the community. In general, the attitude of the Gentile elite seems to be that it is natural enough for the more successful Jews to want to move up socially, but that they have not yet learned how to behave properly. This attitude may be colored by affable condescension, as with one woman, the cultivated

TABLE 3–6 STATUS CRITICISMS OF JEWISH NEWCOMER BY LENGTH OF RESIDENCE AND INCOME AMONG GENTILES

Among those who criticize status behavior of Jewish newcomer	*Gentile respondents Length of residence*			
	10 YEARS OR LESS		11 YEARS OR MORE	
	LEVEL OF INCOME		LEVEL OF INCOME	
	Less Than $20,000	$20,000 and Over	Less Than $20,000	$20,000 and Over
Per cent who mention Status striving and claims	13%	0%	29%	0%
Lack of refinement	17%	50%	21%	44%
Conspicuous consumption	39%	33%	42%	44%
	(23)	(6)	(38)	(9)

wife of a publisher, who dismisses the objection to Jewish wealth as mere envy: "They are very nice little people just like the others. They are friendly and want to be part of the town." As this respondent immediately adds, though, "I don't like some of the women. They wear too much make-up and talk too loud." Other Gentiles of this class are more overtly impatient with the social behavior of the new Jew. A wealthy longtime resident who holds strong religious convictions about human equality relates that:

> A Jew moved into our neighborhood and built a house and had noisy parties. They are noisy. They don't know how to live. They are not used to living in close proximity to a Gentile area. They don't know how to adapt themselves.

However, the responses of the wealthy Gentile natives seldom exhibit the anxiety of those who feel their own social customs and status are being threatened by the Jewish newcomers. Moreover, they remain conscious of their option if worse comes to worst: they can follow many of their former neighbors to the nearby elite communities where Jews have not been able to enter in any numbers. Some of the less affluent and prestigious Gentiles of Lakeville, on the other hand, do apparently feel threatened by the social behavior of the new Jews. This is evident from their concern with the Jewish pursuit of status, particularly by means of a conspicuously expensive life style. Middle-income Gentiles are understandably prone to this reaction. One lifetime resident, an engineer who lives in a relatively unfashionable neighborhood, believes that "most of the Jewish newcomers are very fine, but the bad part about them is that they are pushing their money around." Along with their fear that the lavish expenditures on homes, cars, clothes, swimming pools, and other prestigious items will increase the importance of money as a determinant of status, the middle-income Gentile critic of the *nouveau riche* Jew is also more sensitive to signs of Jewish arrogance and snobbery. "I would say that the Jewish newcomers strike me as social climbers," reports one member of the group, trying to sort out her ambivalent reactions to the new Jewish neighbors who now outnumber the Gentile ones in her area. "They definitely have a feeling of superiority."

CHILD REARING AND THE NEWCOMERS

The status and value anxieties of the Gentile respondent tend to be fairly unfocused and unspecific in relation to his own place in the community. This is not true, however, in the responses that refer to his children. By and large, he views his children rather than himself as bearing the brunt of the problems created by a rising Jewish population. Thus 65 per cent of the respondents who believe that the Jewish influx has created or will create a personal problem for themselves or their families report that the problem affects only their children; 11 per cent say that it affects their children and themselves; and 24 per cent say that it affects only themselves. As we have noted, a small minority of Gentiles regard themselves and their children as a minority and have begun to develop its characteristic mentality. The majority of Gentile parents do not feel that their children are being engulfed by Jews, but many do believe that exposure to the social behavior and values of their Jewish classmates and playmates may have an adverse effect on them.

Of the one out of two who expresses an opinion on the matter, 58 per cent of the newcomers and 67 per cent of the longtime residents disapprove of Jewish practices of child rearing. Moreover, their responses are weighted and pointed by specific examples of their objections and frequently by an emotional tone that reveals a serious preoccupation with the problem.

The major complaint is that Jewish parents give their children far too much freedom and far too little discipline. As young children they are allowed to do as they please, and consequently their behavior is ill-mannered, hectic, and highly obstreperous. A wealthy local merchant with an otherwise affable manner speaks for a good many of our respondents in the following complaint:

> The Jewish parents believe in letting their children do more or less as they please. They let them run wild in the store without reprimanding them. They don't care how much trouble they cause, they don't punish them enough. Children run up and down aisles knocking down merchandise.

A young housewife who is living among Jews for the first time observes that "the few Jewish children I've met are kings and queens of their house." A Catholic who recently moved to Lakeville makes this criticism: "I don't think that Jewish children are being prepared for life in a heterogeneous community. They are taught that they are the 'chosen people' and not disciplined, and they're always Mama's angel."

Such behavior, according to our respondents, continues into adolescence: Jewish teenagers are notable for their arrogance, ostentation, and sexual precociousness. According to a merchandising specialist, most of whose business contacts are with Jews, "Jewish children sass their parents and parents pass this off as a gesture of individualism. In other words, 'How can he become a merchant prince if he knuckles down to me all the time?'" Another respondent who finds that the Jewish children "run wild" remarks that "they make the standard of clothes and cars in high school ridiculous." "I have a friend who works at the high school," remarks a young wife who is studying for a graduate degree in education. "She feels that the Jewish children are very spoiled, have everything they could possibly want [including] their own way, and are difficult to handle." A particular source of grievance is the Jewish girls. "A twelve-year-old Jewish girl wears lipstick and high heels and stockings, while a twelve-year-old Catholic neighbor's child doesn't," observes a former nurse who has four young children. Another respondent, one of the pillars of Lakeville society, deplores the fact that "Jewish girls start going out with boys in the sixth and seventh grades, and parents encourage this with boy and girl parties and kissing games."

The second major ground of criticism is that Jewish parents inculcate their children with grossly material values. Young Jewish children in Lakeville are almost invariably believed to be spoiled by an overly generous allowance and an unlimited supply of playthings, indulgences which in turn engender a false sense of superiority. A young divorcée who works as a magazine illustrator speaks for many of her fellow townsmen in suggesting that Jewish parents

> . . . raise their children to feel superior to Gentile children either materially or else purely defensively. . . . For example, my gun is better than yours. My house is better. They try to give security to their children by this sort of thing, but it's really a fake security.

The complaints on this score proliferate. The Jewish child who receives a dollar allowance at the age of five; the Jewish teenagers who drive their own Thunderbirds, have their own private telephones, give lavish parties, are waited on hand and foot by servants, and judge their Gentile peers accordingly. Meanwhile, the children of our respondents are made unhappy or else have their own values distorted by the Jewish example. As a well-informed businessman who has lived in Lakeville all his life sums up the matter:

> There is a heightened sense of competition within the schools. It's more bad than good. It's competition directed toward the material ends rather than toward education for education's sake. Competition shows itself again in possession of the material things. It creates competition with a distorted sense of values. My daughter came home from a Jewish home and asked why we didn't have seven telephones.

In short, the image of the Jewish child—aggressive, unrefined, hedonistic, and materialistic—is a mirror image of the adult Jewish newcomer. Whatever may be the accuracy of this appraisal of the younger generation of Lakeville's new Jews, it clearly represents a more distinct threat to normative Gentile values in the community than the behavior of the Jewish adults does. Gentile respondents believe that their children are the most vulnerable to "Jewish" manners and values because they are so directly exposed to them at school and because they are the least able to withstand their seductive influence. They also show an anxiety that the disciplined, austere, and responsible way of life which they believe themselves to be inculcating in their children may possibly be vitiated by the changing ethos of Lakeville, which they tend to attribute to the Jewish newcomers.

The ethos of the contemporary American suburb, particularly of its adolescent culture, has been studied and deplored from every conceivable angle in recent years. It is worth noting that objections entered against Lakeville's Jewish newcomers, old and young, are similar to the more general critique of manners and mores in our rapidly changing suburbs. This critique invariably turns upon the dissolution of traditional moral and social values and the emergence of an avid and indulgent ethic that places great emphasis on material possessions, social mobility, and shallowly sophisticated conduct. In other words, the question can be fairly raised whether a certain amount of Gentile anxiety in Lakeville about the influence of the new Jews on his children may not be displaced, and whether the image of the Gentile child—beckoned to give up his sturdy Protestant ethic by the false gods of status seeking, conspicuous consumption, irresponsible license, and the rest—may not reflect, in part, his parents' situation in a rapidly evolving urban society.

4

THE INFLUX OF JEWS AND
THE LONGTIME
JEWISH RESIDENTS

As we noted in Chapter 1, Lakeville had for many years a small Jewish population that was relatively isolated and inconspicuous to the Gentile community. At the time of our study, 19 per cent of Lakeville's Jews had lived there for eleven years or more. Most of them belonged to the prewar community, and some to the original Jewish families that had summered in Lakeville early in the century. Many of the longtime Jewish residents regard themselves as native Lakevillers and choose to identify with the older Gentile residents rather than with the Jewish newcomers. For example, while 59 per cent of the Jewish newcomers believe that they have been a benefit to Lakeville, only 31 per cent of the longtime Jewish residents agree with them, and 40 per cent believe their effect has been noticeably harmful.

The Effect of the Newcomer on Lakeville

In analyzing the attitudes of the established Jews of Lakeville toward the newcomers, it is best to begin with the broadest areas of objection: the size of the influx. Thirty-seven per cent of the critics object to the population growth as such and not merely to its Jewish element, a fact which they are often careful to make clear. An elderly architect who has lived in Lakeville for twenty-eight years quietly remarks, "The influx of Jews has helped to change the nature of the community. Any large influx of any group would cause this. I would be the last person to blame it on the Jews." And he goes on to say of the newcomers, "This is life. They are merely seeking for themselves and their children the qualities I desired when I first came here."

As one might expect, the longtime Jewish residents who deplore the influx of newcomers do so on the grounds that Lakeville is losing its traditional sedate character and rural flavor and becoming too large, crowded, urbanized, overtaxed, and so forth. "I hate to say this, but we love to live in the country, but this is not the country," remarks the wife of an insurance executive who is visibly troubled by her resentment of the newcomers. "We love to have ten or fifteen in classes for our children; now there are seventy." According to another woman who plays an active role in her temple, while admitting that she is "anti-Semitic": "The neighborhood's gotten less friendly. Maybe I'd feel this way if any people moved in. It has turned from a small town into a large city. I never locked my doors before." And as elsewhere in Lakeville, there are the complaints of inadequate facilities and services, hasty construction, high taxes, and the other stresses and strains of rapid growth. As a wealthy manufacturer sums up this attitude: "It has nothing to do with the fact that the newcomers are Jews but that as people they have contributed to the growing pains of the community."

On the other hand, three out of four of the longtime Jewish residents who object to the Jewish newcomer do so either partly or wholly on the ground that he is Jewish. The most widespread concern is that the population balance between Jew and Gentile is being seriously upset. In the words of an elderly widow who has been active in many non-sectarian organizations in the community: "There is not enough of other people in Lakeville now. I do feel a healthier percentage of all kinds—Jew and Gentile—is important. This is also true on boards and clubs. There should be a good percentage." Some of our longtime Jewish residents, in fact, seem no less apprehensive than their Gentile counterparts that the Jewish influx is already getting out of hand and creating a preponderant and predominant majority group. A woman of sixty who has lived most of her life in Gentile communities remarks: "It's not good for any community to be taken over by one religion. I don't think it's good for children to grow up with all Jews." "There are too many Jews here," says a wealthy resident who has considered moving away because her neighborhood has become predominantly Jewish. "They ought to go to another community where there are fewer Jews. When a community becomes 100 per cent Jewish, it's not good for anyone, for children, or for people who live there."

This response is an extreme one. Most of our Jewish respondents who have lived in Lakeville for eleven years or more do not believe that the community is becoming overwhelmingly Jewish. When asked to estimate the percentage of Jews in the present population and to predict that of the coming decade, they produce an *average* figure of 47 per cent and 67 per cent respectively; the average estimate of their Gentile counterparts is 52 per cent and 64 per cent respectively. (The actual percentage of Jews in the present population is approximately 35 per cent.) Most of these Jewish respondents, however, do see a trend toward increasing Jewish proportions, are worried by it, and tend to evaluate the effect in Lakeville of the Jewish influx in terms of its estimated extent. Indeed, there is a strong correlation between speculations about the size of the Jewish population and attitudes toward the Jewish newcomer (see Table 4–1).

TABLE 4–1   Jewish Oldtimers' Response to the Influx of Jews by Their Estimates of the Jewish Population

Per cent of longtime Jewish residents who say that the Jewish influx has been:	Oldtimers' estimates of the present percentage of the Jewish population			
	Less Than 30%	30–49%	50–69%	70% and Over
Harmful to Lakeville	9%	38%	50%	72%
Beneficial for Lakeville	46	29	27	14
Both equally	18	18	19	14
Neither	27	15	4	0
	100%	100%	100%	100%
	(11)	(34)	(26)	(7)

The term that frequently occurs in the response of the established Jewish group is "ghetto"—a word that carries a heavy charge of anxiety. A more or less typical instance of this response comes from a young insurance salesman who has lived in Lakeville all his life:

[The Jewish influx] is harmful only to the extent that the great increase has labeled us, as it will, a Jewish town. I wouldn't like to see that happen. It conjures up in my mind the idea of a "ghetto" and I react against it. I don't know why.

Not all the settled Jews, of course, look upon the newcomers with skeptical or apprehensive eyes. As we have already noted, 31 per cent of this group regards the overall effect of the newcomers as beneficial. Some respondents, for example, believe that the physical character of the town has been enhanced by the new Jewish residents rather than altered and disfigured. A wealthy clothing manufacturer who has lived in Lakeville for twelve years and identifies strongly with the town believes that the newcomers "take better care of their homes than anyone else. A certain type of Jew moves out to the suburbs. They desire their own homes. In the old days you owned an apartment with an income." "A lot of areas have been made beautifully residential that we thought couldn't ever be that pretty," says the wife of a real estate lawyer who takes particular pride in her own gardening. Another respondent who has lived in Lakeville for nearly twenty years and has worked hard to improve his own property believes that the "large influx shows that Jews can live in harmony at least on the surface with non-Jewish neighbors to make the area more beautiful."

Other longtime residents point to the fact that the new Jewish residents have raised property values throughout the community. Moreover, they have injected new energy into Lakeville's economy, a fact which tells in their favor with a fourth-generation German-Jewish resident who otherwise deplores the influx because his neighborhood has become overpopulated with Jews "who have only materialistic values." An elderly salesman who has lived in the town for eighteen years notes that "the newcomers tend to spend more money, live higher, trade higher." The same respondent goes on to observe that the newcomers are also more interested in spending money on the social and cultural welfare of the community.

This point is frequently made by the settled residents who have a positive or relatively balanced attitude toward the newcomers. "Just as Jews take real pride in their homes," says a middle-aged businessman who has lived in Lakeville all his life, "so they will back all civic improvements to the hilt. They will raise money for schools because it is good for children, and [they] won't gripe like the Gentile." This respondent also believes that the "Gentiles still look at Lakeville as a little village. I like the newcomers better. They like progress." Another respondent, who has lived in the town for thirty-four years and belongs to one of the most distinguished and civic-minded of the Jewish families in the area, identifies most of the recent improvements in Lakeville— "better schools, the city manager system, and so forth"—with the influx of Jewish voters. Several other longtime residents are pleased by the broader political changes that have transformed Lakeville from a Republican and conservative stronghold into a more liberal, two-party community. Finally, the positive responses of the older Jewish residents center upon the increased resources and improved leadership that have accrued to the Jewish community itself and strengthened its religious as well as social life.

The Character of the Jewish Newcomer

As analysis of the negative responses of the established Jews shows, their composite image of the Jewish newcomer is strikingly similar to that of the Gentile community, particularly that of the longtime Gentile residents. Though the objections of the established Jews are often uneasy rather than hostile, the themes of criticism are nonetheless the same as those of our Gentile respondents in Chapter 3. "I am forced to say that it is slightly possible that some harmful effects have come about," says a serious, well-informed housewife who is active in Jewish as well as non-sectarian organizations. Appraising the new Jewish population in Lakeville, she goes on to say, "I am dismayed at seeing lots of Jewish names, and also the kind of Jews—the *nouveau riche,* the ostentatious, the materialistic, and the overly Jewish."

Such a response sums up much of the prevailing opinion among the settled Jews of Lakeville concerning the new breed that has come into their midst. Over half consider them to be a serious problem. Like their Gentile counterparts, these critics view the Jewish newcomer as seriously lacking in propriety, as unduly concerned with material wealth and possessions, as capable of misusing power, and finally as stand-offish and ethnocentric. When asked to describe in detail the "kinds of Jews [that] pose a serious problem for the Jewish community in Lakeville," one out of two of the critical longtime residents mentions those whose behavior is socially improper, while approximately one out of three mentions the materialistic, the power-oriented, or the un-assimilated Jew.

In ranking the frequency of these themes, we find a great deal of similarity between the responses of the longtime Jewish residents and those of the Gentile community at large. For example, longtime residents of both groups who have high incomes tend to object most often to the Jewish newcomer's lack of manners. The only significant difference in the two groups is that Gentiles tend to attach somewhat greater weight to the Jewish newcomer's use and abuse of power, though again this objection is more prevalent among the lower-income rather than the higher-income members of both groups.

If anything, Jewish criticisms of the newcomers' impropriety tend to be more detailed and specific than the criticisms on this score made by Gentiles. "One Saturday I went into the delicatessen," says a woman who belongs to one of the oldest and most aristocratic Jewish families in Lakeville. "I was floored by the people there: their costumes, their accents, their grammar, the yelling of the fishwives for this and that. Also I don't like what I see at the beauty shop. Did you ever see them in those shorts?" "Nonconformist" dress seems to be a major source of complaint, particularly sports clothes that are too blatantly expensive or scanty. "I'm disturbed by those who wear gold leather jackets, gold jeweled sandals," reports the wife of a psychiatrist. "This is the sort of thing you'd expect to find in Miami Beach, which is not what Lakeville has been like." Another longtime Jewish resident, who would prefer his neighborhood to be 100 per cent non-Jewish, speaks of the "loud-mouthed noncomformists" (these two traits are frequently tied together in our respondents' replies) who "feel that because they are living in the suburbs they don't have to care about their appearance. Women who weigh 300 pounds come in stores in bras and shorts and with painted toenails." In a somewhat more charitable tone, a cultivated woman living in a neighborhood that has become predominantly Jewish ascribes the peculiar dress of the newcomers to their being "overanxious to be casual and countrified," but she still views this group as one whose behavior is more appropriate to Miami Beach than to Lakeville.

Somewhat less common are the objections and apprehensions about the values, aggressions, and ethnocentricities of the new Jews. Though these are also taken as signs of nonconformity, they are somewhat less immediately visible and presumably do not weigh quite as heavily on the minds of the established and accepted group. Again, the comments of these respondents often resemble in content and tone the objections of the Gentile critics of the new Jews. For example, a middle-aged woman active in community affairs complains of the spoiled Jewish children in terms that might very well have appeared in our previous chapter on Gentile opinions:

> The Jewish newcomers have harmed the future young people in Lakeville. When my children went to school they used to work summers and buy a jalopy. Today children have Cadillacs. It hurts them and makes them materialistic and distorts their sense of values. Just take a look at the parking lot of Lakeville High.

Similarly, there are the typical observations on the aggressiveness of the newcomers, "who demand a lot of things when they have no right to demand them"—a remark which comes from a successful physician who has little use for the old German-Jewish elite circles and, except for this criticism, sympathizes with the hard-working, ambitious newcomers. Antipathy to Jewish behavior in such matters as the traditional celebration of Christmas in the schools is by no means confined to Lakeville's Gentile population. A Jewish saleswoman who has lived in Lakeville for two decades remarks:

> The Jews move in and try to take over. One example is the way they try to have the Christmas carols removed from the schools. After all, there has been Christmas carol singing in the Lakeville schools for a lot more years than the Jews have been living here. A Jew should not move in and suddenly demand that the old customs be dropped and the new ones be put in to suit him.

Or again, there is the annoyance of the longtime residents over the political behavior of the "Jewish" faction, which can be resented as keenly by a Jew as by a Gentile. A young mother who grew up in Lakeville after her family had fled from Nazi Germany finds that:

> The pushy kind causes the biggest trouble. They want to take over right away. When the PTA was formed out here, everyone wanted to say something. Generally, people are elected for office, but here each person got up and gave credentials about themselves and asked you to vote for them. They told you what college they came from, their degrees, and how capable they were. A Gentile told us he was asked to run but when these big loudmouths got up and spoke for themselves he backed out.

And, finally, there are the settled and highly integrationist Jews of Lakeville who express concern about "the Orthodox Jews with great orientation toward Israel," in the words of a wealthy industrialist who contributes heavily to Jewish causes. Or more generally, they criticize the Jewish newcomers "whose orientation is entirely Jewish," in the words of a chemist who is active in the American Council for Judaism. He complains, "They put Jewish causes before Lakeville causes, even separate their children from the community."

The Anxieties of the Established Jewish Resident

In the eyes of these critics, the undesirable newcomers do not threaten the Jewish community as such but rather its relations with the Gentile community. Only 21 per cent of those who allude to these effects are worried that the newcomers may seriously disturb existing relations among Jews, while 79 per cent believe that they may damage the existing relations between Jews and Gentiles. By their "loud and flashy" dress and deportment, their "arrogant display of possessions," their overly sensitive and pugnacious natures, their tendencies toward "self-segregation," the Jewish newcomers are felt to arouse the disdain, envy, or hostility, as the case may be, of Lakeville's Gentiles. The net result, according to a member of the local school board, is to "encourage a split in the community that was once well-integrated interdenominationally at the high school level," or more generally, according to an active clubwoman, "turn a small, friendly community into a larger divided group." And not very far back in the minds of some of our established Jewish respondents is the fear, in the words of a lawyer who has worked hard for thirty years in Lakeville to improve Jewish-Gentile relations, that "these kinds of Jews may arouse anti-Semitism and it could blow wide open."

Such threats are by no means remote to a majority of the longtime Jewish residents. Some 61 per cent believe that the attitudes of "most Gentiles to the Jews in Lakeville" are now unfavorable; only 19 per cent believe they are favorable, while the rest believe they are neither one nor the other. Their dismay at this new state of affairs is reinforced by the fear that their own record of adjustment to Gentile norms counts for little. They have little faith that the average Gentile distinguishes between acceptable and unacceptable Jews, the settled community or the new one. Speaking of the newcomers, the wife of a stockbroker, who claims to have trouble only with her Jewish neighbors, believes that when "non-Jewish neighbors judge them, they judge us all." This may be due to "the natural tendency toward anti-Semitism which exists among Gentiles," according to a merchandising executive who conducts his business life largely among Gentiles, or simply to the force with which the blatant aggressiveness, impropriety, and clannishness of the new-comers evokes traditional stereotypes. These, in turn, obscure any positive image that may have been created and "distort the picture of the Jews," as a young woman who grew up in Lakeville and was educated at Pembroke remarks. Once the Gentile community begins "to lose respect for this kind of Jewish newcomer," the continuing heavy influx of such Jews serves to extend and exacerbate ill-will until finally "the entire community will feel all Jews are this way."

The Gentile Image of the Established Jews

While it is not surprising, then, that the established group of Jewish residents in Lakeville believe their hard-earned status and security is being compromised and threatened, their own picture of Gentile attitudes appears to be considerably more distorted than is the prevalent Gentile picture of them. The truth is that many Gentiles in Lakeville do distinguish between the older group of Jews and the newcomers. Moreover, the longer they have lived in Lakeville the more inclined they are to make this distinction (see Table 4–2).

TABLE 4–2 GENTILE DIFFERENTIATION OF JEWS BY LENGTH OF RESIDENCE

Do Jewish people who have lived in Lakeville a long time seem to be like the Jewish new-comers	*Gentile respondents Length of residence*		
	5 Years or Less	6–10 Years	11 Years or More
In most respects?	46%	28%	18%
In some respects?	34	25	29
In virtually no respects?	20	47	53
	100%	100%	100%
	(35)	(28)	(103)

Furthermore, such distinctions are almost invariably made in favor of the established Jewish group. Indeed, Gentile respect for its qualities is such that it functions as the norm of Jewish acceptability. In other words, a favorable image of the Jewish newcomer is usually related to

his degree of similarity to the longtime Jewish resident, while an unfavorable image of him is almost invariably related to his degree of
dissimilarity to the longtime Jewish resident (see Table 4–3).

TABLE 4–3 GENTILE ATTITUDES TOWARD AND
DIFFERENTIATION OF JEWISH
RESIDENTS

	Gentile respondents who say Jewish oldtimers are like the Jewish newcomers		
	In Most Respects	In Some Respects	In No Respects
Per cent whose attitude toward Jewish newcomer is			
Favorable	72%	35%	3%
Neutral or balanced	16	29	12
Unfavorable	12	36	85
	100%	100%	100%
	(43)	(49)	(74)
Per cent whose attitude toward Jewish oldtimer is			
Favorable	73%	74%	94%
Neutral or balanced	16	20	3
Unfavorable	11	6	3
	100%	100%	100%
	(37)	(49)	(73)

As we might expect from our survey of Gentile attitudes toward the
Jewish newcomer in Chapter 3, the positive group image of Lakeville's
Jews turns upon their being of "the better class of Jew," usually with
respect to their education and income. And, again as in Chapter 3, the
Gentiles who approve of Jews—whether they are of the older or newer
group—tend to value highly their progressiveness and zeal in community affairs. By and large, the profile of individual responses is
virtually the same.

A Gentile who distinguishes between the older and newer Jews of
Lakeville is likely to have a fully elaborated and favorable image of the
former, along with the highly reductive and negative image of the latter
which we described in Chapter 3. The chief ground of contrast is in the
context of class behavior and status, just as the most frequent theme of

opinion is the propriety of the longtime Jewish residents. In order to analyze Gentile responses to this group, we have made use of the same four contexts and themes which were employed in Table 3–5 to analyze the responses to the Jewish newcomer. The results appear in Table 4–4.

In the eyes of these Gentile respondents, it is now taken for granted that virtually all the members of the older group belong to the established social and economic elite of Lakeville. "The old settlers are people of means and background," says an articulate reading therapist who has been living in Lakeville for five years. "The newcomers just came up the ladder from a furnished room. Their attitudes differ." According to a longtime resident, the wife of a local grocer who has recently moved into a neighborhood where there are a number of Jewish newcomers, "There is a difference between the two. It's one of class. [The new Jew] doesn't have as much money," which explains why he is objectionably forward and bold. "Newcomers want more for their money. They are out to get all that they can." Or again, in the words of a drugstore owner who grew up in Lakeville and has "many friendly contacts with Jewish merchants," "the longtime residents are the money people and they are wonderful."

It is not the older Jews' wealth that is decisive to most of these Gentile respondents, however; it is their background of established wealth. Explaining why "Jewish longtimers don't get along with the incoming Jew," a salesman married to a native Lakeville woman says that "the Jews have had money for a long time, and newcomers have just made theirs and think they are big shots." An advertising man who lives in a low-prestige area and is himself a newcomer to Lakeville puts it this way: "The older Jew comes from a wealthy, well-established family. New ones are a class or so below the older ones. The new Jew is about the same class as we are."

In general, Gentile responses tend to gravitate toward two polar images. In direct opposition to the crude, aggressive, *nouveau riche,* ethnocentric newcomers, recently arrived from the ghetto, the longtime resident is imagined to be an aristocratic figure. He is seen as belonging to one of the elite Jewish families in town that have earned the respect of the community over the years by their unostentatious wealth, culture, and refinement and by their fastidious deference to the Christian customs and mores of Lakeville. Thus, speaking of the longtime residents in general, a Gentile newcomer who sees a good many Jews in her social activities quickly associates them with this elite segment. "We have some of the finest old Jewish families here," she says. "They won't

TABLE 4-4 THEMES AND CONTEXTS OF FAVORABLE GENTILE REFERENCES TO JEWISH OLDTIMERS

Theme	Status relations	Interpersonal relations	Community	Family	Total who mention theme
	Social contexts				
Manners	*Refined, high social status* 52%	Considerate of others 12%	Respects traditions 5%	Family-minded; trains children to be considerate 6%	63%
Money	*Established wealth; simple style of life* 42%	Not material-istic; generous 9%	—	Doesn't over-indulge children; cares for home and property 2%	50%
Power	Treats people as equals 20%	Not aggressive 19%	Not power hungry; accepts status quo 8%	—	40%
Group orientation	Not clannish; mixes with Gentiles 16%	Not prejudiced against Gentiles 6% More acculturated and accepting of Gentile values 20%	Integrated in community; civic-minded 9%	—	41%
Total who mention context	78%	47%	19%	8%	100% (132)

have anything to do with these newcomers, you can bet." "The old Jewish settlers . . . seem to be more refined," says a longtime resident, whose deceased husband refused to associate with Jews. "Probably it's the names. You know that their families are so respected that you just sort of feel that way. I really didn't come into contact with them, just knew that they were here." And in the eyes of a sophisticated club-woman who has herself lived in Lakeville for thirty-three years, "the Jewish oldtimers are all people of many generations and of background . . . a great addition to any community. I personally couldn't get along without them. They make every possible effort to make their community a better place to live."

As a result of this identification with the prominent and accepted Jewish families, the image of the longtime residents takes on the qualities of a "genteel," "responsible," and "conservative" class. Having earned his status in the community by his record of highly respectable and tactful behavior and by his good civic deeds, he does not try to buy status by means of conspicuous consumption. Instead he lives simply, modestly, tastefully. He takes pride in his possessions, but it is the pride of cultivation and maintenance rather than of mere ownership and display. At the same time he can afford to be casual in his life style because he is attuned to the relaxed rhythm and informal tone of Lakeville's suburban social climate. Having been raised in an atmos-phere of culture and responsibility, he can take his attainments for granted and implement his interests in the fine arts and civic affairs without being aggressive. Also, according to the Gentile image of him, he does not adopt an arrogant air of superiority, because he is con-fident of his acceptance by the Gentile community. He regards his fellow townsmen as equals and does not make class distinctions, except between himself and the Jewish newcomer.

In Gentile eyes the solid, respectable quality of the longtime resident's social behavior also extends to his private life. He trains his children to be respectful, diligent, and unassuming; since he is not viewed as regard-ing his Jewish identity as a stigma, he has no need to arm his children against rejection by means of arrogance and money. Finally, our Gentile respondents who distinguish between the two groups of Jews are par-ticularly impressed by the longtime resident's acceptance of the indi-vidual Gentile, by his adaptation to Gentile customs such as Christmas trees and cards, and by his desire to preserve Lakeville's traditional way of life against the depredations of the newcomers.

Given this gloss of Gentile statements about the longtime Jewish resident, it is not surprising that many of our Gentile respondents should see little or no difference between him and themselves. "I know a number of oldtimer families," reports a sixty-seven-year-old spinster, "and I never even think of them as being Jewish. They seem like the rest of the people who have been here a long time." "There is no difference between the old Jewish settlers and the Gentiles," says a resident of thirty years who belongs to the DAR. "I've never had any friends among them; however, I feel that they are people we've been used to throughout our whole life. They are polite, considerate, and generous." Or, as another Gentile respondent sums up the prevailing opinion of the established Jews of Lakeville: "They are more Gentile and not so pushy."

The Rise of the Older Jewish Group

The image we have been developing of the older Jewish residents would probably come as a surprise to many of them. One of the principal reasons why they are so much concerned about being tarred by the brush of Gentile contempt and animosity toward the new group of Jews is that their own position as an accepted, indeed an elite, class in the community has been only recently won. Indeed, so recently won, that they tend to be quite unaware that they have won it. While there are no community studies of Lakeville's Jews before the influx of newcomers, their status appears to have been much more problematic and marginal than the picture that is currently painted by our Gentile respondents. For example, one of our Jewish respondents, a fair-minded lawyer who has been a close observer of Jewish–Gentile relations in Lakeville for the past twenty-five years, observes that, paradoxically enough, "it was not until after World War II that Lakeville's Jews had any kind of decent place in the social community or were permitted any." It seems evident, then, that if only a few of the old-guard, wealthy, and aristocratic Jewish families were able to gain some measure of acceptance in prewar Lakeville, many more of less prominence must have been at best tolerated, and the Jewish community itself, which was not integrated into the social fabric of Lakeville, must have had little prestige or influence in the life of the town.

The new-found acceptance, esteem, and good will that pervade the present image of the older Jewish residents would seem to be due to the presence of that very figure in their midst—the Jewish newcomer—who arouses so much anxiety among them about their status and security. There is little doubt in our minds that the objectionable traits of the new Jews—presumed or otherwise—have deflected latent anti-Semitism among Gentiles from the settled Jew and have at the same time high- lighted his social virtues—presumed or otherwise. In the same way, the antipathy toward the Jewish newcomer as an aggressive interloper, as well as a Jew, reinforces the image of the older residents as repre- sentative of the traditional life of Lakeville. Apparently, then, acceptance of the older Jew is a necessary counterpoise in the minds of a good many Gentiles to their rejection of the newer ones, a fact which perhaps explains why so many of our Gentile respondents are quickly moved to assert that the settled Jews dislike the newcomers as much as Gentiles do. Be that as it may, the differences between the two groups of Jews have become inordinately exaggerated to produce in many Gentile minds the diametrically opposed images which we have observed.

The new acceptance and prestige of the settled Jews are not the only benefits that have accrued to them through the influx of their fellow Jews. Their influence in the community has also noticeably increased. First of all, the influx of Jews and the subsequent exodus of many of the elite class of the Gentiles has changed the power structure in Lakeville, so that the prominent Jews in the town, formerly an insignificant minority, now find themselves at least equal in numbers to the remaining Gentile elite. Moreover, as more Jews have entered the community, pressure for Jewish representation in its civic life has mounted. It goes without saying that for Gentiles the more acceptable Jewish candidates have been from the older group, and Gentiles have accordingly helped to elect them to positions on school boards, the city council, and the local judiciary. Furthermore, the longtime Jewish residents have inevitably assumed a number of ambassadorial functions between the Jewish and Gentile communities, a role which has also increased their status in the community.

The negative responses of the majority of longtime Jewish residents to the Jewish newcomer were described earlier in this chapter. There is irony in the fact that they owe to him a good deal of their emergence from relative obscurity and isolation in the community to positions of general acceptance and individual prominence.

5

THE RESPONSE OF
THE JEWISH NEWCOMER

The new Jews of Lakeville are not unaware of the cold reception they have received from the established Gentile and Jewish communities alike. They understand that the postwar transformation of the town is viewed as largely their doing. They also realize that the public image which is held of them tends to be a harshly critical stereotype. At the same time, most of the newcomers are quick to acknowledge that their influx has created structural and cultural problems in Lakeville and that there are individuals in their midst who foster the image of all the new Jews as an aggressive, pretentious, and defensive group.

However, the Jewish newcomers insist upon making and emphasizing distinctions between their positive and negative effect on community life, between the pressures of growth as such and the effect of any "Jewish" influence, between the acceptable and unacceptable newcomers, and, finally, between adjusting to cultural differences and being completely absorbed by them. Thus, while the Jewish newcomers are far less homogeneous in their backgrounds, traits, and attitudes than their Gentile and Jewish critics suppose them to be, they do exhibit a number of representative tendencies in their assessment of themselves and of their relations to both the Gentile community at large and the group of settled Jews who preceded them in Lakeville.

The Jewish Influx and the Changing Community

Most of the Jewish newcomers resist the view that they have damaged the character of the community. On the contrary, they regard themselves as the main agents of its recent progress and enlightenment. Some 59 per cent of them assess their total effect on the community as beneficial; only 12 per cent believe that it has been mostly harmful. (The comparable figures for the longtime Jewish residents are 31 and 40 per cent respectively.)

Speaking of their impact on Lakeville, the majority of our Jewish respondents who have lived there for five years or less believe that they have noticeably improved the economy of the town. Quite simply, as the young wife of a sales executive puts it, "A great many of us have brought money in. As a result, business has improved." Moreover, as a mechanical engineer who came to Lakeville two years ago points out, "With the influx of Jews there has been a growth in property values, and this has increased the wealth of the community." Finally, and most important in the eyes of the newcomers, they have had a progressive influence on the allocation of the town's fiscal resources. A young executive with two small children remarks, "The type of people moving out here want improvements for themselves and for their kids." More specifically, according to the wife of a municipal financial consultant, who belongs to two PTA groups and is also active in the League of Women Voters, "We have supported such things as an expanded police force, parking meters, and bond issues for schools." A furniture manufacturer, who says that he moved to Lakeville seven years ago because of the superior school system, sums up the matter in these words:

> I think the Jews have been prime leaders in trying to get taxes raised to pay for services needed for a growing community. This cuts through all things, especially education. Without their fiscal support the community would be overburdened, with insufficient funds to pay for these services. If Jews didn't move in then someone else would have, but I don't think they would have been as willing to pay bigger taxes as Jews are.

According to the Jewish newcomers, their effort to finance better services in Lakeville is part of the generally beneficial impact they have had on the civic and organizational life of the community. An elderly lawyer who has been living in Lakeville for a year is impressed by the "young, vigorous Jewish people who have moved in" and whom he characterizes as "generally well informed and intensely civic-minded and community-minded." Or, as a middle-aged technician who spends most of his leisure in adult education courses puts it, "I like to feel that the community is more alive and dynamic now. These people insist on better government." "The newcomers have been more dynamic than those already here," says a graduate of Antioch who is married to an entymologist. This woman is much involved in the Girl Scouts and a PTA group of which she is an officer. She elaborates her image of the new Jews as follows: "They work actively for better leadership and are generous in giving time, money, and effort. Their caliber is higher in intellectual and educational abilities, and they want a better community and they work for it."

Responsible, energetic, creative citizens: this pretty well sums up the image that the Jewish newcomers tend to have of themselves. They take particular pride in their activity in improving the public schools, a primary feature that attracted them to Lakeville and a major outlet for their civic zeal and individual aspirations. "Jewish people want the best for their children," says the wife of a dress manufacturer, who in her four years in Lakeville has become an officer in its League of Women Voters. "They work and work for the best schools they can get." It is worth noting that 59 per cent of all the women who have moved to Lakeville in the past five years belong to the PTA.

The majority of Jewish newcomers believe that the detrimental changes in Lakeville, which they minimize, have resulted from a heavy increase in population rather than from a Jewish influx as such. They also believe that the beneficial changes, which they emphasize, have been due in some part to new Jewish wealth, civic-mindedness, and enlightenment. It is hardly inconsistent, then, that they should be less troubled than older Jewish residents by the Jewish complexion of the influx. As we noted in Chapter 4, there is a definite correlation among the longtime Jewish respondents between their estimate of the percentage of Jews in Lakeville and their judgment of the newcomer's overall effect on the town. Among the newcomers, however, those who estimate that Jews now make up about 50 per cent of the population are no less positive about their value to the community than are those whose estimates only run to 30 per cent: in each group, three out of five consider their effect beneficial. Only those newcomers who estimate the present Jewish population to be 60 per cent or more of the total are quantitatively less positive about the Jewish influx. Their percentage of favorable reactions (47 per cent) is similar to the percentage of the longtime Jewish residents who estimated that Jews currently make up no more than 30 per cent of the town's population. In other words, our data suggest that the typical Jewish newcomer is comfortable in a community which is 30 per cent more Jewish than the community the older Lakeville Jew prefers to live in. This difference is also reflected in the ambivalent responses of those newer residents who disapprove of a Jewish majority but often immediately add that "the Jews are more responsible people," or that "they are family-conscious and have good homes and an interest in the community."

Such qualifications also reflect the general unwillingness of the Jewish newcomers to regard their influx as more harmful to the community than not. Only 12 per cent of our respondents in this group do so. The rest are apparently pressed to justify their record in the community by their awareness of the hostility toward them that we have described in Chapters 3 and 4. How, then, do they explain the gap between their achievements and their status, between the positive civic image they have of themselves and the negative one that exists in the minds of a majority of Lakeville's established Gentiles and Jews?

The Objectionable Newcomer

The principal explanation one might expect is that the unpopularity of the newcomers is due to their sheer numbers. And indeed most of the newcomers would agree with the "impression" of a lawyer who has lived in the community for seven years: "Most of the non-Jews have been here longer than we have and they feel they're being invaded and overwhelmed. Two [Gentile] friends of mine who are broadminded and liberal have said jokingly, 'Now we're in the minority group.' The rest of them may feel worse." However, many of the newcomers believe that the size of their group is a less important factor than is the individual behavior of some of their members. Far from corresponding to the town's hostile image of them as *nouveau riche* emigrants from the "ghetto," these newcomers tend to repudiate those Jews who conform to it and to see them as the main agents of intergroup tensions. Indeed, the responses of the two out of five newcomers who believe some Jews do pose a serious problem to the Jewish community closely resemble those of the oldtimer and often are virtually indistinguishable from them (see Table 5–1).

TABLE 5–1 CHARACTERIZATION OF PROBLEM JEW BY JEWS ACCORDING TO LENGTH OF RESIDENCE

	Jewish respondents Length of residence		
Per cent who describe the problem Jews as	5 Years or Less	6–10 Years	11 Years or More
Those who lack manners	46%	57%	50%
Those who exaggerate the importance of money	43%	50%	34%
Those who misuse or abuse power	23%	19%	32%
Those who do not integrate themselves into the general community	17%	16%	32%
	(97)	(58)	(44)

The most frequent term of criticism which newcomers use for the problem Jews is "ostentatious" or its variants, connoting behavior that is not only unduly proud and tasteless but also highly visible. Such responses cut across the various categories of behavior. Thus we hear of "ostentatious [Jews], four Cadillacs, velvet shoes, smoking cigars," or "they push you around and make themselves too ostentatious and important," or "the ostentatious type . . . who don't wait to be accepted," or "uncouth . . . ostentatious Jews who make it known they are Jews," or "they tend to be cliquish in a way that is too obstrusive . . . a louder and more apparent display." As with the veteran Jewish residents, the newcomers' most frequent objection is to the impropriety of behavior of certain newcomers, and the second most frequent complaint concerns their materialism. In the words of a thirty-three-year-old president of an advertising agency who prides himself on his independence and sophistication: "The problem Jews are the kinds of people who present a threat anywhere. The Miami Beach type. . . . I just don't like them any more than I like their counterparts in other areas of humanity." "Sort of degrading," says a resident of eight years, whose husband also heads an advertising agency, in speaking of the Jewish women "who walk around Lakeville looking dowdy and with dirty children." The wife of an investment counselor also finds that the problem Jews are "physically unattractive" ("they wear shorts even though they are fat") as well as loud and rude in public places. A resident of three years who is active in three civic groups complains of "uncultured, unpolished Jews," and also objects to their "indifference to the welfare of the whole community. They have money but are no asset to the town . . . they're only concerned with their house and their own family."

On the other hand, as indicated in Table 5–1, some of the newcomers (though 9 per cent less, proportionately, than among the longtime residents) complain about the power motives of the objectionable Jews. According to a housewife whose activities include the PTA and the Cub Scouts, "the biggest problems are with those Jews who are overbearing, pushy, and aggressive. It makes for unpleasantness on projects and committees." Another respondent, whose husband and circle of Jewish friends identify with the anti-Zionist viewpoint of the American Council for Judaism, singles out the "group that wants to abolish Christmas in the schools. I think it's the worst thing they can do. . . . This is a predominantly Protestant country." A young high school teacher who is active in the Democratic party points to the presumptuous political ambitions of a "Jewish man who ran for office after living here one year. . . . He knew nothing of the community and its problems and made a fool of himself."

Finally, there are some Jews—though half as many newcomers mention them as do longtime Jewish residents—who give offense by their vaunting display of religious and cultural differences: the Jews who, in the words of a woman active in the Conservative temple, "are so Jewish that they make no effort at all to liberalize their thinking toward the non-Jew." Such newcomers, according to a young sales manager who was raised in Germany and whose best friends tend to be Gentile, are "the first generation of Eastern European ancestors who are clannish and who don't adapt to the American concepts of living." The technician who was quoted earlier in praise of the Jewish newcomer's intelligence and zeal takes particular exception to "the type who feels that they must throw their Jewish culture at you right and left. . . . I hate what they do in schools, stopping Christmas carols, having Hanukkah. Everything must be for the Jews."

As well as producing a typology of the problem Jew which is similar to the typology used by the longtime resident, those two out of five newcomers who believe some Jews pose a serious problem are much like the longtime residents in holding that the main damage done by problem Jews is to Jewish–Gentile relations. Approximately 8 out of 10 of these newcomers (more or less the same ratio as among the long-timers) say that the problem Jews—whether through their impropriety, their flagrant materialism, their misuse of power, or their ethnocentrism—pose a threat to the Jewish community by their effect on Gentiles. As the longtimers do, these newcomers tend to believe that "Jews as a whole are judged by one Jew in this Christian world," as a respondent asserts who was educated at one of the more exclusive Eastern women's colleges. They feel, as the same respondent explains, that the objectionable Jews create "resentment and ill-will" among the more accepting Gentiles and "give the wrong kind of Gentiles ammunition in the form of classic examples of anti-Semitic stereotypes." In general, the newcomers believe that Gentiles, whether friendly or hostile, do not draw distinctions between acceptable and unacceptable Jews or between individual behavior and group characteristics. Such responses as that of a supervisor of music programs in the metropolitan school system who claims that ostentatious Jews "give a bad impression to the public, who condemns the group as a whole," or that of a Jewish clubwoman who remarks that Gentiles "will not look at quiet, refined Jews but will judge us by the rest of the undesirables," are just as typical of the newcomers as of the oldtimers.

These newcomers, however, are generally even more alarmed by the problem Jews because they feel they are more readily associated with them. Accordingly, they often dissociate themselves more sharply and vehemently than do the longtimers. A typical example comes from the wife of a successful obstetrician who is highly assimilationist in her views:

> I don't want to be identified with them [*nouveau riche* or unintegrated Jews] by non-Jews because I don't like what they stand for. Non-Jews would think less of me, and more important, I'd think less of myself if I were associated with them.

The Longtime Jewish Residents

The problem Jew in their midst is not the only grievance found among the newcomers. Many of them also complain of the settled Jews of Lakeville, whom they may even regard as a more serious obstacle to their acceptance and well-being in the community. The vulgar or aggressive or unassimilated Jews may arouse Gentile resentment, which in turn affects the general social atmosphere in which the newcomers live;

however, this problem is felt to have a more indirect effect on their lives than the snobbish, discriminatory behavior which they claim they encounter among the old-guard Jewish elements in the community. Since most of our respondents tend to be more concerned about being accepted by Jewish country clubs and other Jewish social groups in Lakeville than by those in the Gentile community, and since they are less prepared to experience rejection by fellow Jews than by Gentiles, their reaction to Jewish prejudice and discrimination is doubly bitter. Apparently, too, the newcomers find that Jews are more inclined than Gentiles to discriminate against them: 48 per cent say that they know of cases in which discrimination was practiced by Jews, while only 28 per cent know of cases in which Gentiles were the offending party. One out of three of these respondents has had personal experience with discriminatory Jews in Lakeville, while only one out of ten has encountered the same problem with Gentiles.

A young dentist who moved to Lakeville four years ago states that discrimination among Jews rests upon the "basis of wealth." He refers particularly to the older, elite Jewish families who live in the high-prestige area near the lake. "Those people take pride in wealth and look down on those who don't have their material possessions." This group is usually referred to as the "Wildacres crowd" after the name of the country club to which most of them belong. "They're bluebloods," scoffs the wife of an appliance store executive who has lived in Lakeville for ten years. "They wouldn't have anything to do with me. They can trace their ancestry back to the Mayflower." A young public relations man speaks of discrimination at social gatherings in his neighborhood which he partly attributes to "the mutual dislike of German and Russian Jews for each other." Whether they are based on wealth or lineage, the discriminatory practices of the Wildacres Club are widely acknowledged and objected to by the newcomers.

Moreover, the snobbery of the elite group has apparently helped to foster a great deal of status consciousness throughout the Jewish community. "There are six Jewish country clubs," reports a furniture manufacturer whose own income is more than $50,000 yearly, "which are rated according to the wealth and prestige of its members. Each club has its own snobbery, and they turn down people who want to join because they say these people don't have the proper social background." Other respondents report that status consciousness has spread throughout the Jewish community. A department store executive in his middle thirties whose income also exceeds $50,000 observes that "one group looks down on the other; some admit newcomers, others don't. I feel that a small segment of my own social club doesn't accept me."

The other major complaint about the longtime Jewish residents is their lack of Jewish identity and loyalty. Rather than establishing and maintaining a coherent Jewish group and fostering a pluralist community, the older Jewish residents are felt to be either indifferent or hostile to Judaism and to be unduly assimilationist in their social behavior. Such a pattern, some respondents claim, raises problems for newcomers who wish to strengthen Jewish group life and to maintain the Jewish identifications of their children. One respondent who is president of a local chapter of ORT, a Jewish welfare group, remarks that:

> I feel oldtimer Jews who don't like us present a problem. They are people with Jewish self-hatred. They pose a Christmas problem. I want my child to understand she's Jewish, but if Jewish people have Christmas trees, it makes it difficult to bring her up. I don't feel comfortable with these people. I feel more comfortable with the Catholic neighbor who doesn't appear resentful. If she didn't like it, she would move. These people don't like it and don't move either.

Or again, according to a well-educated young housewife whose father was a rabbi:

> I have always felt that a Jew who tries to escape Jewishness is a threat. He degrades Jewishness and draws us down in the eyes of the Christian. He becomes like anti-Semitic Christians, a threat to us. Many Jewish people have Christmas trees. That's not very salutary.

The effects of this attitude are described by a housewife who maintains a strong interest in Israel:

> Those Jews who resent other Jews and who believe the neighborhood is getting too Jewish break down the unity of the Jewish community. The Gentile gets a confused picture of us. We should have more similar ideas and not be a two-headed monster.

In the minds of these newcomers, the worst offenders are the elitist Jews who are associated with the anti-Zionist position of the American Council for Judaism. A housewife who has a graduate degree in art and belongs to two synagogues observes that:

> The other problem group are the Jews from the Einhorn Temple. They are very active in discussing anti-Zionism with their non-Jewish friends. They stress that interest in Israel is un-American. This can cause a lot of misunderstanding and produce bad relationships between Jew and non-Jew

because it leads to confusion about the loyalties and Americanism of Jews with non-Jews, and it causes quite a split in the Jewish groups between the pro-Zionists and the adherents of the Einhorn Temple.

It is not surprising, therefore, that 13 per cent of these newcomers—as contrasted with 2 per cent of the oldtimers—believe that the overly integrated Jew represents a problem to the Jewish community that affects its own group identity as well as its relations with Lakeville's Gentiles.

The Jewish Newcomer and the Gentile

The newcomers' feelings toward the Gentile community tend to be more complicated than those evoked by the *nouveau riche* newcomers or by the snobbish and disloyal longtime resident. Contrary to what his critics believe, the newcomer is disturbed by the negative image of him that has developed among Gentiles, and he tends to be both concessive and defensive about his own responsibility. He admits, for example, that the influx of Jews may have unfairly imposed hardships on Gentiles. However, as we have already noted, he is much more reluctant to concede to or sympathize with the opinion that it is the Jewishness of the newcomers which has harmed the community. As a result, some newcomers attribute Gentile discontent to economic rather than social causes. A typical response comes from a housewife who has lived in Lakeville for five years:

> It's not being a Jew that is at the heart of the ill feeling about the influx. It's the fact that builders have put up small buildings and the tax load these people carry is not proportionate to the cost of sending their children to school.

Other newcomers, as we have noted, attribute Gentile disesteem to the presence of the vulgar, ethnocentric Jew who confirms anti-Semitic stereotypes or to the elite old guard who either make all expressions of Jewishness unacceptable or else disorient Gentiles by their lack of group loyalty. Nevertheless, whether as cause, effect, or attendant condition, the newcomer recognizes that there is deep-seated tension, for which both groups are responsible, between Jew and Gentile in Lakeville. Thus, according to a young housewife who prefers living in a non-Jewish neighborhood: "As many Jews are anti-Gentile as Gentiles are anti-Jewish." On the one hand there are the touchiness and defensiveness of the Jews; on the other, the coolness of the Gentiles. A respondent who is an officer of the local League of Women Voters believes that:

> The Jews have a chip on their shoulder. When an act is bad and Gentiles don't like it, we're too quick to say it's anti-Semitic. We don't make an effort to invite our Gentile friends. On the other hand, the Gentile resents the Jew.

A similar observation comes from a housewife who is active in the Conservative synagogue and maintains a strong Jewish identification:

> Now I think we Jews also contribute to the problems between the Jews and Gentiles. We also use retaliatory things. On our street two neighbors talked against Gentiles. My father even looks down on the Goy [Gentile]. . . . One neighbor, European-born, has a similar outlook. He is definitely retaliatory. He jumps to the conclusion that anything that happens may be anti-Semitism. Gentiles, on the other hand, are also downright unfriendly. One neighbor's wife is friendly, but he won't talk to anyone. Sometimes we misinterpret the behavior. We assume anti-Semitism when it may be a personal thing.

The result is either overt hostility or, more commonly, the absence of genuine social intercourse. "Jews are too cliquish and Gentiles are too cold," is a common reaction among the newcomers. Or, as a salesman who works in a "Gentile industry" sums up the matter: "The biggest problem is the social separation that exists between Jews and Gentiles. It's not real unfriendliness, just lack of friendship." And the fact that newcomers believe the responsibility for this state of affairs to be equally divided is borne out by the following comparative figures for the three groups of Jews (see Table 5–2).

The complexity of the Jewish newcomer's response to his situation in Lakeville is perhaps most concretely manifested by the specific issue of Christmas and Hanukkah. Many of those who are sensitive to this problem protest that their position has been misrepresented or incompletely understood. Contrary to the criticisms leveled against them, they do not wish to overturn community traditions or offend Gentile sensibilities. At the same time, they remain disturbed by the religious overtones of Christmas celebrations in the schools and are concerned about the lack of consideration that is shown for *their* sensibilities.

Of course, individual responses can vary widely, since the newcomers comprise a far from homogeneous or united front. There are a few who believe that Jews should not protest at all. One point of view is expressed by a father of two children who is active in the PTA:

TABLE 5–2   ASSESSMENT BY JEWS OF RESPONSIBILITY FOR
INTERGROUP UNFRIENDLINESS ACCORDING
TO THEIR RESIDENCE

Are Jews more or less respon-sible than non-Jews for any unfriendliness existing between them?	*Jewish respondents* *Length of residence*		
	5 Years or Less	6–10 Years	11 Years or More
Per cent who say			
Jews are more responsible	22%	30%	44%
Jews are less responsible	20	17	12
Responsibility about equally divided	58	53	44
	100%	100%	100%
	(208)	(100)	(73)

> Some Jewish mothers felt that Christmas shouldn't be celebrated. Others said it was okay, but they should give Hanukkah equal billing. I think the whole thing is ridiculous. It annoyed me. We live in a non-Jewish country and Christmas is its most important holiday, so it's idiotic to expect Gentiles not to recognize it in schools.

A more moderate position of conformity is that of a housewife who mixes easily with her Gentile neighbors:

> The PTA president [Jewish] told me about mothers who come to her and object to religious songs at Christmas. I feel that I had these songs in my day, and when you are in a minority group you should go along with the majority group, in public at least. Simply because they sing these songs, the children don't turn to another religion.

On the other hand, there are newcomers who would cope with the problem by celebrating Hanukkah as well as Christmas in the schools. According to a young mother of two children who is concerned with giving her children, as she says, a "Jewish background":

> My child's teacher made a great deal out of Christmas as a religious holiday and nothing out of Hanukkah. I thought it would have been fairer to do so, especially since a big percentage of the class is Jewish. The teacher is known for being like this and making a definite religious thing out of Christmas.

A positive experience along the same lines is reported by a lithographer who was himself raised in a Gentile neighborhood and who has become actively committed to Judaism:

> My son's teacher handled the whole problem tactfully. There was a school discussion about Christmas, presents among kids, and at the same time our son told the story of Hanukkah. I approved of this.

However, neither of these alternatives seems satisfactory to other Jewish newcomers. A housewife who more or less accepts the *status quo* still registers the divided attitude that is common among our respondents:

> The schools made a concession to the Jews. They sing one Hanukkah song to ten Christian ones. Many Jews resent this approach and consider it strictly a Christian approach. There's been no attempt to keep the celebration on a non-religious basis. Well, this is okay with me, since I was brought up as a minority. Furthermore, the PTA is run by Christians. Some Jews are in it, but they show visibly that they are more interested in the general community than in the Jewish one. We have to conform to the Gentiles. I think myself that this can be done graciously and with taste, but Jewish people should be consulted. Personally I would like to see the world friendship idea stressed in the celebrations, the brotherhood theme rather than Christ in the manger. The prevailing idea seems to be to have something for Jews and something for Christians. However, this stresses differences. I think they should stress common ideas and goals.

Other newcomers believe that this thorny problem can be resolved only by de-emphasizing religious observances—whether Christian or Jewish —in the schools. A typical response is provided by the young wife of a history professor:

> I heard from neighbors a few years ago that a delegation of Jews went to one of the schools and complained about the emphasis on Christmas and on Jewish children having to be angels. I have been told that they increased the amount of Hanukkah. I can see both sides of the matter. From what I gather I frankly feel that there is too much emphasis on both Christmas and Hanukkah. I feel religious things can be emphasized more at home. Not so much energy should be devoted to the religious aspect.

Much the same sense of an earnest conflict and a hoped-for resolution is apparent in the remarks of a chemical engineer who is active in Jewish affairs:

My boy came home singing Hanukkah songs. I was amazed. When I was a kid I suffered with "Silent Night." I felt like a traitor to the Jews. I can't see any objection to Christmas songs today, but they shouldn't ask kids to draw pictures of Christ. On the other hand, we blow up Hanukkah out of all proportion and historical significance. I guess we have to counteract the Christmas influence. But anyhow I feel that church and state should be separate.

"I am mixed up," confesses the mother of two school-age children:

I still remember not singing the word Jesus while singing carols at school. But I don't see how you can do any explaining of the parallels between Hanukkah and Christmas without bringing religion into the school. As to that, I would prefer keeping it out.

Behind the majority of responses, then, is a recurring theme: Some compromise should be worked out which would be equitable to both Jew and Gentile and yet allow them to maintain their group identity and dignity. The wife of a lawyer who has lived in Lakeville for three years and is active in both Hadassah and the PTA provides a particularly vivid example:

We had quite a fuss last year. My daughter got into a hassle with some of the girls at lunch because she refused to sing Christmas carols. Some of the girls said she should just mouth the words. There were tears, words. Her teacher called me. I spoke to the rabbi. He was going to call the principal. This year she accepts it. She has made compromises, sings certain ones, but others she won't. She also took Hebrew songs to music class and a menorah and demonstrated how to light it. The teachers were understanding and very sympathetic. It disturbed us that she was having problems. When I was a child I had some problems too but I was not as vocal. Here it was Jewish kids who were convincing her that she should cooperate. We support this. We tell her that she doesn't have to flaunt her Jewishness or wear it as a chip, but she is very proud of it.

To put the situation of the Jewish newcomer to Lakeville in somewhat sharper focus, it should be apparent from the individual responses of the newcomers and from the identifying details about them that they are a far more diverse and generally acculturated and enlightened group than is envisioned either by their Gentile or Jewish critics. Moreover, they tend to be much more sensitive to the interplay of economic, social, and ethnic conditions that create intergroup tensions in the new Lakeville than are either of the older groups of Jews or Gentiles who rely upon simplistic and distorted images of the newcomers to explain their impact on the community.

If there is a prevailing image of the newcomer which emerges from this chapter, it is that of a well-educated and adaptive citizen who is more or less at home in contemporary American society. Far from being insensitive to the impact he has had on the community, he is aware of the various difficulties that have been created by the heavy influx of Jewish residents. However, he does not feel that his Jewishness should be held responsible for most of the undesirable consequences of change, and he is anxious to dissociate himself from his fellow Jews who provoke this response. On the other hand, he believes that he has made a significant positive contribution to Lakeville without completely submerging and subordinating his Jewish identity and interests to Gentile expectations. Finally, of the different groups we have been studying, the Jewish newcomers appear to comprise the one that is most drawn to the possibilities of genuine pluralism, and the one that is most aware of its absence in Lakeville.

III

SOCIAL INTEGRATION

In the previous chapters we have been concerned mainly with the impact of the large number of Jewish newcomers upon the traditionally Gentile community of Lakeville. For the most part, our findings have led us to focus upon the underlying prejudices, tensions, and conflicts which have been fostered by the rapid expansion of the town and by the alteration, to some extent, of its social as well as physical character. Along with disturbing the pattern of peaceful, if superficial, relations that previously prevailed between Lakeville's Jews and Gentiles, the wave of newcomers has also stimulated or confirmed widespread stereotypes of the Jews as aggressive misfits who threaten the traditional manners and customs of a town such as Lakeville. This in turn has contributed to the tacit but deep-seated estrangement of the newcomers, who are likely to feel at best tolerated rather than accepted by the community at large.

However, we must bear in mind that intergroup relations in Lakeville had been subject to unusual pressure during the decade preceding this study. At the time of our survey the shock of change had already noticeably worn off, and the municipal structure of the community had been successfully adjusted to cope with the increase in population. The question which now presented itself, and which will occupy our attention for the remainder of this study, is that of the social adjustment of Jew and Gentile—the problems of divisiveness that still lie before them, and the resources, both in the individual respondents and in the areas of intergroup relations that exist in the community, by which these problems may be accommodated, reduced, and eventually resolved.

The size of the present population, the transformation of neighborhoods, the expansion of facilities, and the similarities of interests make it virtually inevitable that most Jews and Gentiles in Lakeville will have considerable contact with each other. Their paths are bound to cross in the stores, in the streets, in their backyards, and at the public beaches, concerts, and organization meetings, as well as in their vocations outside the community. Many of these contacts are, of course, fleeting and superficial; others are more continuing, such as being neighbors or members of the same PTA. However, all provide the experience of living, working, or playing together that can foster more informed and positive intergroup attitudes and more personal relations. However, for these attitudes and relations to develop there must be a willingness to overcome differences and to associate with each other.

In the following four chapters we shall examine the setting and the character of the Jewish and Gentile will to relate. We shall be particularly concerned with the attitudes, beliefs, and feelings that reinforce or inhibit a willingness to associate with members of the other group. Then in Part IV we shall attempt to explore the specific channels of social intercourse which currently bring Jews and Gentiles together.

6

THE SETTING FOR
SOCIAL INTEGRATION

The Patterning of Leisure

Before portraying the specific Jewish and Gentile attitudes toward acculturation and integration, on the one hand, and separatism on the other, we shall briefly survey the behavior of Jews and Gentiles in the two dominant spheres of general community activity—leisure and organizational work.

As we noted in Chapter 1, Lakeville has traditionally been a leisure-oriented community. More specifically, it has developed different models of leisure interests and activities which conform to its class structure. One such model reflects Lakeville's history as a summer colony of an elite Gentile group. The most visible institution of this model is the country club, which Lakeville has in much larger numbers than one normally finds in communities of its size. The major activity of such clubs is golf. Lakeville's heritage in music and the theater also springs from its elite interest and tastes, and its Center for the Performing Arts is still the central symbol of this concern. Another leisure model reflects Lakeville's past as a home-centered small town in which a person of relatively modest means spends his leisure time in tinkering around the house and garden, or in hunting and fishing.

107

THE GENTILE AND LEISURE

In Lakeville today only the Gentile men of high income ($20,000 a year or more) are likely to be attracted to both models. On the one hand, they tend to be involved in elite activities: golf is their most popular sport; bridge their preferred game of cards; and half or more attend concerts and the theater and express a liking for classical music. On the other hand, they name sports and home-centered activities as their favorite leisure pursuits instead of the performing arts and card playing, and this is in accord with what Gentile men of low and middle incomes also prefer. In addition, the men of high income are almost as likely as men of more moderate means to go fishing and hunting. However, they do not share the latter's interest in bowling, which the men of more moderate income like at least as much as golf, or in poker, which is the favorite card game of men in the low-income bracket (less than $10,000 annually). Furthermore, the home-centered hobbies of the affluent men are of a less practical nature, such as photography or collecting stamps and coins. Those of the low- and middle-income men are practical ones—fixing implements and making household repairs, tending lawns and gardens.

In turn, low- and middle-income Gentile men show little inclination to adopt any of the elite activities; only one out of four low-income men, for example, attends concerts. The only exception is the preference of middle-income men ($10,000 to less than $20,000 a year) for bridge and for going to the theater; their response to these activities resembles that of the high-income men.

Among the Gentile women, the differences between classes are much more clear-cut. The women of high income, for example, are much more committed than are their male counterparts to a distinctively elite model of leisure. Their primary interests are in the performing arts: four out of five attend concerts and the theater and like classical music. Their most popular sport is golf, and their favorite card game is bridge. Unlike the men, though, they care little for activities that are relatively popular with the low-income person. Thus, they have virtually no interest in bowling or in playing canasta or pinochle. They are only half as likely as women of low and middle income to consider home-centered activities their favorite leisure pursuits, and one-fourth as likely to regard activities like knitting and sewing as a hobby.

By the same token, the low-income women are not particularly attracted to the things that the high-income women do. They are much less interested in sports and in playing golf. They pay little attention to the performing arts; in fact, they go to concerts no more frequently than low-income men do. They are also much less inclined to play cards in general or to prefer bridge in particular; only one out of four considers it her favorite card game, in contrast to seven out of ten women of high income.

Middle-income women occupy an intermediate position between the other two. They like bridge and some of the performing arts virtually as much as do the women of high income; at the same time, they retain significant ties to home-centered activities and have little interest in golf.

THE JEW AND LEISURE

How do the leisure activities of Lakeville's Jews compare with these two patterns? In general, most of the preferred activities of Jewish men fall into one or the other of the Gentile models and also correlate with levels of income. Jewish men in the low-income bracket tend to pattern much of their leisure life along the same lines as their Gentile counterparts. They are as broadly interested in sports, for example; and only about the same proportion of those who participate in sports—one out of three—plays golf. They favor home-centered activities, though with a somewhat greater emphasis on hobbies such as photography and a lesser interest in manual crafts and gardening. Even with respect to the performing arts, the low-income Jewish men are no more active in attending concerts, operas, or dance recitals, though they are more likely to prefer classical music and to attend plays. They are also more likely to play bridge.

In some respects, then, the Jewish men who have not entered the affluent class differ from their economic peers among the Gentiles in preferring leisure activities that are characteristic of the wealthier class. This tendency becomes more pronounced among Jewish men in the middle-income bracket. Most significantly, in this bracket there is a loss of interest in home-centered activities and a marked increase of interest in the performing arts. Thus, many more men in this group attend concerts, operas, and dance recitals, and more consider the performing arts to be their favorite activity. No less striking is their attraction to golf: 57 per cent of those who participate in sports in this bracket play the game, as contrasted with 33 per cent in the low-income bracket, and also as contrasted with the negligible increase of interest in golf that occurs between the low- and middle-income Gentile men. Moreover, respondents in the middle-income group show a marked increase in selecting one or another sport as their favorite leisure activity and approach the level of the middle-income Gentile males in this preference.

Among high-income Jewish men, the adoption of an elite style of leisure has become virtually complete. Sports, especially golf, and the performing arts become the mainstays of their leisure: 71 per cent of the Jewish men who earn $20,000 or more a year attend concerts; 97 per cent attend the theater; and 77 per cent of the sportsmen play golf. Also, seven times as many men in this bracket go to the opera and to dance recitals as do Jewish men in the low-income group. Indeed, more Jews than Gentiles at the high-income level appear to have a distinctively elite leisure style; for, unlike the Jews, wealthy Gentiles are more likely to retain significant ties to home-centered activities.

If the elite model of leisure in Lakeville is more attractive to Jewish men at a lower level of income than it is to the Gentile, it is even more so to the Jewish women. Indeed, there is little significant deviation from this model among the three income levels. Interest in the performing arts, whether in concerts, dance recitals, or the theater, is much the same for the three. So is the interest in sports, though as with the men, participation in golf tends to rise with the respective levels of income. On the other hand, slightly more women in the low-income group prefer bridge than in the upper-income groups. Finally, the percentage of women in the low-income bracket who prefer home-centered activities is as small (7 per cent) as it is for the wealthier Jewish women. Thus the elite model, which among Gentile women is preferred mostly by those in the highest income bracket, is widely distributed throughout the classes of Jewish women. It is not too much to say that Jewish women in Lakeville provide the broadest base of support for the traditional elite culture of the community.

THE DIFFERENCE IN APPROACH

Just as Jew and Gentile differ in their attraction to the leisure models in Lakeville, so are they different in the range of activities in which they become involved. Characteristically, both Gentile men and women appear to cultivate a few interests intensively, while Jewish men and women are more inclined to spread themselves out in their leisure activities. For example, the average Jewish resident participates in and watches a larger number of different sports than does the average Gentile, and also plays a greater variety of card games (see Table 6–1).

TABLE 6–1 THE AVERAGE NUMBER OF ACTIVITIES BY RELIGION AND SEX

	Gentile Men	Jewish Men	Gentile Women	Jewish Women
Average number of different sports that are played by those who play some sport	1.89	2.34	1.94	2.23
Average number of different sports that are watched by those who are a spectator at some sport	2.84	3.78	2.31	2.76
Average number of different games of cards that are played by card players	1.76	1.95	1.57	1.96

Adding significance to this differing approach to leisure is the fact that Gentiles are more inclined than Jews to devote themselves to a sport only if they have a strong personal liking for it. Thus where Jews and Gentiles consider sports to be their favorite leisure activity, each is almost as likely as the other to play some sport. But at lower levels of interest the gap between the two groups increases, so that among those respondents who profess no interest in athletics at all, only 7 per cent of the Gentile men participate, while 35 per cent of the Jewish men do so. A similar pattern is found among the Gentile and Jewish women. In short, Jews are much more likely than Gentiles to play a given sport even if they are not interested in it (see Table 6–2).

Similarly, Jews are much more likely than Gentiles to attend concerts, even if they do not particularly like classical music. Among the college-educated high-income persons, who comprise the group of most avid concertgoers, 52 per cent of the Jewish men and 74 per cent of the Jewish women who lack interest in the music attend concerts, in contrast to only 33 per cent and 52 per cent of the uninterested Gentile men and women, respectively. Of the people who like classical music, however, Gentiles are almost as likely to attend concerts as Jews. Among the men, for example, differences are very slight; 86 per cent of the Jews and 80 per cent of the Gentiles attend. Among women, Gentiles are even more likely to go than the Jews are; the figures are 85 per cent and 76 per cent respectively.

TABLE 6–2 INTEREST AND PARTICIPATION IN SPORTS
BY RELIGION AND SEX

Per cent who play some sport among	Level of interest in sports		
	Most-Favored Activity	Interested in But Not Most-Favored Activity	Not Interested
Gentile men	93%	67%	7%
	(42)	(54)	(14)
Jewish men	98%	81%	35%
	(64)	(110)	(34)
Gentile women	95%	75%	6%
	(19)	(56)	(65)
Jewish women	100%	95%	25%
	(17)	(130)	(76)

The best explanation for this greater diversification of leisure activities among Jews, and one which is borne out by our subsequent discussion of organizational affiliations, is that it reflects a central desire and tension common to Lakeville's Jews: the desire to establish themselves within the general mores and values of the community and at the same time to maintain some of their distinctive identities as Jews. Nowhere is this more apparent than in their athletic activities. As we have already noted, Jews tend to opt for games that are popular and prestigeful in the American culture; however, they do not usually abandon the games that can be said to be characteristic of the Jewish subculture, such as handball and table tennis. Nine out of ten men who play these games also play golf or bowl. Among Gentile men, an active interest in hunting and fishing—the sports that can be said to be most confined to this group—tends to preclude the likelihood of their also playing golf or bowling; only one out of two who hunts or fishes also plays these games.

Much the same point is suggested by our data on card playing. A majority of Jews who play gin rummy, poker, or canasta also play bridge; among Gentiles, a much sharper split is found between those who play bridge and those who play pinochle, poker, or canasta. In sum, even in card play the Jew who maintains a distinctively Jewish or sex preference also adopts a high-status game associated with acculturation. The Gentile is more willing to confine his card games to those that most appeal to him, even though they may not carry the social cachet of the community.

Thus, in performing a leisure activity the Jews introduce considerations other than mere interest, and what may help to make these other considerations so important is the homogeneity of the Jewish subcommunity. As we have already seen in Chapter 1, the Jews in Lakeville resemble each other in age, in income, and in education much more than the Gentiles do. This sociological difference between the two subcommunities can be expected to foster greater awareness and agreement among Jews than among Gentiles as to what the norms of appropriate behavior are—and also greater pressure to conform to them if a person wishes to be accepted by others.[1] And since many of these Jews are relatively new to the community and are seeking to secure such acceptance, there is an added incentive for them to conform to what is expected even though personal preference and interest may be lacking. The Gentiles, comprising a more heterogeneous subcommunity and also drawing their leisure models from two separate sources, have a greater number of alternatives to choose from. Thus the Gentiles are in a better position to do what they want to do and not merely what others expect them to do.

Still another factor which may influence the behavior of the Jews is that many—because of their own backgrounds and because of the immigrant backgrounds of their parents or grandparents—have only recently been introduced into the leisure world of sports, hobbies, bridge, and the like. As a result, they have had neither the time nor the tradition to develop any abiding commitment to a specific set of activities, as the Gentile has. And to the Jew, the intrinsic character of the activity may seem less rewarding than certain extrinsic functions such activities perform.

We have already alluded to several of these extrinsic functions. One other may be the sociability function: such activities bring people together. And it may well be that the social gratification he attains is more important to the Jew than the satisfaction intrinsic in the activity itself. Certainly the activities that Jews prefer, such as golf, bowling, and bridge, lend themselves to social intercourse more than do the Gentile's fishing and hunting, which are more individualistic and isolated activities.

Whatever motivates their differing approach to leisure, the question

[1] To determine the extent to which this homogeneity factor helps account for the differing leisure approaches of Jew and Gentile in Lakeville would require a comparative analysis with another community—presumably one in which the Gentile is the homogeneous and the Jew the heterogeneous group.

remains: How does the adoption by many Lakeville Jews of the Gentile elite model of leisure affect intergroup relations? So far, at least, it represents the adoption of a life style rather than an active form of social integration and assimilation as such. For the country club remains the dominant institution of the elite model, and its membership is still segregated sharply along ethnic lines as well as by class and income levels. Similarly, these self-selective tendencies operate in the more informal social arrangements that are developed as part of leisure activities. Thus at each level of income, when eight or nine out of ten Jewish respondents play cards, they do so predominantly with other Jews.

As will be seen in Chapter 11, however, there has been emerging in Lakeville a new pattern of recreational and cultural facilities which are formally organized and open to the public. These facilities have helped to breach the self-segregating habits and institutional barriers of leisure activities that lie between Lakeville's Jews and Gentiles, for in the new pattern, members of both groups participate together and individual friendships begin to develop. But for the present, leisure in Lakeville is more likely to provide opportunities for acculturation than for integration.

Organizational Affiliations

Leisure in Lakeville is also traditionally devoted to membership in organizations, the numbers and variety of which are typical of the highly complex and differentiated group life that is found in the modern suburb. These groups range over a broad spectrum of interests and needs and serve a variety of functional and expressive purposes. Some are closely related to the community structure: its schools, hospitals, welfare programs; its religious and cultural institutions. Others are devoted to neighborhood and community planning or to participation in the political parties and processes. Still others serve the economic interests of the town's commercial and professional class. Finally, there are the groups organized around social and cultural tastes and interests. In all, we have been able to distinguish eight major categories of organizations, whether within or outside the community, to which Lakeville residents belong. They are youth-serving associations such as the PTA, political and community groups, health and welfare, business and professional, cultural, fraternal, patriotic, and social.

In analyzing the organizational affiliations of our Jewish and Gentile respondents, we find that these follow much the same pattern as their leisure activities. Jews at all levels of income have developed some organizational tie, while among Gentiles this is generally true only of those who are in the middle- and high-income brackets. Moreover, at each level of income, affiliated Jews tend to belong to more organizations than affiliated Gentiles do (see Table 6–3).

TABLE 6–3 MULTIPLE GROUP MEMBERSHIPS BY RELIGION, SEX, AND INCOME

Per cent of affiliated residents who belong to four or more groups among	*Level of income*		
	Less Than $10,000	$10,000–19,999	$20,000 and Over
Gentile men	21% (33)	53% (32)	65% (26)
Jewish men	31% (16)	68% (84)	72% (92)
Gentile women	17% (59)	48% (31)	57% (21)
Jewish women	48% (29)	63% (108)	82% (79)

It is also worth noting that just as Jewish leisure activities tend to be more general and less confined to specific personal interests, so too their more numerous array of memberships does not mean that they necessarily take more of an interest or devote more time than Gentiles do to organizational work. As Table 6–4 indicates, only the low-income Jews of both sexes and the middle-income Jewish women spend more time in these activities than their Gentile counterparts; Jewish men in the middle- and upper-income brackets spend less, and Jewish women of high income spend about the same. In fact, at the upper-income level, virtually the same proportion of Gentile women who belong to few organizations (56 per cent) as Jewish women who belong to many (52 per cent) devote four or more hours weekly to them. In other words, organization and group participation reflects the same pattern of generalized as against specialized involvement that we observed with regard to leisure activities.

This pattern continues to reveal itself within the spread of organizational type preferences. Apart from the "social" organizations, which are popular among all four groups, we find, not unexpectedly, that Jewish and Gentile women in Lakeville are most concerned with youth and welfare work and men with their business and professional associations. Jewish women, however, tend to join these organizations earlier

TABLE 6–4   PARTICIPATION IN GROUP ACTIVITIES
BY RELIGION, SEX, AND INCOME

Hours per week spent on group affiliations and volunteer activities among	*Level of income*		
	Less Than $10,000	$10,000– 19,999	$20,000 and Over
Gentile men			
None	45%	18%	19%
1–3 hours	33	38	38
4 or more hours	22	44	43
	100%	100%	100%
	(42)	(34)	(21)
Jewish men			
None	39%	29%	30%
1–3 hours	28	45	46
4 or more hours	33	26	24
	100%	100%	100%
	(18)	(91)	(95)
Gentile women			
None	35%	27%	14%
1–3 hours	51	38	38
4 or more hours	14	35	48
	100%	100%	100%
	(72)	(34)	(21)
Jewish women			
None	10%	22%	16%
1–3 hours	70	36	37
4 or more hours	20	42	47
	100%	100%	100%
	(30)	(111)	(78)

in life and to maintain membership over a longer period of time. Although nine out of ten women in both groups belong to a youth-oriented group while their oldest child is in elementary school, one out of three Jewish women (in contrast to one out of eight Gentile women) joins before her child has entered school, and 85 per cent continue membership when their youngest child is in junior or senior high school, as opposed to 36 per cent of the Gentile mothers. Similarly, 70 per cent of the Jewish women become involved in health and welfare groups before the age of fifty; in contrast, only 25 per cent of the Gentile women do so before they reach this age, and 54 per cent do so after fifty. Thus Jewish women are more inclined to be involved in both types of group work, while Gentile women tend to confine their interest to activities which are most immediately related to their stage of life. Moreover, only the elderly Gentile women whose husbands' incomes are at least $20,000 show the same percentage of membership in welfare groups that one already finds among the younger Jewish women of middle income.

Though we would normally expect youth-serving work to be attractive mainly to females, our findings show that it is the third most popular organizational activity among Jewish men. Some 66 per cent of those who have children in elementary schools belong to one such organization, as contrasted with 38 per cent of the Gentile men. Jewish men, particularly in later life, also participate more in health and welfare organizations: approximately three times as many of them in the upper-income bracket are members of such organizations (33 per cent) as are found among their Gentile counterparts. Thus while Gentile men remain essentially aloof from the main organizational activities of their wives, Jewish men in substantial numbers either participate with or support their wives in youth and welfare work, an activity which has deep roots in traditional Jewish culture.

The most important of the distinctively male organizations are the business and professional ones. Proportionately many more Jews than Gentiles belong to these groups. One reason is that proportionately many more Jews are in the professions or in white-collar and managerial positions—occupations in which group associations are likely to occur. However, even in the professions Jews are more likely to belong to an organization that represents their economic interests than are Gentiles: the percentages are 82 and 57, respectively. On the other hand, the organizational affiliations of Jewish and Gentile businessmen vary rather sharply. Of the Gentiles in business who earn less than $10,000 annually, 10 per cent belong to economic associations, while 82 per cent of those who earn $20,000 or more annually belong to them. The comparative figures for Jewish businessmen are 25 and 56 per cent respectively.[2] Thus, only at the highest level of income are Gentiles more likely to be members of these organizations than Jews are.

Fraternal, civic, and social affiliations also reflect differences between

[2] Among businessmen who earn $10,000 to less than $20,000 annually, 38 per cent of the Gentiles and 49 per cent of the Jews belong to economic organizations.

Jews and Gentiles. The wealthier Gentiles who belong to trade or professional associations, for example, are not as likely as their Jewish counterparts to be involved in fraternal organizations as well. Once again the distinction between the particularistic orientation of the Gentile and the more general one of the Jew asserts itself. Furthermore, among Gentiles, membership in social and civic organizations rises sharply at the different levels of income. The proportions among Gentile women in the lower, middle, and upper brackets are 43, 65, and 86 per cent respectively for social organizations, and 12, 37, and 48 per cent respectively for civic organizations. But for the Jewish respondents, membership in these types of organizations is relatively unaffected by income, and the extent of participation is such that the low-income group compares favorably in memberships with the high-income Gentile group.

Organizations and Ethnicity

The elaborate organizational structure in Lakeville is also differentiated in terms of sectarian and non-sectarian sponsorship. Since they are an ethnic group, Jews are much more likely to belong to nonreligious sectarian organizations than Gentiles are; Gentiles are more likely to find sectarian activities within their churches than Jews are within their synagogues and temples. Furthermore, such sectarian organizations, whether they are religious or ethnic, by no means subsume the activities of Lakeville's Jews. Only about 5 per cent of the Jewish men and women who are affiliated with some organization belong to sectarian groups exclusively; the rest belong to somewhat more non-sectarian groups in the community than Gentiles do (see Table 6–5).

TABLE 6–5 NON-SECTARIAN GROUP AFFILIATIONS BY RELIGION AND SEX

Number of non-sectarian group memberships of the affiliated	Gentile Men	Jewish Men	Gentile Women	Jewish Women
None	3%	6%	13%	5%
1–3	59	52	61	61
4 or more	38	42	26	34
	100%	100%	100%	100%
	(94)	(196)	(114)	(219)

Thus among Jews, membership in sectarian groups goes hand in hand with membership in the non-sectarian ones: 79 per cent of the women and 71 per cent of the men belong to both. This is in contrast to 19 per cent of the Gentile men and 35 per cent of the Gentile women who report some affiliation; most of the Gentiles belong to non-sectarian groups only. However, among residents who belong to both types, Gentiles are much more likely to devote time to each than Jews are; many of the Jews spend time on only one, if that (see Table 6–6).

It is therefore apparent that the Gentiles place greater emphasis on active participation rather than on mere membership in an organization. Jews, however, tend to associate themselves with both sectarian and non-sectarian organizations even though theirs may be only a nominal

TABLE 6–6 PARTICIPATION IN SECTARIAN AND NON-SECTARIAN ACTIVITIES BY RELIGION AND SEX

Per cent of those with membership in both sectarian and non-sectarian groups who spend time on	Gentile Men	Jewish Men	Gentile Women	Jewish Women
Both kinds of activities	90%	44%	75%	52%
Sectarian only	5	17	8	15
Non-sectarian only	0	16	8	20
Neither	5	23	10	13
	100%	100%	100%	100%
	(18)	(140)	(40)	(172)

membership. This pattern reflects once again their dual wish to belong both to the Jewish community and to the community at large.

The remaining question is how non-sectarian in membership, as distinct from purpose, are the groups to which Jews belong? Unfortunately, most of our answers will have to be approximations, inasmuch as the only data that are available for most of these groups were obtained from Jews alone. These respondents were asked to estimate the percentage of Jews in each of the groups to which they belong.

If all non-sectarian groups had a uniform percentage of Jews as members, we would expect Jews to comprise somewhat over one-third of the membership of each—the proportion of Jews in the total Lakeville population. However, most groups have either many more or many less Jewish members. At the one extreme are the patriotic and economic groups: Jews comprise an estimated 11 per cent of the former and 25 per cent of the latter. At the other extreme are the organized social groups and circles of close friends: respectively, these have 78 per cent and 86 per cent Jewish membership. Between the two are the relatively mixed civic, cultural, welfare, and youth groups (see Table 6–7).

TABLE 6–7   Jewishness of Membership
of Non-Sectarian Groups

Non-sectarian groups	Estimated per cent of Jews
Patriotic	11%
Economic	25%
Fraternal	37%
Civic	44%
Cultural	46%
Health and welfare	51%
Youth-serving	54%
Organized social	78%
Circles of close friends	86%

Only the fraternal groups' proportion of Jews appears to correspond to the population parameter. But on closer inspection, this is more apparent than real, for most have a predominantly Gentile membership, and one, a Masonic lodge, has a predominantly Jewish membership. The average figure masks the bimodal tendencies of fraternal group memberships.

Similar variability exists within many of the other general organizational categories; however, we do find specific groups within these categories that reflect this parameter fairly accurately. These are generally community-wide organizations with relatively specific functions—civic groups such as the Lakeville Civic Association and a homeowner's association, and health and welfare groups such as a community-wide mental health association. In addition, groups which support important community institutions also show some correspondence with the population parameter. This is true of some auxiliaries and volunteer groups associated with the local hospital, and even more so of groups which support such local cultural institutions as the library, community concerts, and the local symphony. The Jewish membership of these groups is estimated at somewhat less than the population parameter.

Other local community groups, however, are much more mixed in their composition and approach a 50–50 division in membership. In other words, more Jews belong to them than would be expected on the basis of the Jewish proportion in the local population. The most outstanding examples of these are the PTA's, the League of Women Voters, some neighborhood community clubs, and formally organized cultural groups with community-wide appeal, such as the local art league and the film society.

In part, the mixed nature of these groups reflects differences in the composition of the Jewish and Gentile populations. For example, the greater youthfulness of the Jews increases the likelihood of their having school-age children and therefore of their being attracted to the PTA. Because of their higher level of income and education, more of them are interested in civic and cultural affairs. And, since the residences of Jews are not randomly distributed throughout the community, the number of Jews in groups which are organized on a local basis varies with the neighborhood. Accordingly, the percentage of Jews in the local PTA's increases as the neighborhood becomes more Jewish.

However, the selective preferences of Jews are even more important than these population factors. As we have already noted, Jews are more attracted to these community organizations than Gentiles are—especially at the lower levels of income and education and in the younger age groups. Since few such organizations exclude Jews from membership, most succeed in gaining admittance—a fact which probably makes the groups even less appealing to Gentiles and therefore further compensates for the imbalance between Jew and Gentile in the general population.

Sometimes, however, these Jewish selective preferences are diverted into sectarian channels, so that Jewish interest in these activities does not result in the higher representation in non-sectarian groups. This is especially true of health and welfare affiliations. Almost twice as many Jewish as Gentile women belong to such groups; yet we have been unable to identify any non-sectarian welfare group in Lakeville that has a truly mixed membership. Even non-sectarian welfare groups with a predominantly Jewish membership appeal to only a small number of Jews. In other words, most Jewish women with non-sectarian welfare affiliations belong to groups with few Jews or at least with no higher a percentage of Jews than is found in the local population. The reason is fairly obvious: Their sectarian affiliations siphon off most of their interest in welfare activities. The same point applies—though on a lesser scale—to the fraternal affiliations of Jewish men. There too, more Jews than Gentiles belong to such groups, but their sectarian affiliations satisfy most of them, and those who belong to non-sectarian fraternal groups are primarily found in predominantly Gentile ones.

Many other groups in the community also reveal a highly skewed distribution of members: they are composed predominantly of Jews or of Gentiles. If they have explicit community functions, their skewed distribution may reflect their lesser appeal to the other group. Jews, for example, show little interest in the American Legion and other non-sectarian patriotic groups, and even less interest in Republican political groups. Or a skewed distribution may result from a selective recruitment of membership within special subgroups of a larger organization. For example, one Masonic lodge in Lakeville is predominantly Jewish; most others have relatively few Jews. A local unit of the Red Cross is reported to have a predominantly Jewish membership; others are predominantly Gentile. One chapter of the Infant Welfare League is mostly Jewish; other chapters are mostly Gentile. Skewed distributions are also found in groups with specific functions that are relatively small in size and not too formally structured. This is especially true of small cultural groups such as literary and book clubs or drama and play-reading groups, and small health and welfare groups such as those which raise money for cerebral palsy or multiple sclerosis organizations.

In general, however, the most consistently skewed groups are those which are organized around the social and personal interests of their members. Thus, the more formally organized country or city clubs are predominantly Jewish or Gentile. So are the garden clubs, the sports groups, the bridge clubs, and especially the informal social groups. This does not mean that no members of a given club come from the other ethnic group. The proportion, however, is considerably higher in those groups that are closely associated with public institutions and with organized community activities. For example, almost 40 per cent of the members of the women's public golf league are Gentile, as contrasted with only an estimated 1 or 2 per cent in the various bowling groups in which Jewish women predominate. Similarly, almost half the membership in the community-wide duplicate bridge group is Gentile, as contrasted with only an estimated 7 per cent in the more informally organized bridge clubs. In other words, the groups that are privately organized, and especially those that have a traditional structure such as country and city clubs, are more likely to have few, if any, members from the other ethnic group.

In large measure, this distribution results from the tendency of people with similar backgrounds to associate with each other. However, it is frequently reinforced by a conscious or unconscious effort to exclude those who may actually be similar to the present members in respects other than their ethnic identity. No group is more visibly exclusionary than the country clubs. This is clearly reflected in the responses of our Jewish respondents to the question about the kinds of discrimination being practiced by Gentiles against Jews in Lakeville. They point to exclusion from Gentile country clubs as the most prevalent form; next in importance is exclusion from the Lakeville Woman's Club; and 59 per cent of all complaints of discrimination deal with one of these two. However, just as Jews still do not become members of the major Gentile country clubs in Lakeville, so Gentiles do not become members of the major Jewish ones.

Thus, the composition of the country clubs reflects, first of all, the general tendency of Lakeville Jews to adopt the elite model of leisure in the community. At the same time it also reveals that the more personal their affiliations, the more likely both Jews and Gentiles are to remain separate. These findings will take on increasing significance in subsequent chapters which explore in more detail the moods of acculturation and integration of the Lakeville Jews.

7

THE JEW AND INTEGRATION

Our findings indicate that integration is a central value among the Jews of Lakeville. Despite the trait of clannishness that is attributed to him, the Jewish newcomer is as likely to be convinced as the older residents that he should not confine his social interests and associations to Jews and to the Jewish community. The emphasis placed by both newcomers and longtimers on becoming part of the larger society is reflected by the fact that two out of three of our respondents say that to be a "good Jew" one must promote civic improvement in the community. Of the remaining Jewish respondents, all but 4 per cent consider civic involvement to be a desirable, if not essential, aspect of Jewishness. Along with participation in general community affairs, the good Jew, according to the majority opinion, is also obliged to build good personal relations with Gentiles, particularly those who are his neighbors, and to win their respect.

The Mixed Neighborhood: The Common Basis of Integration

Positive relations with Gentile neighbors require their presence in the immediate environment. The mixed neighborhood is also part of the ideology of the Lakeville Jew. All but 1 per cent of our respondents

124

want a substantial number of Gentiles in their neighborhood: indeed, half of them would prefer to live in a neighborhood that is 50 per cent Gentile. This figure is even more striking when we realize that 60 per cent of those who choose it live in a neighborhood where Jews are presently a majority, while only 15 per cent live in a dominantly Gentile neighborhood.[1] Moreover, only 6 per cent of our Jewish respondents say that they are indifferent to the ethnic composition of their neighborhood.[2]

The desire of our respondents to have a substantial proportion of Gentile neighbors represents a decisive break from the world of their ancestors. While few Jews in past historical eras preferred enforced segregation, they had a definite preference for a Jewish neighborhood. In fact, the Jew whose occupation required him to live among Gentiles felt himself to be in a kind of double Diaspora, and was regarded so by other Jews. Not only was safety and security a factor in choosing a neighborhood, area, or town populated predominantly by Jews, but the choice was preferable on other grounds as well. A Jewish neighborhood afforded the Jew easy access to Jewish facilities. Even more important, it facilitated the preservation of his way of life. Finally, since the Jew assumed that his way of life was not only different but superior, to live among Gentiles did not confer distinction upon him.

On the other hand, in explaining why he wants 50 per cent of his neighbors to be Gentile, the typical Lakeville Jew reveals the strong attraction of the world outside the Jewish community. It is an attraction, however, that is more often primarily of the "head" rather than of the "heart." Approximately 60 per cent of those who prefer a parity

[1] While there are well-defined community areas in Lakeville, the lack of a grid system or other uniform pattern and the presence of hills and other distinct topographical features in certain parts of the town made the use of the term "street" or "neighborhood" in the conventional sense unrealistic. We therefore developed an arbitrary definition of "neighborhood" that could be applied uniformly to all respondents but would still be rooted in the realities of the local situation. After a preliminary investigation, we decided upon the twenty houses nearest to the respondent. Thus, we asked our Jewish respondents: "Let's consider the twenty houses nearest to yours . . . about how many are occupied by Gentile families?" (If the respondent said that fewer than twenty houses were in the area, he was asked for the relevant figures.) Gentile respondents were asked a similar question, except that the word "Jewish" was substituted for "Gentile." The term "neighborhood" is used in this special sense throughout the book.

[2] The extent of concern among Jews about the composition of their neighborhood is further suggested by the fact that 43 per cent of our Gentile respondents claim to be indifferent about the ratio of Jews to Gentiles in their immediate environment.

of Jewish and Gentile neighbors are mainly interested in the benefits of social learning, while the rest are mainly motivated by the desire for more direct and personal relations with Gentiles.

Speaking of the educational benefits of such a neighborhood, a young high school teacher, who grew up in a predominantly Jewish neighborhood, explains, "I suppose I don't want to be too insular. It limits you in outlook. You become narrow and prejudiced." A young mother of three children who was active in interfaith activities at Ohio State similarly observes: "I feel this figure [a 50–50 neighborhood] can give our children and ourselves a better viewpoint toward living, a more true viewpoint, a more wholesome view into what life is." "I am a woman of the world, not only a Jew," says an accomplished painter who is troubled by the constraint between Jews and Gentiles in her predominantly Jewish neighborhood. "As a result, I feel I'd like to know Gentile people more, because they have different attitudes and ways of thinking and I would like to incorporate that into my way of life." Along with freeing oneself from a narrow, ethnocentric perspective and developing new social and moral awareness, some respondents also see a positive gain in group relations. A young used-car dealer who has lived in Lakeville for three years sums up the matter in these words:

> I feel that I'd like for my own personal feelings to get rid of the sense of difference. It's important to be in contact with other faiths without losing your identity. Specifically, it's important for Jewish people to dispel the stereotype notions of Jews held by Gentiles and to get a broader outlook.

The general value of Jews and Gentiles learning to live with each other in a mixed neighborhood is frequently affirmed by those respondents who are conscious of the divisiveness that exists in Lakeville. "You learn to get along better with other people," observes a housewife who has also recently moved to Lakeville. "And when they get to know you, their prejudices lessen. I know the woman next door was very worried when she learned Jews were moving in, but now she is very happy." Or again, another newcomer who has had little to do with Jews until now remarks: "I think it's a better community, better for both. People might then get together and get to know each other's beliefs and learn to respect each other." As well as reducing intergroup tensions, such a neighborhood also answers to the democratic dream that continues to have a powerful appeal to Jews as one of the more recent immigrant groups. A parity of Jews and Gentiles is "certainly democratic," says a woman active in liberal politics. Or as another woman who devotes her free time to ORT "because I am Jewish" and to the League of Women Voters "because I am a citizen," puts it, "I feel this percentage is important for democratic integration."

The mixed neighborhood is particularly desirable to respondents who are interested not only in their own integration and acculturation but in that of their children. Indeed, a number of respondents, such as a middle-aged engineer, say that "it's primarily because of the children that I'd want this percentage." As this respondent goes on to remark, "I'd like them to have contact with the problems they'll face in later life, but as an adult I'd prefer an all-Jewish neighborhood." Whether as an education in the realities of ethnic differences or in the possibilities of democratic pluralism, the open and balanced community is felt to be the best type of milieu for the Jewish child. One respondent speaks of an "interchange of habits, values, ideas"; another of mutual "understanding and respect"; another of a "more rational idea of what the world is like"; another of "preparation for the bumps they'll get." "Even a high-class ghetto I wouldn't like," says a salesman who grew up in a non-Jewish neighborhood and who wants his children "to develop an understanding of other people and other religions." In many such responses, it is clear that one of the chief advantages which the Jewish parent is anxious to bestow on his child is the experience of living among Gentiles and relating freely to them. The wife of a manufacturer speaks on this point in the following manner:

> I like this figure [50 per cent] for the simple reason that children should be raised in a neighborhood where there are Jews and Gentiles. When they get out into the business world, they will find that there are many Gentiles, and I'm afraid they won't all be kind. If my children are going to be called a "Dirty Jew," I would like it to be when they are young and it can be explained. I know that when I was of high school age, I was sent away to a private school where another girl and myself were the only Jews in a class of about sixty. We really were pushed around; I remember the pins being knocked out from under me; I almost think it left me with a complex about Gentiles. Sometimes I think I must be prejudiced against Gentiles.

It is worth noting that the preference for parity of numbers and cultures frequently expresses the respondent's wish to protect the security and integrity of his children as Jews as well as to introduce them to the mixed society in which they will live. In other words, a 50–50 neighborhood provides for pluralism while guarding against assimilation. A self-made man who regards himself as an atheist still speaks for many of our respondents when he says, "I think this percentage provides a healthy atmosphere. It meets the purpose we had in mind when we moved here. We feel that the child should know his origins but should also know differences as well." Or as a lawyer whose teen-age son dates Gentile as well as Jewish girls puts it: "It's just that I feel that I want my son to know both; not, in other words, to be afraid to understand them, and yet not to forget his own people." Or again, another lawyer who grew up in Russia provides a more extended statement of the same attitude:

> My child should be exposed to the experience of meeting with Gentiles. For we are a minority in this country and one could get an erroneous idea of the role of a minority group if one didn't live with Gentiles. In school if the pupils were all Jewish it wouldn't be best for my child. Yet, if she were the only Jewish child with all Gentiles, it would be equally bad; she might not have a sense of belonging or might become assimilated. I don't want to have that. I want her to have a feeling of Jewishness too.

It is thus apparent that the 50 per cent figure has assumed a deep symbolic significance for a majority of Lakeville Jews. It expresses their view of a model community, one which guarantees the best opportunities for social learning while preserving the opportunities for Jewish identity. In other words, it envisions a solid middle ground of pluralism that lies between ethnocentrism on the one hand, and assimilation on the other.

The other 44 per cent of Lakeville's Jews who express a preference do not find this magical potency in parity of numbers and instead favor a majority–minority arrangement in their neighborhoods. They split almost evenly, however, over which group should be in the majority. Approximately one out of four Jews in Lakeville wishes Gentiles to be the preponderant group. Accordingly, slightly less than half of these respondents (46 per cent) prefer to have more Gentiles than are presently in their respective neighborhoods, 43 per cent want the same proportion that currently exists, and only 11 per cent want fewer Gentile neighbors.

Though their notions of a favorable imbalance range from 60 to 90 per cent, the respondents who prefer a majority of Gentiles usually offer much the same explanations. They are more committed to the experience of adaptation than are those who prefer parity, for they wish their neighborhoods to reflect the fact that Jews are a minority in Lakeville and in the society at large. A native of Lakeville who elects a

60–40 split remarks: "As a minority group [Jews] should realize that there are certain inherent disadvantages when a minority group nationally becomes a majority group locally. Accordingly, I'd like to see, other features being equal, the Jews remain a minority group in Lakeville." A manufacturer dislikes the "parochialism" of his Jewish neighborhood and prefers a neighborhood that is 90 per cent Gentile: "I'd like the proportion to resemble a cross section of the country in order to acquaint my children with all kinds of people." "I feel that [70 per cent] is more representative of the distribution of the population," says a civil engineer who is active in his temple but is disappointed by the fact that most of his neighbors are Jewish. "It's better for the children. You want kids to be used to the majority to face up to the world as it is. I don't like the tendency for Jews to congregate in certain localities. It is no good for the Jewish community."

What tends to distinguish this group from the respondents who want a neighborhood closer to parity is a more marked interest in developing personal relationships with Gentiles. Approximately 60 per cent say that they are primarily interested in the social relations rather than the social education of living among Gentiles. (This priority is reversed by nearly the same percentage among those who prefer a balanced neighborhood.) "I like it as it is—75 per cent non-Jewish," says the young wife of a realtor. "I feel that I'd like to be friendly with non-Jews and also that I'd like my children to know both. We'd get a little too clannish and cliquish if it were more Jewish."

Most respondents in this group, however, do not wish the percentage of Jews in their midst to drop to the point where they would comprise a scanty and isolated minority. Their model neighborhood in the matter of religious-ethnic distribution is much closer to the Lakeville of today than to the prewar community in which Jewish residents made up a small marginal group. According to several of our respondents—who are satisfied with being in a minority of 25 or 30 per cent—a smaller percentage would create a misleading image of modern society, or separate the two groups and weaken the ground for friendly relations, or foster an undue amount of assimilation. An executive who grew up mainly among Gentiles expresses this attitude as follows:

I don't want Jews to be the majority nor only 5 per cent of the population either. I want enough to give my children some security so that they can understand, for example, that those who celebrate Hanukkah are different from those who celebrate Christmas and that the latter are the majority. I want, in other words, enough Jews for collective security but not enough for a majority.

Indeed, there is often a certain ambiguity in the responses of this group which results from a desire to maintain a security in numbers and at the same time avoid an unrepresentative cluster of Jewish residents that smacks of a "ghetto." This tension is expressed by a housewife who wants her neighborhood to be 40 per cent Jewish. "I want to create a proportion akin to that in the world. On the other hand, I want enough Jews to create an atmosphere where I have my own identity. We should also have Catholic friends too."

The desire for the reassurance of numbers is much more pronounced among the Lakeville Jews—20 per cent of the total—who prefer a Jewish majority in their neighborhood. So, too, is their preference for social relations with other Jews. As an accountant who comes from an immigrant Jewish background remarks: "For security, comfort, and ease I'd want mostly Jews. A stranger who is Jewish can't be the same kind of threat that a stranger who is non-Jewish can be." An attorney who grew up among Gentiles agrees: "It's more comfortable and more pleasant with more Jews around."

However, only 26 per cent of this group want fewer Gentiles than actually reside in their neighborhood. And an even smaller proportion— 1 per cent of the total Jewish respondents—would be content with an all-Jewish neighborhood. The rest are convinced that they want a significant minority of Gentiles. Three out of five are satisfied with the *status quo* in their neighborhoods, and another 14 per cent desire more Gentiles than are presently living there.

By far the prevailing reason for this choice is the benefit of social learning that will accrue to their children. As with the other Jewish respondents, those who prefer a majority of their co-religionists as neighbors are mindful of the need to educate their children in the realities of a mixed society. For example, a wealthy young housewife who is active in the Girl Scouts observes: "It's good for children to come into contact with non-Jews and to see the differences and to know the differences and not to think too much of them. They'll have to face such matters all their lives because they'll never live in a world of all Jews."

It is evident, then, that the general acceptance of integration leads our respondents to believe that they ought to live in some sort of mixed environment. The issue is the relative proportions of such a mixture. As we have already seen, the preference for parity or for a majority of

Gentile neighbors is in part influenced by how much support and satisfaction respondents receive from the presence of other Jews. But what
also determines these choices is the extent of their acceptance of Gentile
values. It goes almost without saying that those respondents who prefer
a majority of Gentiles tend to go much further in their acceptance than
do those who would retain at least parity in the neighborhood. This is
most clearly seen in the attitudes toward Christmas trees: respondents
who prefer a majority of Gentiles are much more likely to approve of
Jews having a tree or to have one themselves (see Table 7–1).

TABLE 7–1 RESPONSE OF JEWS TO CHRISTMAS TREES
BY NEIGHBORHOOD PREFERENCES

*Response to Christmas trees**	Percentage of Gentiles that Jewish respondent would prefer in his neighborhood		
	Less Than 50%	50%	More Than 50%
Approves of Jews having Christmas trees in their homes and has one in his own home	23%	32%	46%
Either approves or has tree in home	7	13	12
Doesn't approve and doesn't have tree in home	70	55	42
	100%	100%	100%
	(86)	(216)	(97)

* These items were used: (1) "In general how do you feel about a Jewish family having
a Christmas tree?" (2) "What about yourself? Did you have one last year?"

Christmas Trees: The Upper Limits of Integration

Unlike preference for the composition of one's neighborhood, the
question of displaying a Christmas tree is a highly charged issue in the
Jewish community. It taps deep emotions, particularly among those who
object to adopting this practice. They do not consider the issue one of
taste but of principle: a Jew should not display a tree because it is a
Christian symbol. As a second-generation Jew who is a college teacher
puts it: "I think it's an affectation and a mistake to have a Christmas
tree. It's an attempt to adapt something from a culture which has a
different ritualistic and religious significance. There is no place for it
in Judaism." Or, in the words of a young accountant: "I don't think it's

right for the same reason that I don't think it's right for the Christian to have a Hanukkah menorah. The Christmas tree is the religious symbol of Christ's birth; he is their God, not ours."

There is also the question of motive. According to their critics, Jews who place a tree in their home at Christmas are guilty of evasiveness and bad faith. "It's very repulsive to me to display a tree," says a salesman from an Orthodox background. "If you are a Jew, be proud of it. Too many Jews are trying to be like Gentiles, so they have Christmas trees. It's strictly a Gentile religious custom." An engineer who fled from Vienna in the late 1930's registers his disapproval in these terms: "It is hypocrisy when you try to steal a nice portion of a religious holiday that doesn't belong to you. It's an easy way out for parents to avoid pointing out to children the difference between the Gentiles and Jews." Evidently the celebration of Christmas in this overt form marks to many Jews the abandonment of one's commitment to Judaism as a distinctly separate religion. "If they had a picture of Christ, it would be the same thing," says an accountant who also comes from an Orthodox family, though he is non-observant himself. "Both are symbols of Christianity. . . . Jews who have trees are denying their faith." Or again, an educational psychologist asserts that having a tree "shows lack of understanding of the Jewish religion, and it shows that they are trying to apologize for being Jewish."

In a community where acculturation, integration, and secularism are proceeding at a rapid rate and the distinctions between the two faiths tend to blur, it is not surprising that Jews with strong feelings of loyalty should seize upon some specific practice as marking the boundary of acceptable accommodation to community mores. Apparently the display of a Christmas tree serves this function.

The arguments of those Jews who defend and/or practice the custom mostly rely upon denying the basic premise of their critics: they do not consider a Christmas tree to be a symbol of the Christian religion, though it does have some symbolic meaning to many of them which is in keeping with the values they place upon integration. Most often the tree represents an important bit of Americana, a symbol which in turn reflects the fact that Christmas has become a national holiday, so secularized that it is devoid of any religious significance. Consequently, Jews can and should celebrate the occasion with a tree because they are Americans. "I think Christmas should be treated and celebrated as Fourth of July," says a lawyer from a highly assimilationist background. A more explicit justification is provided by a fourth-generation German

Jew: "I feel it's important that Jews have a tree because I think that Christmas is more of a national holiday than a religious one, and it's about time for all Jews to become American as long as they wish to live in the United States." Or again, a young woman who belongs to the same Reform temple as these two men, and who shares their opposition to Zionism and Israel, goes so far as to say, "I don't think that Christmas has anything to do with Christ's birth."

Other respondents justify their tree on the ground that it was initially a pagan symbol of the season only later adopted by Christianity. They therefore see no reason why a Jew is not also free to adopt it—provided he bears in mind its original symbolism. This argument is typified by a professional woman who prides herself on her enlightened, liberal views:

> The tree is a lovely thing. You know, it didn't start as a religious symbol. It was a pagan one in Germany. I think it's a shame that so much fuss is being made about it. It's been made into a religious symbol by my Jewish friends. They claim that we lose their respect by showing it.[3]

A more popular and expressive symbolism for the holiday and tree is developed by those respondents who abstract qualities which have universal moral meaning and which accordingly make the holiday worthy of observance. Peace, good will, fellowship, and brotherhood are seen to be the dominant meaning of the holiday, which the Jew can celebrate because of his ties to humanity. Thus a young housewife whose husband is a native of Lakeville and who has no temple affiliations believes that "Christmas trees belong to all people without religious significance. The principles of good fellowship which are so strong at Christmas can't hurt anyone; its moral aspects are good and

---

[3] It is worth noting that a small number of Jews do not rely on a symbolic explanation for defending the Christmas tree and are content with aesthetic reasons. A poised and cultivated woman whose mother was a convert to Christian Science remarks as follows:

> I feel it's fine having a tree. I guess I just feel that Christmas is a beautiful thing and since we are part of a community which enjoys this beauty, I feel we too may partake of it. I think Christmas is the most beautiful fairy tale there is. It's more inspiring to give one's children than the Mosaic concept. I don't feel this way for adults that are ready for ethical concepts.

Or again, a second-generation Jewish woman of Eastern European descent says, "I would like to have a tree primarily because of its beauty. Oh, it's only an evergreen with lights to me, but it is also pretty. I don't associate it with religion." However, in rebutting this point of view, a local rabbi has remarked, "If a Jew wants to display a Christmas tree merely because it is beautiful, then he should do it in July instead of December."

fine." Moreover, the desire for easing interfaith tensions and for bridging the divisions between neighbors finds a natural object in the celebration of Christmas. As such, participating in its customs becomes another form of the social education that brought many of our respondents to Lakeville. Even a man from a religious home who does not go so far as having a tree himself takes this position: "Christmas is a universal celebration. It's very nice—good will to all. If anyone feels like they want a Christmas tree to show good will to their neighbor, it's fine; but I wouldn't have it." Much the same point is made by an engineer who is the product of a mixed marriage: "Having a tree and observing Christmas tend to accentuate similarities rather than differences between people, and I approve of this." Then, too, there is the development of the children to be considered. "I approve of the tree because I think Christmas is a wonderful holiday" says another fourth-generation German Jew. "It develops a feeling of good will toward man and if handled right can help our children to realize the responsibility we have to others."

Finally there are those respondents to whom Christmas symbolizes reaffirmation of family pleasures and solidarity, which have traditionally been major values among Jews and which transvalue any other meaning the season may have. "I see nothing wrong with Christmas," says a young housewife who has spent most of her life among Gentiles. "Any occasion that brings a family together is good, provided it's a good experience. Christmas is warm and enriching." Another respondent approves of the tree "as long as it is not used as a religious symbol but as a symbol of pleasant family get-togethers; then it's no more religious than is a Thanksgiving turkey or an Easter egg."

The Range of Integration-Mindedness

The crucial dispute, then, in the Lakeville Jewish community is in defining the upper limits of integration. In other words, the value of integration is uniformly accepted, but opinion on the extent to which one should participate in civic affairs, foster good intergroup relations, and adapt to the predominantly Gentile life style and customs of the community have been seen to vary quite sharply in some respects.

The range of Jewish responses to this issue can best be analyzed by classifying and combining individual reactions to the various items bearing on the matter. Thus we have developed an index of "integration-mindedness" based on the key items that pertain to Jewish attitudes and behavior vis-à-vis the Gentile community. Table 7–2 shows the distribu-

TABLE 7–2   RESPONSES TO COMPONENT ITEMS FOR SCORE VALUES ON INDEX OF INTEGRATION-MINDEDNESS

Score on index of integration-mindedness	Civic involvement and/or winning respect of Gentile neighbors are essential to being a good Jew			Membership and/or participation in non-sectarian groups		
	Both	Either	Neither	Both	Either	Neither
	(2)*	(1)	(0)	(2)	(1)	(0)
9	80%	20	0	100%	0	0
8	88%	12	0	96%	4	0
7	67%	31	2	83%	17	0
6	66%	19	15	76%	23	1
5	60%	20	20	61%	34	5
4	43%	27	30	56%	39	5
3	32%	30	38	35%	43	22
2	10%	13	77	27%	46	27
1	0%	23	77	0%	46	54

Score on index of integration-mindedness	Neighborhood preferences: Gentiles should comprise			Participates in distinctively Gentile leisure activities		Approves of and/or has Christmas tree		
	More Than 50%	50%	Less Than 50%	Yes	No	Both	Either	Neither
	(2)	(1)	(0)	(2)(1)†	(0)	(2)	(1)	(0)
9	80%	20	0	100%	0	100%	0	0
8	64%	32	4	56%	44	96%	4	0
7	38%	60	2	37%	63	83%	11	6
6	35%	54	11	34%	66	48%	21	31
5	18%	66	16	27%	73	29%	12	59
4	12%	60	28	22%	78	9%	11	80
3	3%	60	37	17%	83	0%	10	90
2	3%	50	47	3%	97	0%	7	93
1	0%	23	77	8%	92	0%	0	100

* The figure in parentheses refers to the score value of the category.
† Only 7 Jews engage in two or more distinctively Gentile leisure activities (score value 2).

tion of the responses for the component items of those respondents in each score level, ranging from 0 to 10.

In Table 7–3 we find that the distribution of score values for integration-mindedness describes an almost symmetrical curve; only a fraction of the respondents—10 per cent or less—are at either extremity; the rest cluster around the middle values.

The average Lakeville Jew—whose score value is 4.9—does not differ from the less integration-minded respondent in the items he prefers; he merely combines a greater number of them. Thus, almost two out of three respondents not only belong to but also participate in nonsectarian organizations; they believe that *both* civic involvement and gaining the respect of the Gentile are essential; and they are much more likely to be convinced that a 50–50 ratio in the neighborhood is desirable.

Further, no respondent is devoid of all the characteristics that indicate some degree of acceptance of integration (no respondent has all of them, either). Thus, even those who score lowest on the scale are likely to belong to some non-sectarian organization, *or* to consider 50 per cent a desirable proportion of Gentiles in the neighborhood, *or* to consider either gaining the respect of the Gentile or civic involvement extremely important for the Jew.

TABLE 7–3　Distribution of Scores of Jewish Respondents on Index of Integration-Mindedness

Score value	Per Cent of Jewish Respondents
Highest 10	0%
9	1
8	5
7	12
6	19
5	20
4	19
3	14
2	7
1	3
Lowest 0	0
	100%
	(432)

MEAN SCORE VALUE: 4.9

At the same time, relatively few of the respondents who score in the average range prefer distinctively Gentile leisure activities or have Christmas trees in their homes. Only among the most integrated do these two characteristics become widespread, as does the wish to live in a predominantly Gentile neighborhood instead of one with a 50–50 ratio.

Thus in the kinds of items he endorses, the average scorer appears to differ more from the highly integrated Jew than he does from the less integrated. This is still another way of seeing that the major cleavage in the Jewish community is at the upper limits of integration, where today the crucial questions of Jewish identity within the context of a Gentile-dominated community sharply pose themselves.

8

THE JEW AND
SOCIAL CONTACT

Irrespective of the diverse limits that Lakeville Jews place
upon integration, their common desire to establish some degree of contact with individual Gentiles and with the general community inexorably
draws them into a problematic area of experience. For not only do most
Jews in the community wish to belong to non-sectarian organizations, to
participate in community affairs, to adopt new styles of leisure, and to
live in a mixed neighborhood; but in addition, they are drawn to the
possibility of direct personal relations with Gentiles. However attractive
the latter contacts may seem, they create marked anxiety among some
50 per cent of our Jewish respondents, who find that they are apprehensive, defensive, or otherwise ill at ease in the company of Gentiles.[1]

The Bases of Discomfort

The anxiety with which Jewish respondents approach social relations
with Gentiles appears to stem from three major sources: (1) fear of
general anti-Semitic prejudice—hostility, denigration, rejection; (2) un-

[1] The question asked was "In general, do you find that you are less comfortable
with non-Jews than you are with Jews?" These respondents said "less comfortable
with non-Jews." Some 48 per cent of the respondents said there was no difference,
while 2 per cent said they were less comfortable with Jews than with non-Jews.

certainty as to how Gentiles perceive and judge them; and (3) awareness of sharp differences in background, behavior, and values between Gentiles and themselves. Table 8–1 provides a breakdown of these responses.

TABLE 8–1   REASONS FOR THE DISCOMFORT OF JEWS IN THE PRESENCE OF GENTILES

What makes the respondent feel uncomfortable in the presence of a Gentile?	*Jewish respondents who feel less comfortable with Gentiles than with Jews*	
Fear of General Negative Attitudes or Behavior toward Jews		54% *
Expectation of hostility	32%	
Expectation of rebuff or rejection	27%	
The Gentile's Image of Respondent		31%
Uncertainty about Gentile's image	13%	
Belief that Gentile sees respondent as a Jew and not as a person	20%	
Differences in Style of Life and Values		47%
		(214)

* Respondents could offer as many reasons as they wished; therefore the percentages within each category exceed the total for that category, and the sum of all percentages exceeds 100 per cent.

THE FEAR OF ANTI-SEMITISM

Central to the first concern, and perhaps basic to the others as well, is the belief—specifically expressed by 32 per cent but implied by a much larger number—that many, if not most, Gentiles do not like Jews. The wife of a physician who has never had very much to do with Gentiles explains that "I'm not comfortable with non-Jews because of their general anti-Semitic feelings. I can't stand it when they say 'some of my best friends are Jews.' " Or again, according to the wife of a salesman who has lived among Gentiles all her life, "I feel less comfortable with non-Jews because sometimes I feel that there is an underlying prejudice. Unconsciously there probably is." "I don't act natural when I'm with non-Jews," says a young dentist who experienced anti-Semitism in his childhood, professional training, and service in the Navy: "I am worried about whether they are going to say anything antagonistic against us Jews. This happens when they have a few drinks." The fear that underlying anti-Semitism will reveal itself when the normal social inhibitions are weakened is graphically expressed by a young businessman who associates mainly with Jews though his work is mainly with Gentiles:

> I went on a trip to a steel mill with a group taken by one of our suppliers. I was the only Jew among seven or eight fellows. We left in the afternoon, got there at night and spent the day being wined and dined. . . . One of the fellows was a big jovial Irishman I know through business. Throughout the course of this drinking bout I had a very strange feeling that in his drunkenness he would make anti-Semitic remarks. It occurred to me that it would be embarrassing to the fellow who was my host. He's a high-type, clean-cut, Gentile boy. I will never go again.

Or there is a stockbroker active in a Jewish community-relations group who claims to be more anxious about his own aggression: "I'm uncomfortable with non-Jews only because I'm liable to pull the trigger if someone made a remark against Jews. I knocked a guy down once who called a friend of mine a 'dirty Jew' in front of me."

It is worth noting that our respondents need not have recently experienced anti-Semitic hostility to feel anxious in the presence of a Gentile. For example, 47 per cent of those who say they have not encountered any anti-Semitism in recent years claim to be uncomfortable with Gentiles—a figure that is only 5 per cent lower than that found among respondents who report recent anti-Semitic incidents. Presumably the former respondents have had earlier experiences with anti-Semitism. But whether they have or not, it is clear that the *expectation* of hostility is enough to make them anxious in Gentile company and that this expectation is equally shared by many Jews, irrespective of their actual exposure to anti-Semitism.

A vivid example of this deeply rooted expectation of Gentile enmity is expressed by a housewife who recently moved to Lakeville:

> I'm less comfortable with non-Jews. I feel a certain amount of tenseness—that something may be said against Jews. As a result, I feel that I have to watch what I say, that I can't think or speak as freely. This doesn't particularly come from my experiences with non-Jews; it's just the way I have felt all my life.

Many other respondents report a similar cautionary attitude in relations with Gentiles that have not been clearly defined. In the words of a housewife who has lived in Lakeville for five years without developing any significant contact with Gentiles:

I'm less comfortable with non-Jews because I'm aware of the differences between us, and I wait to see if the person is anti-Semitic or not. Usually you hold off discussions in depth until you see if they sound anti-Semitic in talking.

Indeed, the tension of such ambiguity and apprehension, according to a woman who prefers living in a "more Jewish neighborhood," may lead one to withdraw from contact with Gentiles:

I'm less comfortable with non-Jews. With the new and the unknown I'm not sure how non-Jews stand on the question of the Jews, and I have to feel my way. Once a relationship is established it's okay, but even that is dependent upon the personality and make-up of the person. In the other situations I get a tingling sensation. I get excited and look for strain and for lack of acceptance, and I want to get out.

A second group of Jewish respondents (27 per cent of the insecure) tends to experience its anxiety about Gentiles less in terms of fearing overt aggression than in feeling out of place, alienated, or rejected in the company of Gentiles. A middle-aged housewife who is among the longtime residents in Lakeville explains her feelings as follows:

I have always felt less comfortable with non-Jews. Most of the time I grew up in a Jewish neighborhood, and my parents had no Gentile friends. I always felt that a barrier exists between us. Even at ten years of age I felt it. I never felt completely free and relaxed. I probably have a fear of not being accepted. It's an uncomfortable feeling.

Rather than expecting direct hostility or defamation, such respondents tend to anticipate a chilly reserve, or a politeness that excludes friendliness, in the behavior of Gentiles. As another longtime resident puts it, "I have a cold, left-out feeling when I'm with non-Jews. I feel you are not in their confidence and they won't put things on a close level; the relationship remains strictly impersonal."

Such Jewish respondents typically feel shunned and attribute their feeling to the fact that the offending Gentiles simply do not like Jews and thus keep them at a distance. This sense of alienation "comes out in many small ways," according to a manufacturer who both likes living in an all-Jewish neighborhood and regards the Jewish influx as the most serious local problem. "I feel that I'm on the fringe and am not being taken into the heart of the group. We treat each other politely and cordially, but we can come together so far and no further." Or again, an engineering consultant whose circle of friends is Jewish but who wishes his children to know more Gentiles finds that "I'm less comfortable with non-Jews in social situations [because] they probably have the feeling that we are different and that we are strangers. They don't go out of their way to make us comfortable. I feel left out."

As with the fear of anti-Semitic remarks, the lack of warmth and intimacy with Gentiles produces unduly self-conscious and guarded behavior. A longtime resident who asserts that "I'm less comfortable with non-Jews because I feel that I'm not being accepted as well as I would be if I were a Gentile," finds that "I get more sensitive and reserved with them, although I'm not this kind of person. And I never bring up the religious question." A housewife who has made no Gentile friends in Lakeville says, "I suppose it's inbred to expect rebuff. It seems I've never come across anti-Semitism, but it's a feeling. As a result, when I'm with Gentiles, I try to put my best foot forward." Another respondent, a well-educated artist who has achieved a good deal of objectivity about her feelings, still finds it difficult to behave freely with Gentiles:

> Although it doesn't always hold, in some new situations I do somehow feel a little bit more uncomfortable with non-Jews. Sometimes it's a [self] inflicted kind of thing. We are raised with the feeling that Jews are rejected by non-Jews, so we act in accordance with this belief—justified or not. Although I've had no bad experiences with prejudiced Gentiles, I don't feel wanted or accepted. I withdraw and I can't make contact with these people, and this makes me uncomfortable.

THE GENTILE'S PERCEPTION OF
THE INDIVIDUAL JEW

A more specific source of tension in such relations is reported by a third group (13 per cent of the insecure). This takes the form of worrying whether they are being perceived as the individuals they are or as a stereotyped embodiment of Jewishness. As the young wife of an electrical engineer puts it, "I'm more uncomfortable with non-Jews . . . because I really never know whether they think of me as a person or as a Jew and what their reactions will be." This usually implies the further question: If I am being perceived as a Jew, am I numbered among the desirable or among the undesirable Jews? "You know [Gentiles] feel an antipathy toward some Jews but you're not sure if that includes you or not," says a lawyer who grew up in Russia and "saw people killed because they were Jewish." "Because I really never know whether they think of me as a person or as a Jew, I have to be more on my guard," says the young housewife quoted above. "I have a little more anxiety and self-consciousness. I feel that they may be critical of me because of my religion."

However, one out of five of the respondents who feel uncomfortable with Gentiles has little or no uncertainty on this score: he is convinced that in the eyes of Gentiles he is a Jew first and an individual a poor second. For example, a young housewife who typifies the well-educated and socially aware younger generation that has moved into the community shrewdly observes: "I'm less comfortable with non-Jews because you feel that they think of you as a Jew. Jews don't really think of you as a Jew."

Such respondents are likely to take on the added strain of acting as though they were ambassadors of the Jewish people. Thus the housewife above believes that it is essential to gain the respect of Christian neighbors in order to be a good Jew. Their tendency is to become extremely self-conscious in the presence of a Gentile and extremely aware of being Jewish; in fact, they may come to feel that they do indeed represent the Jewish group and are responsible for its public image. A good example of this attitude is provided by a sales manager who grew up in Germany. Though he has managed, like the housewife above, to make and keep close friends who are Gentiles, and though he is highly integration-minded, he notes that:

> I'm not quite at ease with Gentiles. I'm much more conscious of myself, and I want to leave a good impression because I feel that I am a representative of the Jewish people, inasmuch as Gentiles consider me as such a representative and use that as a yardstick for judging Jews.

Such a fixed attitude of group consciousness and responsibility encompasses the range of manners by which the Jew attempts to alter and redeem the Gentile stereotype. "I have to be careful with my manners, my dress, my expressions," says a middle-aged lawyer. "I'm always on my guard as to whether I laugh too loud or my voice is too shrill," says a board member of the League of Women Voters. "I feel that I have to count my words," says the wife of a chemist. "I hesitate to discuss certain topics, for example, religion," says a wealthy executive still in his thirties. "I must say things well and with meaning."

GROUP DIFFERENCES

Along with whatever other reasons they offer, 47 per cent of our respondents who report that they feel uncomfortable in the presence of Gentiles also attribute it to an acute sense of difference between the two groups. This may take the form of a direct experience of otherness, expressed typically by a recent arrival in the community who relates that "over the Christmas holiday we were invited to [a Gentile's] house, and we were the only Jewish persons there. They sang carols. I felt different, apart, like I didn't belong." Or the sense of otherness may be attributed to the restrictive categories that exist in Gentile minds, as described by a writer who works for a predominantly Gentile advertising firm: "There's a recognizable difference in their minds. They say, 'You are different. You don't celebrate Christmas: you're different.'"

Be that as it may, the sense of difference is not merely an awareness of historical ethnic and religious divisions between Jew and Gentile, but also reflects more immediate and crucial disparities in manners and mores. As the wife of a lawyer puts it:

> I'm less comfortable with non-Jews because I don't feel I have as much in common with them. They don't take cha-cha lessons, and I never heard of a Gentile woman playing mah-jongg. They live differently. They don't have help. They eat differently, and they are stricter with children. I feel I don't know them. Perhaps if I knew them I'd feel more comfortable and wouldn't attribute such differences to them.

Or again, a woman who sees a good deal of Gentiles through her husband's business life reports that:

> I'm less comfortable with non-Jews because, well, they have all that money and never spend it on themselves. They deprive themselves of clothes and things, and I'm conscious of investing in good tailors. It's a peculiar thing but when I'm in the company of Gentiles socially, which is not the usual thing for me, it being only on some special occasion, I find that these affairs are usually a rather stiff thing. We are invited and they serve liquor, and there's nothing to do but stand and drink.

Or, as a young lawyer who pursues a strenuous program of serious reading and adult education courses reports, "I'm less comfortable with non-Jews because at times I think that as a Jew I may stand out as a person who has interests, for example, like books and music that the rest of the group doesn't have." Or more generally, in the words of a woman who has lived in Lakeville for sixteen years, "I don't feel as much at home with non-Jews. There isn't that common interest or feeling of *Gemütlichkeit*. It just isn't there."

Instead of *Gemütlichkeit*, there is the ever-present awareness of disjunction and distance which increases social tension and is felt to be difficult to bridge: "I'm less comfortable with non-Jews because the avenues of discussion are not always mutual," reports a woman who is active in community as well as Jewish affairs. As she goes on to say,

> Jews have a different set of values, and a common ground isn't there unless you meet Gentiles on some basis such as business or similar hobbies. You can't talk about your organizations or your temple. They would never understand. There's an incompatible feeling, and yet I hope we can find a common ground to talk about.

In sum, as a longtime and old-guard Jewish resident puts it, "I'm less comfortable with non-Jews because there isn't as much common ground for discussion. You have to be on guard and careful about subjects you discuss. I don't have the freedom of personality I have with Jews."

Anxiety, Integration-Mindedness, and Social Contact

Small wonder, then, that the respondents who feel uncomfortable in the presence of Gentiles are wary of personal relationships with them. They are more disposed to associate with Gentiles in structured situations, such as non-sectarian organizations, in business, or at formal social affairs where behavior is usually clearly defined. But they remain reluctant to develop these formal and casual contacts into more personal and friendly relations and to participate with Gentiles in more informal social situations. Those who belong to non-sectarian organizations are less likely to go out socially with Gentile members or to entertain them in their homes than are our other Jewish respondents who feel more comfortable with non-Jews (see Table 8–2). The same is true of their contacts with Gentile neighbors. The only apparent exception is in the business world, where as many Jews in the uncomfortable group as in the more comfortable one mix socially with Gentiles and even invite them to their homes. The uncomfortable group does so somewhat less frequently, however: 68 per cent, in contrast to 78 per cent of the more comfortable group, report at least five informal social contacts a year with Gentiles.

Evidently, then, many Lakeville Jews are subject to ambivalent pressures in establishing and developing informal social contacts with Gentiles. On the one hand, their espousal of integration makes them desire these contacts; on the other, their anxiety in social relations with Gentiles inhibits them from carrying out this desire. Accordingly, the

TABLE 8–2   INTERFAITH SOCIAL CONTACTS OF JEWS
BY DISCOMFORT WITH GENTILES

	More uncomfortable with non-Jews than with Jews	
Per cent who report at least one social contact with Gentiles during the past year	No	Yes
Through Non-Sectarian Organizations		
Went out socially	70% (171)	51% (182)
Entertained at home	56% (170)	33% (180)
Through Their Neighborhood		
Went out socially	52% (176)	36% (169)
Through Work or Professional Relations*		
Went out socially	88% (101)	88% (98)
Entertained at home	58% (99)	57% (99)

* Because so few Jewish women in Lakeville are engaged in full-time employment, we have excluded them from this category. In the other categories, however, we have combined the responses of both men and women. This is the practice we shall follow in all tables in this chapter, unless otherwise specified.

We are able to do so because the differences noted in this table persist even when we take into account the sex of the respondent. It is interesting to note, though, that the social behavior of the women is more responsive to their feelings toward Gentiles than is that of the men. Also, the man's social contacts which arise through organizations and through the neighborhood are much more influenced by his feelings of discomfort with the Gentile than are those arising from vocational contacts. This suggests that other factors may play an even more important role in influencing his social behavior in that context; we shall explore this more fully in Chapter 10, Work and Social Contact.

insecure Jew needs to have a strong commitment to integration if he is to overcome his inhibitions sufficiently so that he can develop social contacts with Gentiles whom he meets in his organizations, neighborhood, or business life. As Table 8–3 indicates, this attraction to the world of the Gentile appears to compensate to the extent that such respondents are almost as likely to have social contacts with Gentiles as are those who are less integration-minded but more comfortable with Gentiles.

Not unexpectedly, the most extensive contacts with Gentiles are found among those Jews—only one out of five—who not only disclaim such insecurity but are also highly integration-minded. However, being highly integration-minded apparently has little connection with feeling comfortable with Gentiles. There is some correlation between the two, but less than one might expect if he had assumed that a strong

TABLE 8-3   SOCIAL CONTACTS OF JEWS BY INTEGRATION-
MINDEDNESS AND DISCOMFORT WITH GENTILES

	More uncomfortable with non-Jews than with Jews			
	No		Yes	
Per cent who report at least one social contact with Gentiles during the past year	Level of integration-mindedness†		Level of integration-mindedness†	
	High	Low	High	Low
Through non-sectarian organizations				
Went out socially	75% (76)	65% (95)	60% (73)	44% (109)
Entertained at home	63% (76)	50% (94)	43% (72)	27% (108)
In their neighborhood				
Went out socially	62% (71)	46% (105)	39% (57)	34% (112)
Per cent who report five or more social contacts with Gentiles during the past year				
Through work or professional relations*				
Went out socially	90% (38)	72% (63)	80% (39)	59% (59)
Entertained at home	32% (38)	28% (61)	27% (40)	20% (59)

* As we have already shown, the frequency of social contacts and not their presence or absence varies within the context of work.
† "High" includes scores of 6 or more; "low," scores of 5 or less.

desire to associate with Gentiles would have led these respondents into relations which would have alleviated their anxiety (see Table 8–4).

There is a more distinct relationship, however, between the level of the relatively insecure Jew's integration-mindedness and several specific areas of disturbance in his personal relations with Gentiles. The Jew who is more integration-minded is less likely to believe that differences in life style are a leading source of his difficulties. One explanation is that his tendency to accept Gentile values would make him less inclined to see any great degree of difference in his own way of life. But despite this greater attraction to and ease with things Gentile, he is even more worried about the possibility of the hostility or the chilliness of anti-Semitism; evidently the problem of prejudice becomes an even greater source of anxiety. Accordingly, he is no less insecure about the Gentile's image of him than is the less integration-minded Jew.

TABLE 8–4 DISCOMFORT WITH GENTILES BY
INTEGRATION-MINDEDNESS

	Index of integration-mindedness*		
	High	Moderate	Low
Per cent who say that they are less comfortable with a non-Jew than with a Jew	47%	50%	53%
	(161)	(167)	(103)

*In all other tables we include the moderates (score values 4 or 5) in the Low category. Moreover, if we separate this composite index into its component parts, we find that only the category which deals with neighborhood preferences bears any significant relationship to respondents' feelings about being in the presence of Gentiles: those who want a predominantly Gentile neighborhood are least likely to be uncomfortable with Gentiles. This suggests that those people who want to live in such neighborhoods are not only expressing a strong attraction to the Gentiles but have also taken into account any personal feelings of anxiety about living in such surroundings.

The Socially Comfortable Jew

If integration-mindedness does not appreciably diminish this general anxiety, what then helps the other 50 per cent of our respondents to feel relatively comfortable in relating to Gentiles? Approximately one out of three of these respondents attributes it to his history of contact and association with Gentiles, particularly if he was reared in a preponderantly Gentile neighborhood. As the son of an Eastern European immigrant family explains:

> I don't feel any different when I'm with Gentiles than when I'm with Jews because as a child I grew up in a neighborhood where there were more non-Jews than Jews, and this helped to make me comfortable with both groups.

However reasonable this explanation may seem, it is also apparent that other Jews who also lived in predominantly Gentile neighborhoods do not share this equanimity. Indeed, the milieu of our respondents in their earlier years—whether it was mostly Gentile or mostly Jewish— bears no significant correlation to the present feelings they report about Gentiles. In each case, approximately one out of two claims to be as comfortable with Gentiles as he is with Jews.

Some of our secure respondents, however, go a step further and say that they are able to relate easily to Gentiles because of a history of friendly and intimate association. As another newcomer to Lakeville puts it, "I don't feel any different with Gentiles, because all my life I've had non-Jewish friends." This association may have begun in their home, where friends of their parents may have been Gentile, or it may have begun in public schools and neighborhoods where they may have mixed with Gentile children and found close friends among them. If these early experiences were in predominantly Gentile circles, then, as indicated in Table 8–5, they do indeed foster a greater ease with Gentiles in later life.

TABLE 8–5   Comfortableness with Gentiles by Heterogeneity of Parental and Teen-Age Friends

	When you were growing up, how many of the close personal friends of your parents were non-Jews?	
	Half or More	Less Than Half
Per cent who say that they are not any less comfortable with non-Jews than with Jews	60% (52)	49% (376)
	When you were a teen-ager, how many of your close friends were non-Jews?	
	Half or More	Less Than Half
Per cent who say that they are not any less comfortable with non-Jews than with Jews	63% (159)	43% (271)

Along with reducing anxiety, a history of intimate association also produces a greater acceptance of integration in many cases. Some 48 per cent of those whose close friends were mostly Gentile are highly integration-minded, in contrast to 31 per cent of those whose friends were predominantly Jewish.

By promoting these beliefs and attitudes, a predominantly Gentile background increases the likelihood of a respondent developing personal relations with Gentiles in Lakeville. It is interesting, however, that a Jew who does not have a history of intimate association, but who is nevertheless integration-minded and relatively free of anxiety, is just as likely, if not more so, to develop social relations with Gentiles in Lakeville as the Jew with such a history (see Table 8–6).

It is evident, then, that a Jew who is integration-minded and free of anxiety does not need a history of intimate association to help him establish personal relations with Gentiles today. His motivation will lead him out sufficiently into the Gentile community, and his social poise will allow him to develop friendly contacts with Gentiles. However, if he lacks either or both of these qualities, then a social history of intimate association does make a difference in his present-day relationships with Gentiles. Thus those Jews who are not attracted to Gentiles, either because they are disturbed by such relations or because they are not particularly integration-minded, evidently still find that the habit and experience of association which they retain from the past enable them to overcome their present indifference or resistance. Having been in these situations before, they are less apt to consider them as upsetting and difficult as do those who have always related mainly to Jews.

Another 14 per cent of the group who are comfortable with Gentiles attribute their equanimity to their general social confidence and adaptability. So speaks a widow who sells real estate in Lakeville and belongs to a mixed bridge group: "I don't have any feeling of difference between Jew and non-Jew. Well, I don't know why. But that's just the way I feel. I can get along with anyone." Or, in visible contrast to the fearful, hypersensitive, or socially diffident respondents we have seen earlier in this chapter, there are Jews like the self-made factory owner who retorts, "There's no reason to feel any different. I'm a tough guy to begin with. I don't give a damn about anybody. If someone's not nice they'll hear from me." Or a good deal of experience may be combined with a strong ego: the wife of an architect who has lived in Lakeville for three decades and has been very active in its cultural affairs has this to say:

> I don't feel any different being with a Gentile from being with a Jew, because I'm not an uncomfortable person. I'm secure. I've always had Gentile friends at school, at college. I even had a non-Jewish husband [whom she divorced].

Those Jewish respondents, then, who do not feel nervous in social situations, whose moods are not easily influenced by people around them, and who are untroubled by feelings of inferiority, are less likely to experience anxiety in intergroup situations. In short, the less a Jew suffers from general feelings of social sensitivity or inadequacy, the less likely he will be to report a specific anxiety in connection with Gentiles (see Table 8–7).

TABLE 8–6 SOCIAL CONTACTS OF JEWS BY INTEGRATION-
MINDEDNESS, DISCOMFORT, AND TEEN-AGE
FRIENDSHIPS

Per cent who have had five or more social contacts with Gentiles during the past year	*Jewish respondents who are highly integration-minded, and/or relatively free of discomfort with Gentiles, or neither*		
	Both	Either	Neither
Through non-sectarian organizations			
Went out socially			
Among those whose close teenage friends* were mainly			
Gentile	63% (46)	50% (58)	38% (26)
Jewish	70% (30)	49% (110)	22% (83)
Entertained at home			
Among those whose close teenage friends were mainly			
Gentile	39% (46)	30% (57)	12% (26)
Jewish	40% (30)	17% (108)	10% (82)
Through their neighborhood			
Went out socially			
Among those whose close teenage friends were mainly			
Gentile	38% (42)	41% (56)	27% (26)
Jewish	41% (29)	24% (106)	21% (86)
Through work or professional relations			
Went out socially			
Among those whose close teenage friends were mainly			
Gentile	85% (20)	79% (38)	74% (19)
Jewish	95% (18)	72% (64)	51% (39)
Entertained at home			
Among those whose close teenage friends were mainly			
Gentile	30% (20)	33% (36)	26% (19)
Jewish	33% (18)	25% (65)	15% (39)

* Those who said half or more of their close teen-age friends were non-Jews were included in the Gentile category; the rest were included in the Jewish category.

TABLE 8–7 DISCOMFORT WITH GENTILES
BY SOCIAL SENSITIVITY

	Index of social sensitivity*				
	(Highest (sensitivity 4	Score values 3	2	1	Lowest) sensitivity) 0
Per cent who say that they are less comfortable with non-Jews than with Jews	59% (39)	57% (83)	50% (131)	46% (104)	40% (72)

* This index includes responses to the following questions:
"Is your mood easily influenced by people around you?"
"Do you consider yourself a rather nervous person?"
"Are you ever troubled with feelings of inferiority?"
"Are your feelings hurt more easily than most people's?"
For a "yes" response to any of the items, a respondent was given a score of 1. The maximum he could get for all items was 4; the minimum, 0. For purposes of convenience we shall henceforth consider those with a score value of 2 or more as having a *high* degree of social sensitivity; and those with a score value of 1 or less as having a *low* degree of social sensitivity.

However, the specific, rather than the general, sensitivity is the more important determinant of a Jew's behavior toward Gentiles. In fact, among the less integration-minded Jews, general feelings about their social capabilities and sensitivities have little direct bearing on their behavior once we take into account specific feelings toward Gentiles (see Table 8–8).

Among the highly integration-minded, however, the psychological situation is much different. Inasmuch as they are strongly attracted to relations with Gentiles, a reduction in their social inhibitions and self-doubts, whether with Gentiles specifically or with people generally, allows them to express this attraction more fully in behavior. As such, a respondent's general confidence in his social abilities has an effect independent of his specific feelings toward Gentiles. Such a socially confident person believes that he can cope with the various contingencies that frequently arise in social situations and is therefore more willing to take the chances that might be involved in associating with Gentiles than are those who lack confidence.

In addition, a feeling of self-confidence also provides reassurance for those who express some anxiety about being with Gentiles. It allows them to act on their desire to associate with them because they evidently believe that they can manage their anxiety effectively.

Other integration-minded Jews claim to handle the problem of differ-

TABLE 8-8   SOCIAL CONTACTS OF JEWS BY INTEGRATION-
MINDEDNESS, DISCOMFORT, AND
SOCIAL SENSITIVITY

Per cent of respondents who report at least one social contact with Gentiles during the past year	*Level of integration-mindedness*			
	High		Low	
	More uncomfortable with non-Jew		More uncomfortable with non-Jew	
	No	Yes	No	Yes
Through non-sectarian organizations				
Went out socially				
Among those whose level of social sensitivity is				
Low	83% (29)	65% (23)	66% (50)	48% (42)
High	70% (47)	58% (50)	64% (45)	42% (66)
Entertained at home				
Among those whose level of social sensitivity is				
Low	69% (29)	48% (23)	52% (50)	25% (40)
High	59% (47)	41% (49)	48% (44)	28% (67)
In their neighborhood				
Went out socially				
Among those whose level of social sensitivity is				
Low	70% (27)	44% (18)	51% (53)	31% (45)
High	57% (44)	36% (39)	40% (52)	36% (66)

ences between Gentiles and Jews by attempting to ignore them. In so doing, they believe, they are able to avoid any marked feelings of anxiety. (Approximately 33 per cent of those who express no greater discomfort with Gentiles than with Jews offer this as an explanation.) A young woman who recently graduated from Bryn Mawr and is married to a bank executive remarks, "I don't feel any different in the presence of Gentiles than in the presence of Jews, probably because I don't make any differentiation between them. I don't think of the distinction between Jew and non-Jew." Instead of ethnic and/or religious categories, they adopt universalistic ones in relating to people. As another young housewife remarks, "I don't feel any different because I don't think about the religion of the person. I wouldn't care if his skin was yellow or black. I don't think in those terms." Their "terms," they believe, allow them to judge men as individuals and not as religious representatives; consequently, there is no reason for them to feel different with Gentiles than with Jews.

Important though this belief may be for these respondents, it has little distinctive bearing on the extent of their social relations with Gentiles, particularly in their neighborhood and organizations. In effect, their social behavior does not differ consistently from that of the Jew who offers other reasons for not being overly insecure with Gentiles; both, however, show an appreciably higher level of contact with Gentiles than do those who suffer much discomfort.

What increases the social contacts of these Jews with the Gentile, then, is not the reason they give for their feeling[2] of being comfortable with Gentiles, but the effect of the feeling itself. However, this effect does not in and of itself ensure maximum contact, which requires a high degree of integration-mindedness as well as of social confidence.

Our main finding, then, is that Lakeville Jews do not have to train themselves to believe that differences between themselves and Gentiles are nonexistent, or are to be totally disregarded, in order to associate more frequently and personally with Gentiles. What they must do is to make their consciousness of these differences less forbidding.

---

[2] Among the less integration-minded, there is one kind of social situation in which belief in the insignificance of group difference does have an independent effect on social behavior. This is in relationships with Gentiles that develop from work or professional contacts. The same effect does not occur, however, among the highly integration-minded.

9

THE GENTILE AND HIS ACCEPTANCE OF THE JEW

As we have seen in the previous two chapters, "integration" is a major value of the Lakeville Jews. It expresses both their intense wish to become part of the main stream of American society and their conviction that to do so they must learn how to live among and associate with Gentiles.[1] For Lakeville's Gentiles, on the other hand, there is no value of comparable scope and force which commits them to live among and associate with Jews. Even though a Gentile may feel strongly that he should participate in neighborhood and community affairs, he does not thereby consider that his civic responsibility obliges him to become involved with Jews.

The reason for this difference is obvious enough. Gentiles simply do not need to be accepted by Jews in order to establish themselves in the community. Lakeville's Protestants have always been the dominant group there as well as in the society at large. This is only somewhat less true of Lakeville's Catholics, who took their place in town earlier than did the Jews. And to the extent that Catholics, who comprise somewhat

[1] It is no less apparent that "integration" also expresses the concern of many Lakeville Jews with their Jewish identity.

155

over 20 per cent of the population, consider themselves a minority, they do not need to be accepted by the Jews but only by the Protestants in order to secure their identity and participation in the life of the community. Thus, the key to understanding the attitudes and behavior of Gentiles in their relations with Jews is to be found in their willingness or unwillingness to accept the presence of Jews as a substantial minority and to establish contacts with them.

That such acceptance is not always offered has already been indicated in our earlier chapters on the Gentiles' reaction to the Jewish newcomers. However, we have still to treat the problem as it relates to the life situation of the individual Gentile in sufficient depth to obtain an adequate understanding of the sources of Gentile reluctance or readiness to develop significant relations with Jews.

The Gentile and His Neighborhood

The difference between the respective social situations of Lakeville's Jews and Gentiles and the values that come from these stations is immediately apparent in the responses to our question concerning the preferred composition of their neighborhood. Overall, some 46 per cent of our Jewish respondents who express a preference want more Gentiles in their neighborhood than presently live there, 37 per cent are satisfied with the present number, and only 17 per cent want fewer Gentile neighbors. Among our Gentile respondents who express a preference on the matter, there is no comparable passion for living among and relating to Jews. Indeed, 50 per cent of them want fewer Jews in their neighborhood, and only 13 per cent want more.[2] Similarly, the prospect of having an equal mixture of Jews and Gentiles in their neighborhood has nothing like the same appeal for Gentiles as it has for Jews. Only somewhat more than one out of ten chooses this proportion, in contrast to five out of ten Jews. On the other hand, the most common response of Gentile respondents to this question is not that of opposition but of indifference, particularly among the Catholics (see Table 9–1).

[2] It is worth noting that Protestants and Catholics are in close agreement on this matter. Neither group is particularly interested in having more Jews in their neighborhood, though Protestant respondents are slightly more inclined to want fewer Jews.

THE SELF-SEGREGATING GENTILE

By far the most pressing concern to the one out of five Gentiles who does not want Jewish neighbors is that of maintaining his way of life. It must be remembered that the average Gentile respondent believes that

TABLE 9-1   PERCENTAGE OF JEWS PREFERRED AS NEIGHBORS AMONG PROTESTANTS AND CATHOLICS

Preferred percentage of Jews as neighbors*	Protestants	Catholics
0%	19%	22%
1–49%	27	16
50%	17	6
51% or more	1	2
Don't care	36	54
	100%	100%
	(154)	(83)

* The actual question was "If it were up to you, what per cent of the people living in this neighborhood would you like to be Jews?"

Jews already make up one-half of Lakeville's population, rather than the one-third that they actually comprise. Since approximately two out of five of these respondents still live in all-Gentile neighborhoods, this preference is frequently expressed as a contentment with things as they are. As a waitress who has lived in Lakeville for twenty-three years puts it: "I like it the same as it is [no Jews]—well, because I'm so used to everyone around here. They're just wonderful, and it's because I'm a Gentile." Or the wife of a cabinetmaker who also lives in central Lakeville opts for the *status quo* without even contemplating it as a distinctly Gentile choice: "I like it the same as it is because it's a pleasant neighborhood. It's still the same as it used to be, and I don't think I'd like it different." Indeed, such a preference may be couched as a resistance to change rather than to Jews. The wife of an electrician from a similar neighborhood remarks: "In the last twenty-three years, I've lived with Gentiles. I'd have to get accustomed all over again to a lot of new things and people if I were to live with Jews."

Those respondents who prefer an exclusively Gentile neighborhood but presently live among Jews tend to be more explicit. The average respondent in this group lives in a neighborhood that is 40 per cent

Jewish and estimates that the population of Lakeville is 60 per cent Jewish; thus the issue is of more than academic interest to him. Generally speaking, their reasons for preferring a solidly Gentile neighborhood stem from one of two attitudes. The first is a disposition toward living with one's own kind of people and is expressed, for the most part, fairly dispassionately. "I suppose we all prefer Gentiles," says a well-educated widow who has had friendly relations with a good many Jews. "To be honest, I'm very happy to have Gentiles as my nearest neighbors. You have to be honest with yourselves, don't you? They're more or less your own kind of people in thinking and in the things that you do together." Though he also prefers an all-Gentile neighborhood, a local physician finds that "I don't have too much feeling about it, but I suppose I would like it because of the similarity of religious backgrounds and of common social interests, church, and so forth." And an engineer expresses his preference with not a little self-irony. "If I had my way, my neighbors would all be just like me and think just like me on every subject. [Laughs.] That's a facetious answer. I was only kidding. But I suppose everyone would prefer to have neighbors that are somewhat like themselves."

Other responses tend to pinpoint specific values that motivate or reinforce Gentile exclusiveness. "I don't know why but I suppose I feel more relaxed with a Gentile," says a popular schoolteacher. "The Gentiles are more on our level," says an engineer who lives in a predominantly Jewish neighborhood. "I can feel I'm just as good as they are. They're more friendly." "I prefer no Jews for reasons of sociability," says a young housewife who fears that Lakeville will be virtually all-Jewish in ten years. "You play bridge back and forth, and the children play together."

A particular consideration that figures in this, as in most matters in Lakeville, is the welfare of the children. To this group of respondents, cultural uniformity and consistency represent a distinctly more valuable learning experience for their children than do otherness and diversity. It is interesting, for example, to compare the following response with those in Chapter 7 which were made by our Jewish parents, who typically opt for the mixed neighborhood in order to expose their children to Gentiles. The respondent is a retired schoolteacher:

> I want my children to grow up as much as possible with children who are raised the same way and afforded the same principles. All the kids around here come from the same type of homes. They are allowed to do the same things. Their parents are home, and all observe Christmas. It's just nice.

It saves so many questions as to why at Christmas, for example, the other kids are getting or not getting presents. It's hard on Jewish kids too.

More than half the respondents (54 per cent) who want no Jews for neighbors, however, are not only concerned about the advantages of a uniformly Gentile environment but also mention explicitly the disadvantages of living among Jews. There are several distinct sources of objection to Jews, which parallel the criticisms of the newcomers to Lakeville that were discussed in Chapter 3.

Indeed, many of these respondents simply restate their earlier general objections to the Jewish influx. "Back to the aggressiveness of the Jews," says one such respondent, a young designer who came to Lakeville three years ago, "I don't know that I'd want them for close neighbors." Or again, a woman who has lived in Lakeville for fifty years and who knows no Jews says, "I don't want any Jews because they're bold and arrogant, as I've already said. They tell you how to run your affairs. They just take over, period." The fear that the presence of aggressive Jews would eventually mean their dominating the neighborhood is expressed as follows by an elderly hardware store salesman:

> From what I hear and from what I've seen of [Lake City] and from my past experiences with Jews, I'd like to see all Gentiles in my neighborhood, because I feel that the Jews override the Gentiles. However, I have never heard personally about anything like this happening right around here.

Or there are the reiterated complaints about Jewish clannishness ("Jews are nice people all right, but they stick to themselves") and Jewish impropriety ("We never used to have difficulty with disrespect for property. Jews have no hesitancy to utilize your lawn and to take your fruit") or merely Jewish difference ("Jews are more foreign to me. I mean, they don't speak our language. I feel this way because the religious customs and habits of the Jews are not very close to mine and to the way I was brought up"). In a few cases, there is an additional resistance which is particularly provoked in matters having to do with neighborhoods: the fear that the presence of Jewish families signals the advent of Negro ones. "It's just a feeling I have," explains a longtime resident from a low-income neighborhood. "But when Jews come in, then colored people follow."

Whatever their reason, one out of five of our Gentile respondents is in favor of self-segregating neighborhoods. It is worth noting that however extreme their choice, their defense of this choice tends to be moderate and equable in tone. Far from the markedly prejudiced tone

one might expect, most explanations for preferring self-segregation take the matter-of-fact approach illustrated by the response of an automobile mechanic who has lived in Lakeville all his sixty-four years.

> Let Jew and Gentile live by themselves and there won't be any conflict, because basically they are different social units. What I like to do, the Jew doesn't like to do. It's like with Irish and Germans. They get along all right separately, but it's a more strained feeling if they live together.

Still, the fact that self-segregation is attractive to so many of these respondents helps to illuminate a basic difference between Gentiles and Jews in social orientation. For the Jews of Lakeville, segregation is almost exclusively negative: it raises the specter of the "ghetto" and defeats one of their essential purposes in coming there to live, which is to locate themselves and particularly their children in a mixed society. Even though he may be no less self-segregating in his choice of friends, country club, or charity work, the Jew will still want the opportunity to learn to live in the dominant culture and to feel a part of a modern American community. The Gentile, on the other hand, perceives little conflict between his self-segregating tendencies and his place in the society. The fact that Lakeville is a rapidly changing community in an increasingly pluralist society does not make him want to expose himself and his children to the new problems and possibilities that these transformations have created. In fact, as we have seen, he may even believe that the exclusion of Jews safeguards his social identity and welfare and provides the best basis for his children's social education.

THE JEW AS A NEIGHBORHOOD MINORITY

Most Gentiles in Lakeville are willing to admit Jews into their neighborhood, but this does not mean that many are less concerned than the self-segregating respondents about maintaining their traditional way of life and its dominance in the community. The 23 per cent of Gentiles who prefer a minority of Jews in their neighborhood differ from the advocates of self-segregation mainly in believing that they could still maintain control of a mixed environment. It is not that they see any positive advantage in heterogeneity. A saleswoman who has lived in Lakeville most of her life wishes to return to the 10 per cent Jewish minority of the past: "I like the proportion as it was when we first moved here. It was friendly then. [Why?] I suppose because I like Gentiles better, inasmuch as I'm one too. It's just that we're all Gentiles

and we are afraid of what would happen if more Jews were present."
Another longtime resident is willing to go up to 25 per cent: "If we had
this figure I feel we could control the type of schools we have and the
type of social life the children would enjoy. We could, in other words,
keep these at our standards." A well-read widow in her sixties who opts
for a 30 per cent Jewish neighborhood discusses the maintenance of
standards in these terms:

> I like this figure because the United States was originally a Protestant
> country of English descent and was founded on that basis, and I'm used
> to it. Our customs are based on that. Why change it to some Oriental cul-
> ture, which is what it [Judaism] is? The culture of Jews is just not the
> same as ours. It may be some day.

Or again, there is the preference for a Gentile plurality that would ensure the social benefits of like-minded neighbors: "I like this figure
[25 per cent] because I would then be able to enjoy having a close
neighbor who would be much more apt to run in for a cup of coffee in
the morning, and I'd be able to have a close association with the home-
makers of families." Or more specifically, in the words of a high school
teacher who is willing to accept a 40 per cent Jewish neighborhood:
"Well, I think the main thing is Christmas. I wouldn't want to live
where Christmas wasn't celebrated. I don't suppose you like to be a
minority group ever." Some respondents who are already in a minority
would be content to see the current proportions reversed:

> I'm afraid it's the other way around now, with 40 per cent Gentile. Being
> a Gentile, I'd rather have it 60 per cent Gentile and 40 per cent Jewish.
> I guess I don't want to feel that I'm a minority. When I look around in all
> the stores and I'm the only Gentile, I don't feel that I'm in the right
> community.

The attitude of many respondents in this group is that their numerical
superiority would prevent their being engulfed by the objectionable
group behavior which they, no less than the self-segregating respondents,
attribute to Jews. Much the same comments about Jewish aggressiveness,
impropriety, and clannishness can be found in both of these Gentile
groups. The difference between the two groups on this score is that the
respondents who are willing to accept a minority of Jewish neighbors
have a somewhat less monolithic image of Jews. In fact, only one Gentile
in this group insists that he would restrict the number of Jews on the
ground of their general unacceptability: "Frankly, a percentage of 25
per cent of undesirable persons in the neighborhood is about all I could

gracefully stand." Otherwise, the prevailing opinion is that some Jews are much more preferable than others: "Some Jews are so nice," says a registered nurse whose preference is for 30 per cent Jews, "but the rest are so awful." A few of our respondents appear to believe that a particular percentage of Jews will help to provide acceptable neighbors. "I don't want any more Jews than this," says one who chooses 40 per cent, "because I'd be afraid of what type of family they'd be."

More commonly, the respondent will settle the question on the basis of individual merit. A housewife who is a native of Lakeville typically remarks, "It depends upon the people personally [as to whether I want them in the neighborhood]. I hate to lump them into one group." However, a respondent who bases his choice on the person rather than his group identity need not be particularly receptive to Jews. The above respondent wants no more than 10 per cent of her neighbors to be Jewish. A young Catholic engineer stops at 15 per cent, saying, "I like it the same as it is. I feel that I'd rather look into the person's habits and home than into their religion." A department store buyer who believes that Jews are generally not socially acceptable acknowledges that "if the Jewish families were as equally acceptable as the Gentiles, that is, if they were not loud, boisterous, and antagonistic, then I'd say they'd be perfectly okay in the neighborhood."

In general, this group of respondents appears to believe that relatively few Jews would meet these requirements; their average preference is for a neighborhood that is just over 20 per cent Jewish. "That figure would give a chance for the fair-minded and well-meaning Jewish people to live here," as one respondent puts it.

Obviously these percentages and specific responses demonstrate little attraction to Jews. Usually they reflect no more than a compromise that has been made with recent realities. Most of the respondents now live near Jews,[3] and 35 per cent of them have framed their preference to accord with existing percentages in their neighborhood. Of the rest in this group, 47 per cent prefer even fewer Jews than are presently in their neighborhood, while only 18 per cent would like more.

In general, the respondents who accept a minority of Jews and say they would regard them as individuals do not see any particular advantage for themselves in a mixed neighborhood. This is not to minimize the significance of their choice, but rather to indicate that with little or no positive motive for it, the Gentile is more likely to tolerate than

[3] The average person in this category lives in a neighborhood that is 35 per cent Jewish.

to accept and relate to Jewish neighbors. In contrast, a few Gentiles (approximately one out of ten of those who would accept a Jewish minority) look upon Jewish neighbors affirmatively, if somewhat luke-warmly, because they believe that associations outside their own group are valuable. The wife of a dentist who would accept a 35 per cent Jewish neighborhood observes that "everybody likes his own group to be predominant. Yet I definitely think it's a nice thing to have another kind. I don't want to be without contact with them." "I think we should have a mixture," says a woman active in youth work, though she immediately adds, "Frankly, I wish there were fewer Jews." It should be noted that this respondent would want only a 15 per cent Jewish neighborhood. Another respondent finds enough group differences in a 10 per cent Jewish neighborhood: "Right now it's mixed enough. There are enough nationalities here so that not all of one nationality is living alone." Or, somewhat more enthusiastically, a liberal young housewife believes that:

> It's less desirable to live in a neighborhood with any other proportions. With 75–25 you have a better ratio of religious groups. That makes it better and easier to learn about the beliefs and feelings of others. Both Jew and Gentile can do this easily if the Jewish group is not too large.

Another respondent who also prefers a 25 per cent Jewish ratio puts it this way: "I like this percentage because I happen to be in the Gentile group. Still, I like a little bit of any other group that isn't objectionable, just to give your life more interest and balance." Not unexpectedly, such respondents do not share the Jewish interest in the instrumental function of intergroup learning: that is to say, as a means of finding one's way into the society. Instead they emphasize the expressive function of such experience in broadening one's personality and varying his life. Though Jewish influence is by no means negligible in contemporary Lakeville, and though pluralism is becoming an increasingly visible and potent factor in the general political, economic, and cultural life of America, these developments apparently have not yet affected the common assumption of our Gentile respondents that they continue to form the center of the community and the society. As such, they usually feel that a few Jewish neighbors will satisfy their taste for cultural differences.

Be that as it may, we have been able to identify two grounds upon which Gentiles who wish to maintain their dominance in their neighborhoods are willing to accept a Jew as a neighbor. First and foremost is the premise that a Jew may be acceptable as an individual if he shares certain common qualities and standards with Gentiles. The second, and much less frequently expressed, premise is that a Jew may be acceptable because of his distinctive qualities as a Jew. Each of these bases of acceptance is more fully elaborated and assumes greater ideological conviction among those Gentiles who do not strongly desire to comprise a majority in their neighborhood.

THE DISINTERESTED GENTILE

The most widespread expression of the belief that the character of the individual rather than his group ties should determine his acceptability as a neighbor is found among the strikingly large number of Gentile respondents—43 per cent—who say that they "don't care" how many Jews live in their neighborhood.

Given their response, it is evident that these Gentiles are not preoccupied with the problem of closing their neighborhood to the Jews. It should be noted that almost all of them live in predominantly Gentile neighborhoods. The average figure is 30 per cent Jewish—roughly the same proportion that prevails in the neighborhoods of the majority-oriented Gentiles and in the community at large. However, their indifference to the group ratio is much less a product of apathy than of positive democratic sentiments. For example, a housewife in her middle twenties who is well-educated says forthrightly, "I don't care how many Jews live in this neighborhood, because I don't judge a person by what they believe. That's all." Or again, a young art dealer who has lived in Lakeville all his life speaks out with the same conviction: "I don't care how many Jews live in this neighborhood because how you get along with neighbors should have nothing to do with their nationality or race or however you want to put it."

The main basis of a person's acceptance among these respondents is his possession of specific social virtues, the implication being that these derive from individual character rather than group identity. These virtues tend to fall within the value norms one would expect in a community such as Lakeville: propriety, pleasantness, responsibility, and so forth. A well-informed retired salesman puts it this way: "I don't care as long as they're nice people, people with a little background, education, manners, not out boozing to all hours like a bunch of teamsters. People with a few refinements." Most respondents also tend to emphasize virtues that they believe themselves to possess. A civil engineer active in youth organizations explains his indifference to his neighbors' religion in these words:

> I don't care because I don't have any prejudices about Jews. I'll accept them as long as they're good neighbors. I have a neighbor back there with two lovely children; when they play ball and come into my yard I even lift them back over the fence—which I built before they even moved here.

For an electrician devoted to gardening, the main issue is maintenance of property: "I don't care so long as they take care of their yard and I take care of my yard and we have a chat over the fence. That's all that's necessary." A staid businessman emphasizes a respect for privacy: "I don't care as long as people are nice, mind their own business, and don't bother me. Besides, if I need a favor I can go and ask; my Jewish neighbors always treat me nicely."

Or, the disinterested Gentile may simply accept Jewish neighbors as an expression of his personal commitment to tolerance. "I don't care what percentage of Jews live in the neighborhood," says the wife of a gas station owner. "It would make no difference to me. Well, I was brought up to feel that all people are people, and that went for colored or anyone; so I suppose that's why I feel this way."[4] Similarly, the wife of a banker who belongs to elite clubs that do not admit Jews is satisfied to remain in a neighborhood that has become 50 per cent Jewish: "I don't care what percentage of Jews live in the neighborhood. I'm just tolerant. I take people at their face value. Our neighborhood is all right with me."

Believing as they do in "taking people at their face value"—a phrase that repeatedly turns up in the responses of the disinterested group— it is not surprising that they tend to minimize the significance of group differences. "Why is a Jew so different from a Gentile?" bluntly asks a salesman who lives in a neighborhood that is 75 per cent Jewish. "That's my answer."[5]

The idea that "we're all the same, all equal," or that "there is good

---

[4] It is worth noting that others are not as prepared to accept Negro neighbors. As the young wife of a carpenter insists: "I don't care what percentage of Jews live in this neighborhood as long as they're not Negro. Jews are as nice as anyone else as long as they cooperate as neighbors and are friendly."

[5] Despite their tendency to disregard differences between Jews and Gentiles, it is apparent that most of the respondents in the disinterested group do not completely disregard them in other contexts, as we shall see later in this chapter.

and bad all over," works in two ways in directing the responses of this group. On the one hand, they bypass the possibility that there are specific "Jewish" traits that tend to produce bad neighbors. Even one of the few respondents who admits this possibility is quick to qualify it as follows:

> I don't care how many Jews live in this neighborhood, because people aren't undesirable just because they are Jewish. I suppose if I took the whole Jewish race, though, they might have a higher proportion of undesirables than would be true for other races, but it's not based on whether they are Jewish or not.

On the other hand, in discounting group differences as a reason for excluding Jews from his neighborhood, the disinterested Gentile also generally disregards group differences that would enhance the desirability of Jewish neighbors. Thus only three respondents even speak of the advantages of a mixed neighborhood. One of them, a young housewife whose family has lived in Lakeville for two generations, regards diversity as a positive value in itself:

> I don't think it's good to have only one religion in the neighborhood. If you have others as well, you get a better perspective from different ideas. You find out how other people believe and live. You come in contact with different beliefs. It's good to know why people believe the way they do. It's that the more you talk to a variety of people, the more you understand why there are different religions. You can weigh their religion against your own.

However, the tendency even among these respondents is to justify their preference for a mixed neighborhood on egalitarian grounds. A photographer who emigrated from Germany as a young man says that "I don't care what percentage of Jews live in this neighborhood. If it were up to me I'd like a mixture; half Christian, half Jewish. Actually I'd have an Oriental, one from every race. If we're God's children, as we're supposed to be, we all have equal rights on this earth."

In short, by reducing the problem to that of individual behavior and by minimizing group differences, the Gentile who claims to be indifferent to the percentage of Jews in his neighborhood clears the way for his primary concern—that of having neighbors who are agreeable to him. To the extent that he recognizes the otherness of Jews, it is usually as a function of his opposition to prejudice.

JEWISH-GENTILE PARITY

One can see a significant difference in this respect among the small number of Gentiles (13 per cent) who opt for numerical equality between Jews and Gentiles. These respondents are likely to be very aware of differences in group identities and behavior and of the role these play in neighborhood relations. Unlike the self-segregating Gentiles, however, they do not use these differences to justify living apart from Jews but rather to justify numerical equality between Jews and Gentiles as the best way to control the undesirable effects of tension, discrimination, and clannishness and to promote the positive effects of diversity, stimulation, and social learning.

On the whole, our Gentile respondents in this group seem most concerned about the problems that develop when either Jews or Gentiles are dominant. It is well to bear in mind that among these respondents 50 per cent live in an immediate neighborhood where Jews comprise the majority, 28 per cent in one where there is numerical equality, and only 22 per cent in one where Gentiles are a majority. Thus a good many of these respondents are speaking from a minority point of view on this matter, and most of them from one that has been formed after they have actually experienced the daily realities of a mixed or Jewish neighborhood.[6] Some respondents, such as the wife of a manufacturer

[6] Even though 78 per cent of the Gentiles who prefer numerical equality with Jews already live in such neighborhoods or in ones where they are the minority, they comprise only three out of ten of all Gentiles who live in these neighborhoods. The other seven out of ten are almost entirely divided among respondents who do not want any Jews, those who want only a minority, and those who are disinterested.

It is worth noting that length of residence in these neighborhoods has very little to do with the preference for equality. The majority of respondents who favor parity are longtime residents, as is the majority of those who prefer no Jews and the majority of those who are disinterested in the matter. Respondents who prefer a minority are more evenly divided in their length of residence, though the main difference here is the middle range—five to ten years of residence. Only three respondents who say that they would be willing to live as a minority among Jews can be characterized as newcomers, and only two of these three presumably moved into their neighborhoods after it had already become heavily Jewish, since the Jews could not have reached their present proportions in these neighborhoods until recent years.

In other words, most of these Gentiles, despite their varying responses to Jews, have not sought to be part of a Jewish environment but rather have been engulfed by one.

Among Lakeville Gentiles who live in neighborhoods where Jews are a minority,

whose prestigious neighborhood is now almost entirely Jewish, prefer parity "so that I wouldn't feel I'm being a minority." A young copywriter who also lives in a neighborhood with a high percentage of Jews similarly chooses this distribution, "mainly because of my children. I never want any of my children to be a minority."

Most others take a somewhat more reflective position and base their preference for numerical equality between Jews and Gentiles on the ground that it avoids specific problems. An elderly ex-social worker who has lived in Lakeville for thirty-five years observes, "When there's a large percentage of a group either way, there's apt to be discrimination against the minority. I just wouldn't like to see our son doing the discriminating or being discriminated against." "I don't believe in prejudice," says the wife of a wealthy industrialist, "yet anyone is happier if they are not in a minority. You don't have to be on the defensive then."

Other respondents look to the general welfare of the neighborhood and community, which they believe is impaired by minority frictions and factions. A career woman whose immediate vicinity is 60 per cent Jewish finds that Jews are good neighbors, but she still believes that "an even mixture helps avoid neighborhood disputes; also, Jews can't be as clannish as they ordinarily are." Another advantage is that a relatively even split in numbers also fosters a parity in power and control. Thus a physician active in his neighborhood PTA and Boy Scouts believes that "there would be a better chance for collaboration and cooperation with the Jewish group if the leadership were equally divided." A market researcher who regularly plays golf with Jews bases his preference on a shrewd insight into the nature of minority status and action. "The minority by itself does not cause a problem. People permit their minority concept to cause a problem." As he goes on to argue, "If there's a minority, then any controversial issue which comes up is not dealt with on its merits. But if there's a 50–50 split, then when a Gentile and Jew run for office . . . there is a 50–50 chance that either can win, and the issue is based on its merits."

As for the positive advantages of numerical equality, two out of five of the respondents in this group (44 per cent) explicitly state that they derive mainly from the values of pluralism. Unlike the respondents who wish to live apart from Jews or in a majority among them, those who

only one out of twenty prefers numerical equality, nine out of twenty express no preference, and the rest divide equally between those who do not want any Jews and those who would be willing to have some Jews in their neighborhoods.

prefer numerical equality do not feel threatened by group differences but rather tend to accept and prize them.[7] "A mixed place is better than what they call 'your own kind,'" says a corporation executive whose neighborhood is 50 per cent Jewish. "I like it better if I live in a more cosmopolitan community," says an advertising manager who recently moved to Lakeville. "If I had a chance I would like to have a variety of religions for the education of my children," says a housewife who is active in the Mormon Church. Along with the personal preference for living in such a neighborhood, there is often also an active commitment to democratic pluralism. The wife of a policeman whose neighborhood is only 10 per cent Jewish tries to define this relation as follows: "Such a neighborhood is more typically American. I'm sure in my own mind what this means, but it's hard to explain. Anyhow, it's healthy to see how different types of people live and play." One respondent, the wife of a professor of art, carries her commitment to pluralism and her distaste for white Protestant homogeneity far enough to say:

> The only thing that displeases me is that Lakeville is a closed white community. I would prefer more variety within the community, such as Negroes and Mexicans. I think a good healthy mixture which wouldn't exclude me would be fine. Otherwise if the community is entirely white Protestant, it has a stifling and holier-than-thou atmosphere.

Thus there is a quite different emphasis between the group which desires a mixed neighborhood and the disinterested group. A disinterested respondent usually construes equality as allowing Jews equal opportunity to prove themselves capable of conforming to his tastes in neighbors or to general community standards of values and conduct. For the person who expresses a definite wish for a mixed neighborhood, equality tends to be construed as equality of status among groups, whose distinguishing differences he accepts.

---

[7] That these respondents are more accepting of differences in general is evidenced by their political tolerance. Thus they are more likely to permit an admitted Communist to make a speech in Lakeville, to retain his book in the public library, and to permit the Socialist party to publish newspapers in the United States.

It should be noted that these respondents are far from being political radicals. Like the other Gentiles in Lakeville most are registered Republicans. What does distinguish them from other respondents is their greater trust in people and their freedom from the fear of being exploited. In their responses to the statements: "These days a person doesn't really know on whom he can count," and "If you don't watch yourself, people will take advantage of you," they are much less likely than are the other Gentile respondents to agree with either or both of these statements.

THE GENTILE AND THE ACCEPTABLE
JEWISH MAJORITY

Only three among all our Gentile respondents say they are willing to accept a minority status in their neighborhood. None of the three explicitly expresses a preference for this situation; instead their reply, "Same as it is," to the question of how many Jews they would like in their neighborhood, expresses what is basically an adjustment to living among a majority of Jews.

Nonetheless, at least two of the three are content to remain where they are because they are impressed by their neighbors and derive benefits from their contacts with them. One of the three, a former schoolteacher, is married to a successful executive. She particularly admires Jewish perseverance—"Many of the people who don't like the Jews don't have the ambition and therefore don't have the money"— and goes on to say, "Another thing I like about our Jewish friends is that they're always up on what's new. They're doing things, taking lessons. It gets me out to do these things too. I can learn something from them." Accordingly, while she would prefer living in a better-balanced neighborhood, she prefers Gentile neighbors who share her acceptance of Jews:

> If the Gentile wants to move out, let him go. I like the Jews. I like the Gentiles too. And if a Gentile would move in and feel toward Jews like I do, I wouldn't care if it were 50 per cent Gentile. But if Gentiles keep knocking Jews and have no right to, then I'd just as soon they would move out.

The second respondent, a young housewife married to a research chemist, speaks of the friendliness and the kindness that she has found among her Jewish neighbors and that make her feel closer to them than to her Gentile ones:

> Jews have accepted us and our adopted child more than have the Gentiles. They're easier to get along with. When my husband was out of town, they helped me; and especially when my boy was sick, they were of more assistance to me than I would be to them under similar circumstances.

As a result, she too does not particularly mind living in a predominantly Jewish neighborhood. The third member of this group explains her acceptance of the situation on the ground that "I just suppose I accept people for themselves." Despite her apparent effort to minimize group differences, this respondent also admires certain distinctive qualities of her Jewish neighbors which contribute to the general welfare:

> I would say that they are the ones who come here for the excellent schools. They have the background to want this cultural aspect. They send their children to pre-schools, play clubs, and so forth—they can afford to and have full time help, too. That's how they spend their money. They take part in all the recreational programs for children. Jewish people are especially attracted to these things. The rest of us should, but don't always. This makes for a good community, when people are so interested.

The Collective Distinctiveness of the Jew: Gentile Rejection and Acceptance

As we observed in Chapter 3, the attitudes of Lakeville's Gentiles toward its Jewish newcomers are closely related to their individual images of Jewish group characteristics. The same is true of their more specific attitudes about the desirability of living in a mixed neighborhood. In order to explore this relation further, we devised two series of questions that evoke some of the standard positive and negative stereotypes of "Jewish" values and behavior and correlated the Gentile responses to them with the preferences concerning Jewish neighbors. Not unexpectedly, the first series, which tests for the stereotype of the Jew as an unattractive person, shows that this stereotype is more nearly complete the more reluctant the Gentile is to have Jewish neighbors. Thus, Gentiles who would prefer not to have Jews in their neighborhood are the most likely to regard them as spoiling a neighborhood, as being basically unassimilable, as striving too hard to lose their identity, as being less loyal than other citizens, as being unfair and deceptive businessmen, and as being chronically discontented and aggressive (see Table 9–2).

The most interesting of these results are the responses of the disinterested group. They are no more likely to express a significant anti-Jewish bias (three or more assenting responses) than are those who prefer numerical equality in their neighborhood, and on several of the items their percentage is lower. Apparently their general belief that Jews should be judged as individuals makes them no more prone to express prejudice than are those who favor a numerically equal neighborhood, many of whom value distinctively Jewish traits.

TABLE 9-2 BELIEFS ABOUT JEWS BY NEIGHBORHOOD
PREFERENCES OF GENTILES

	Preference for percentage of Jewish neighbors				
	0%	1–49%	Disinter-ested*	50%	More Than 50%
"The trouble with letting Jews into a nice neighborhood is that sooner or later they spoil it for other people."					
Per cent who agree	62%	41%	14%	23%	(0%)
"No matter how Americanized a Jew may seem to be, there is generally something basically Jewish underneath, a loyalty to Jewry and a manner that is hardly ever totally changed."					
Per cent who agree	77%	67%	46%	47%	(0%)
"Some Jews go too far in hiding their Jewishness, especially to such extremes as changing their names, straightening noses, and imitating Christian manners and customs."					
Per cent who agree	62%	55%	38%	35%	(33%)
"In general, do you think that American Jews are just as loyal to our country as other citizens are, or are they less loyal to America?"					
Per cent who say "less loyal" or "don't know"	23%	14%	9%	6%	(0%)
"One trouble with Jewish businessmen is that they are so shrewd and tricky that other people don't have a fair chance in competition."					
Per cent who agree	54%	23%	17%	25%	(0%)
"Most Jews are never content, but always try for the best jobs and the most money."					
Per cent who agree	77%	64%	47%	52%	(50%)†
Per cent who express anti-Jewish sentiments on 3 or more of the above items	75%	52%	29%	27%	(0%)
	(48)	(56)	(87)	(30)	(3)

* We shall exclude from this and the rest of the tables in this chapter the relatively few persons in this category (13 in all) who either offered no reason for their response or said they "didn't care" because of lack of interest in the question.

† We have excluded the response of one of the persons in this category because of our uncertainty as to what it meant. He agreed with the statement, which on the face of it appears to be critical of Jews, but added spontaneously, "If people have intelligence, they should do this."

However, some significant differences between the two groups do emerge once we take into account the composition of the neighborhoods in which they live. Among the respondents who live in neighborhoods where Jews are a minority, those who prefer parity are much less likely to assent to anti-Jewish canards. On the other hand, among those who live in neighborhoods where Jews comprise half or more of the population, the disinterested group are less likely to assent to them than the group who want parity.

It is important to note, though, that this shift is entirely a function of the responses of the parity group. As long as they are dominant in their neighborhoods, they find little about Jews as Jews that is undesirable. But a number of those who are in a minority seem to become convinced that Jews do have some undesirable collective characteristics— a reaction which, as we have already seen, has much to do with the desire for numerical equality. Among the self-segregating and Gentile-majority respondents, we note an appreciable rise in prejudice among those who live in more heavily Jewish neighborhoods, a fact which shows them to be the most prejudiced of all. Thus only the attitudes of the disinterested group seem to be unaffected by their surroundings; virtually the same small proportion is anti-Jewish under one set of neighborhood conditions as under another. Such consistency, as we shall see, characterizes their responses in other areas as well.

Though negative stereotyping declines among Gentiles who are more willing to have Jewish neighbors, this is not true of the tendency to perceive distinctively Jewish traits, as we have already noted. To carry our investigation further we devised a second series of questions which tested for the identification of some fifteen group traits. In each case we asked our respondents whether they agreed that Jews are more likely to have the given trait than most people are.

Questioned in this manner, virtually all our respondents select some traits as distinctively Jewish, the average score being 8. The three traits that are most frequently mentioned are money-mindedness, aggressiveness, and clannishness. Next are the following six in order of frequency: shrewdness as businessmen, ambitiousness, family-mindedness, interest in education and in cultural things, and inclination toward "keeping up with the Joneses." The remaining six are cleverness, fear of physical injury, political liberalism, intellectual superiority, moderate drinking habits, and lack of promiscuity.

Probing further, we asked those respondents who said Jews differ with respect to a given trait: "In general, do you feel favorably disposed or unfavorably disposed to a person who is [each of the traits that were perceived as differentiating Jews was then mentioned]?" As we would expect, the self-segregating respondents score above the average in identifying traits as distinctively Jewish; however, as indicated in Table 9–3, those who prefer an equally mixed neighborhood are even more likely to do so. The group which scores lowest is again those who are indifferent to the number of Jewish neighbors.

TABLE 9–3   GENTILE DIFFERENTIATION OF JEWS
BY NEIGHBORHOOD PREFERENCES

	Preference for percentage of Jewish neighbors				
	0%	1–49%	Disinter-ested	50%	More Than 50%
Per cent who differentiate Jews from most people by 8 or more traits	63% (48)	57% (56)	49% (87)	70% (30)	(67%) (3)

Though the tendency to perceive "Jewish" traits is most marked among the least and most accepting Gentiles, the latter, of course, choose traits which the former frequently omit; moreover, the parity group appraise the traits they select quite differently from the self-segregating one, as can be seen in Table 9–4, which reports the results for the nine most frequently mentioned traits.

Evidently, Gentiles who prefer numerical equality are less disposed to associate Jews with unfavorable traits such as money-mindedness, clannishness, and "keeping up with the Joneses." Moreover, when they mention these traits, they do not consider them to be undesirable as do the self-segregating group. Further, they are more likely to select "favorable" traits such as family-mindedness and interest in education or culture.

When we examine the extent to which the four major groups of Gentile respondents are favorably disposed to the traits they select, we find that those who prefer numerical equality score highest; those who are least favorably impressed by such traits are the self-segregating Gentiles and those who wish to maintain a Gentile majority (see Table 9–5).

TABLE 9-4 EVALUATION OF TRAITS THAT DIFFERENTIATE JEWS BY NEIGHBORHOOD PREFERENCES OF GENTILES

Nine most frequently mentioned traits that differentiate Jews from most people	Gentiles who would exclude Jews from their neighborhood		Gentiles who would at the least afford numerical equality to Jews	
	Per Cent Who Select Trait	Per Cent Who Consider Trait Undesirable	Per Cent Who Select Trait	Per Cent Who Consider Trait Undesirable
Unfavorable traits				
1. Money-minded	98%	63%	79%	59%
2. Clannish	75%	74%	73%	60%
3. Keeping up with Joneses	69%	97%	62%	52%
	Per Cent Who Select Trait	Per Cent Who Consider Trait Desirable	Per Cent Who Select Trait	Per Cent Who Consider Trait Desirable
Mixed feelings				
4. Aggressive	83%	47%	79%	50%
Favorable traits				
5. Ambitious	67%	84%	71%	83%
6. Family-minded	44%	100%	65%	100%
7. Interested in education	56%	100%	65%	100%
8. Interested in culture	58%	89%	65%	100%
9. Shrewd businessmen	81%	65%	67%	65%
	(48)		(34)	

Intermediate between the two is the disinterested group, who, as we have repeatedly observed, are the least likely to perceive "Jewish" traits. Their responses reflect their generally mixed reaction to those group differences that they do perceive: almost as many of them either dislike or are ambivalent about these traits as approve of them. The absence of any clear-cut consensus of judgment suggests once again that these respondents do not tend to conceive of character differences as group rather than individual phenomena.

Another finding is that the longtime Jewish resident does not evoke

TABLE 9–5   The Desirability of Jewish Traits by
Neighborhood Preferences of Gentiles

	Preference for percentage of Jewish neighbors				
	0%	1–49%	Disinter-ested	50%	More Than 50%
Per cent who are favorably disposed toward "Jewish" traits*	35%	34%	58%	73%	(100%)
	(48)	(56)	(87)	(30)	(3)

* This includes all respondents who considered more than half the traits by which they differentiated Jews as desirable; specifically, the cutting point was 60 per cent, inasmuch as the data had been grouped in percentage classes of 10.

a hostile reaction, even from Gentiles who do not wish Jews in their neighborhood. In fact, they are very favorably disposed to him (as are the other Gentiles as well). However, their receptivity does not make them any less opposed to Jews generally. They merely co-opt the old-guard Jewish resident into their own group; for they feel that he is so assimilated in thought, feeling, and behavior that for all intents and purposes he is one of them. As a result, they exempt him from the onus of being considered a Jew, or at least a typical Jew—a label which they apply readily to the newcomer, whom they generally dislike.

The same kind of exemption mechanism also seems to operate among those respondents who wish to maintain a Gentile majority in their neighborhood. However, they are willing to enlarge the category of the exempt to include a fair proportion of newcomers. Yet they too, it must be remembered, consider the typical Jew to be an undesirable person. As would be expected, the newcomer fares better among the other groups of Gentiles: he does particularly well among the "disinterested" group because these Gentiles appear to be just as reluctant to distinguish between categories of Jews as between Jew and Gentile. Thus, they are more inclined than any other group of Gentiles to view the newcomer as resembling the longtime resident—and to describe both as assets to the community (see Table 9–6).

Social Interaction and Gentile Acceptance

In the final analysis the Gentile's preferences cannot alter the reality of the physical presence of the Jews in Lakeville, but they do have a bearing on how he relates to the Jews. The more accepting he is of

TABLE 9-6   GENTILE DIFFERENTIATION OF JEWISH RESIDENTS
BY NEIGHBORHOOD PREFERENCES

Do Jews who have lived in Lakeville a long time seem to be like the newcomers:	Preference for percentage of Jewish neighbors				
	0%	1–49%	Disinter-ested	50%	More Than 50%
In some or most respects	38%	46%	76%	52%	(67%)
In virtually no respects	62	54	24	48	(33)
	100%	100%	100%	100%	(100%)
	(34)	(39)	(57)	(23)	(3)

Jews as neighbors, the more likely is he to become socially involved with them, whether in the neighborhood, in voluntary organizations, or through his work (see Table 9–7).

It may seem remarkable that the disinterested group appear to be

TABLE 9-7   SOCIAL CONTACTS WITH JEWS BY NEIGHBORHOOD
PREFERENCES OF GENTILES

Per cent of respondents who have had social contacts with Jews	Preference for percentage of Jewish neighbors				
	0%	1–49%	Disinter-ested	50%	More Than 50%
In their neighborhood	29%	57%	38%	67%	(100%)
	(34)	(54)	(76)	(30)	(3)
Through the non-sectarian organizations to which they belong	26%	41%	29%	48%	(100%)
	(31)	(44)	(62)	(29)	(2)
Through work or professional contacts	22%	45%	38%	47%	—
	(18)	(31)	(50)	(19)	—
Per cent who have entertained a Jew in their home during the past year	37%	66%	50%	81%	(100%)
	(48)	(56)	(90)	(32)	(3)

* As we would expect, Gentiles who prefer not to have any Jewish neighbors are the least likely to find or to place themselves in situations where Jews are part of their environment. Accordingly, the percentages in this table are computed only for those respondents who presumably have Jews in their neighborhood, organizations, or professional life. Thus the figures are higher than they would be if we computed them by using all respondents in this category. For example, only 21 per cent of the total have had social relations with a Jewish neighbor.

even less inclined to associate socially with Jews than are those who would accept a minority of Jews in the neighborhood. However, once we take into account the basic attitude of these respondents and their individual proximity to Jews, their social behavior becomes more explicable. First, since they believe that Jews are to be treated like everybody else, there can be nothing especially distinctive or attractive about associating with them, just as there can be nothing especially onerous about doing so. In short, the very ground of their acceptance of Jews does not provide any special inducement to seek social relations with Jews, even though they are much less hostile and critical of Jews than the other groups of Gentiles are. As a result, the extent of their social relations with Jewish neighbors is directly influenced by the number of Jews in their neighborhood. If they have only a few Jewish neighbors, less than two out of five develop these relations; if they have many, more than half develop these relations, or about as many as those who accept a minority of Jews in their neighborhood.

We can surmise, then, that Gentiles are more likely to associate with Jews when they perceive them as possessing traits that are distinctive and attractive and when they are willing to treat them as social peers. This inference is also suggested by the responses to a further question in which we asked our respondents to choose whether their experience with the Jew or the Gentile with whom they were most friendly was the more stimulating. As shown in Table 9–8, the respondents who prefer

TABLE 9–8   Jews as Stimulating Friends of Gentiles by Neighborhood Preferences

	Preference for percentage of Jewish neighbors				
	0%	1–49%	Disinter-ested	50%	More Than 50%
Per cent who consider Jewish friend to be as stimulating or more stimulating	19% (48)	24% (55)	36% (85)	52% (31)	(67%) (3)

a mixed neighborhood, and thus are more willing generally to accord Jews as such equal status, are more likely to find their Jewish friend as stimulating or more so.[8]

Further, in examining individual responses, we find that the higher

[8] This holds true even when we control for the number of Jews actually in their neighborhood.

interest felt in the Jewish friend almost invariably derives from an encounter with a new experience, usually of an intellectual or cultural
nature. In contrast, the higher interest felt in the Gentile friend derives
just as regularly from the warmth and intimacy of shared experience,
usually social in nature. Indeed, this difference appears even in the
replies of respondents who choose both the Jewish and Gentile friends.
A hospital supervisor makes the distinction as follows: "I find them
both equally stimulating. However, I suppose that you would say that
I find it more intellectually stimulating with my legal friend [Jew], and
from a social point of view I find it more stimulating with my Gentile
girl friend." Or again, a woman who lives in a predominantly Jewish
neighborhood but sees few Jews socially says that "I find the Jewish
friend more stimulating because she is very brilliant. She's a very well-
read person. The Gentile friend is sweet and easy to be with; she also
seems to appreciate you more."

Typically, the Jewish friend is regarded as more intellectually adept,
curious, unconventional, or otherwise more in touch with a broader
range of experience. "I find my Jewish friend more stimulating," says a
well-informed career woman. "I think it's due to her higher intellectual
level." A widow who has lived in Lakeville for thirty-four years and
formerly associated entirely with Gentiles remarks that the Jewish
friend's "interests are broader. She brings other ideas in the conversation." "He's a good storyteller," says a local dentist in explaining his
choice. "He goes to more places. He knows more people, more dives."
A schoolteacher observes of her Jewish friend, "She does different
things from what I do during the day. I get to hear about the plays and
concerts and things she attends." The added color of Jewish personality
makes the difference for a young salesman: "Well, the other friend, the
Gentile, is a very pillar-of-the-community type guy, but the Jew is a
more exciting type of guy. He used to be a fighter. He has more varied
interests; he is more intelligent and is quite a talker."

Sometimes the distinctive traits of the Jew are combined with differences in his background and orientation that make for relations with
more challenge and impetus to growth. "The Jews are more cultured,
probably, than my Gentile friends," says a sales manager who does much
of his business with Jews. "We're sort of in different worlds or circles." A
businessman who has lived in Lakeville all his life develops this point
as follows:

> I find the Jew more stimulating because there are more controversial sub-
> jects to discuss. We're perfectly frank with each other and discuss these

big subjects. We use them as sounding boards for our opinion. On the other hand, my conversations with Gentile friends tend toward the mundane and prosaic interests of suburban life or business.

Or again, as a newcomer who is living among Jews for the first time in her life puts it: "My friendship with the Jew is more stimulating because it introduces an entirely new set of problems and disagreements that make life interesting."

It is just such an element of controversy and novelty that the respondents who find their Gentile friend more stimulating apparently wish to avoid in their intimate relations. This is particularly evident among the self-segregating respondents. Some make the choice simply on the basis of longevity; for example, the wife of a policeman remarks: "I really don't know why I find the Gentile friend more stimulating but it's probably because I've known her longer. That's all. No other reason." Others explain their choice in terms of the frequency and regularity of the relationship: "I find the Gentile more stimulating because I see him every other day or so. I have more of a chance to socialize with him. He has a lot of interests and works hard. We have mostly the same interests." Many others also relate "stimulation" to mutual interests and background. "I find the Gentile more stimulating because we have more in common," says a longtime resident whose neighborhood is still mostly Gentile. "That's the only answer I can give you. I have nothing in common with this Jewish woman next door at all." "His problems are more nearly my problems," says a longtime resident speaking of his Gentile friend. "The Jew is older and not in my business. The Gentile friend owns boats, we're fraternity brothers, we have similar educations, and our wives get along." Finally, there are the respondents who place their premium on intimacy. "We're closer friends and neighbors," explains the wife of a crane operator. "It probably goes back to his being a better friend," as another respondent typical of this group puts it.

From the thinness of content in the above replies, as well as from the content itself, it seems evident that these respondents require the security of an intimate and familiar relationship in order to be stimulated by it. This, in turn, illuminates the reason why they also prefer a self-segregating neighborhood. However, even among those who are mostly favorably disposed toward relations with Jews, the question of intimacy remains quite distinct in many cases from that of stimulation. Thus while 52 per cent of those who prefer numerical equality in their neighborhood find their Jewish friend equally or more stimulating, only 28 per cent say that they are as close or closer to him. Much the same proportions hold for the self-segregating group (19 per cent and 8 per cent) and for those who wish to maintain a Gentile majority (24 and 7 per cent). Only those who are indifferent to the ethnic-religious makeup of their neighborhood show some degree of correlation between stimulation and intimacy with their Jewish friends (36 and 31 per cent). The question of intimacy between Jew and Gentile will be treated more fully in Chapter 13.

A Typology of Gentile Attitudes

Given the preceding data in this chapter that bear on the relation between the acceptance of Jews and the perception of "Jewish" traits as group differences, it seems worthwhile to speculate about their general significance. As we have found, four out of five of our respondents are willing to have Jews live in their neighborhood, though in sharply varying numbers and for sharply varying reasons. Further, their choice and explanation frequently depend upon their orientation toward Jews, specifically as it involves these three questions: (1) To what extent do they view Jews as being different from Gentiles and as having distinctive group traits? (2) Are these traits desirable or undesirable? (3) How many Jews are typically "Jewish" in their character, behavior, and values? Though we shall have to rely a good deal on speculation, since we did not construct our interviews to measure the broader implications of these responses, we shall suggest a typology that brings into a common frame of reference what otherwise would remain as discrete propositions about Gentile perceptions of and attitudes toward Jews.

To begin with the first question, we have found that virtually all our Gentile respondents believe that Jews have some distinguishing traits. However, there is sufficiently sharp variance in the number of traits which are perceived that we can divide our respondents into two groups, which we shall call the *low differentiators* and the *high differentiators*. The former can be regarded as a separate entity to whom the other two questions have little relevance, since low differentiators perceive and relate to Jews as individuals rather than as "Jews." By and large, the members of this group are found among those who are indifferent to the number of Jews in their neighborhood and who dismiss group traits and differences as a basis either for including or excluding them. Further, since their general attitude is that "people are people," they do not believe that Jews are either more or less inclined to possess the particular qualities which each of them prefers his neighbors to have. In effect, their orientation is an *egalitarian* one, which emphasizes human similarities that underlie group differences and hence insists on the need to relate to and judge people as individuals.

Among the high differentiators, the distinctively "Jewish" traits possess significant meaning. Most answer the second question—concerning the positive or negative value of these traits—by listing both kinds, though there is a large degree of variation not only in the weight they attach to these traits but also in their valuation of certain of them, such as "aggressiveness" or "shrewdness in business." Moreover, these traits are not perceived or judged as discrete entities but rather are organized and weighted by their place in a relatively well-defined image of the typical Jew. Thus a good many of these respondents perceive the typical Jew as aggressive, crude, materialistic, defensive, and clannish.

A smaller number of high differentiators possess a favorable image of the typical Jew. Though this image tends to be less fully and sharply detailed than that of the undesirable Jew, it usually includes the following three motifs: (1) the Jew as an ambitious and energetic man who is willing to work hard to get ahead and who is active in organizational and community affairs; (2) the Jew as a well-informed intellectual who is interested in education and in cultural matters; and (3) the Jew as a family-oriented man, who may overindulge his children but is at least concerned about them.

As for the third question of how many Jews are perceived to be typical, the logic of our typology seems to require a distinction between respondents who view *all* and those who view *most* Jews as typical. Although the realities of our data obscure such a clear-cut division, we can still meaningfully divide those whose image of the typical Jew is unfavorable into two categories.

On the one hand are a large number of respondents whose conception of the typical Jew does not include all Jews and who consider some— even some newcomers—to be better than the rest. Such a conception is most evident among those respondents who say they would not mind having a minority of Jews living in their neighborhood. Examination of their responses indicates that they accept those Jews who in some way or another have lost their Jewishness and have become like Gentiles. In short, these respondents are willing to exempt the non-Jewish Jews from their image of the typical Jew. We can label this type of Gentile as being of the *exemptionist* variety.

On the other hand are those respondents who say they do not wish any Jewish neighbors; they seem to exclude only the small number of longtime residents from the category of typical Jew. As such, these Gentiles would also seem to fall into the exemptionist category. But the pervasiveness of their anti-Jewish sentiments—moderate though many may be—their conception of virtually all Jews as typical, and the self-segregation that they would practice in their neighborhoods, make the response of many of these *exclusionist* in nature. Though few in this category can be considered intensely outspoken or ideologically committed anti-Semites, nevertheless they come closer than do any of the other Gentiles in Lakeville to viewing the Jew as essentially a racial or biological type whose negative traits are so inherently part of his character that few, if any, Jews can be totally free of them.

Those respondents whose image of the typical Jew is favorable provide even more complex responses to this question. In our Lakeville sample we find virtually no Gentile, even the three who are content to live as a minority among Jews, whose orientation is so pro-Semitic that he finds virtually everything Jewish attractive or virtually all Jews desirable. Such a respondent, if he existed, we could label a *Judophile.*[9] Instead we find that the favorably disposed Gentiles place some limits on their pro-Jewishness. Unlike the exemptionist, who accepts only those Jews whom he believes are not really Jews, these respondents accept Jews because of their distinctively Jewish qualities. In short, their orientation is that of a *pluralist,* a person who finds differences challenging rather than threatening and who is attracted and stimulated by them. This does not prevent them from regarding some Jewish traits as undesirable or some Jews as undesirable. However, they are less concerned about the frequency of undesirable Jews than about the influence of a Jewish majority or minority. Accordingly, they prefer a neighborhood in which Jews are numerically equal to Gentiles so that neither can become the dominant group.

In Lakeville the egalitarians comprise the largest single group of Gentiles and the pluralists the smallest (the Judophile being virtually nonexistent). Also, it is the egalitarian who appears to have contributed the decisive influence on the climate of opinion in the community. His

[9] Such a type of Gentile does apparently exist in Lakeville. As reported by our Jewish respondents, some of their Jewish friends have Gentile wives who, though not formally converted to Judaism, have become absorbed into the Jewish group and have virtually assumed a Jewish identity. Such persons, however, do not appear in our sample of Gentiles, for the sample was confined to homogeneously Gentile households.

"live and let live" attitude has fostered a tolerant and peaceful inter-religious atmosphere in the community, but has not encouraged the active attempt to integrate the Jew that might have occurred if the pluralists had been dominant.

Despite the benefits that the community derives from the egalitarian orientation, serious questions can be raised—as Sartre,[10] among others, has done—concerning its reliability. Since it is based upon the perception of similarities often in the face of the facts of group differences, history has shown that in times of social crisis the abstract ties of equality are easily shattered and "Jewish" traits become highly visible and offensive. Under such circumstances the passively accepting Gentile often becomes an exemptionist or an exclusionist, rarely a pluralist.

[10] Jean-Paul Sartre, *Anti-Semite and Jew* (New York: Schocken Books, 1948).

IV

THE CONDITIONS
OF SOCIAL CONTACT

It remains to explore the conditions under which Lakeville's Gentiles and Jews can and do come to know each other well enough to establish meaningful personal relations, or at least to provide a more realistic perception of individual similarities and differences that would alter their inherited burden of group prejudice, defensiveness, and estrangement. Such changes in perception and attitude are not merely a matter of individual good will or even of a favoring social climate. They spring from and are nourished by certain kinds of experience which are part of the daily experience of individual and community life, rather than from abstract principles of religious morality, democratic freedom, or civic fellowship. Such experience is widely available to the citizens of Lakeville, whether through their neighborhoods, their clubs and organizations, or their vocations. The relations between Jews and Gentiles that develop through these experiences are, at least initially, functional or situational ones that can be carried out with little personal involvement. But in time they may also become the basis for friendship precisely because they originate in natural social circumstances that do not overload them with emotional content.

The importance, then, of these casual, pragmatic relations should not be minimized. Even with the climate of tolerance and acceptance that exists in Lakeville, it is unlikely that Jews and Gentiles would have much to do with each other if they did not have to leave the ethnocentric confines of their family, church, club, and intimate friendships in order to pursue other essential needs and interests. In the formulation of Robin M. Williams, Jr., it is those activities and arrangements which are organized around "the principles of achieved, competitive placement rather than ascription by birth, of impersonal universalistic norms, and of highly specific, narrowly defined relations among persons"* that bring Jews and Gentiles into some type of relationship in which tolerance and cooperation work to their mutual advantage.

Moreover, the separation of these relations from the more private spheres of life provides the Jew and Gentile with the open choice of limiting any friendliness that develops between them to an acquaintanceship or of allowing it to ripen into friendship. In other words, their mutual involvement in one sphere does not threaten the privacy or restrictiveness of others.

In Chapters 10 to 12 which follow, we shall explore the relation between functional associations—in jobs, voluntary organizations, and neighborhoods, respectively—and the cultivation of more personal and significant associations between members of the two groups. In Chapter 13, the final chapter of this section, we shall try to delineate the comparative character and limits of these friendships that have grown up between Jews and Gentiles.

* Robin M. Williams, Jr., *Strangers Next Door* (Englewood Cliffs, N.J.: Prentice-Hall, Inc., 1964), p. 356.

10

WORK AND SOCIAL CONTACT

The importance of vocational experience in fostering friendships between Jewish and Gentile men is immediately suggested by the fact that the majority of our Jewish respondents and a substantial minority of our Gentile ones have met the member of the other faith with whom they are most friendly through a professional or business contact. Indeed, such contacts appear to be more conducive to friendship than any other (see Table 10–1).

We shall now turn to a more thorough examination of how these social contacts come about in the vocational pursuits of our Gentile and Jewish respondents.

The Occupational Environments

As suburbanites, most Lakeville men make their living in the city. As members of the complex economic system by which goods and services are produced and distributed in modern urban society, they are also typically involved in a web of relations with employers or supervisors, or with workers they employ or supervise, as well as with peers and colleagues, or with people they sell to or buy from.

Motivated and conditioned by economic needs and occupational re-

187

TABLE 10–1   Source of Friendliest Interfaith
Relationship among Men by Religion

Where did you meet the person of the other faith with whom you are most friendly?	*Respondents*	
	Jewish Men	Gentile Men
Work	57%	39%
Neighborhood	14	31
School	15	5
Organization	5	14
Elsewhere	9	11
	100%	100%
	(170)	(74)

quirements, such ties often take on social and psychological significance as well. As industrial sociologists have repeatedly found, people who work together, particularly in small groups, tend to develop informal and friendly relations which carry beyond the immediate needs of the job, though they also may have a decisive effect on how well the jobs are performed.[1] Further, economic and work relationships increasingly involve quasi-social instrumentalities such as lunches, theatergoing, and other forms of entertainment. Indeed, utilization of these means has become so rampant in our economy that critics such as the late C. Wright Mills fear that our society has become a gigantic "salesroom" in which "sincerity" and "friendliness" become part of the process of distributing goods and services rather than expressions of personal feeling.

Be that as it may, the typically modern organization of economic and work functions brings most Lakeville men into contact with members of the other faith as well as with people who do not live in their community. The latter point applies more completely to the Lakeville Jews, a greater percentage of whom work outside of the community. This pattern reduces the possibility that Lakeville men will associate with

[1] The classic work in this field is, of course, F. J. Roethlisberger and W. J. Dickson, *Management and the Worker* (Cambridge, Mass.: Harvard University Press, 1939). Since then the research in the field has been prodigious; see Conrad Arensberg *et al.* (eds.), *Research in Industrial Human Relations: A Critical Appraisal* (New York: Harper & Row, 1957). For an attempt to apply these findings to the organization of work in our society generally, see Robert Dubin, *The World of Work* (Englewood Cliffs, N.J.: Prentice-Hall, Inc., 1958).

each other during the week, but increases the possibility of intergroup associations. In other words, by working in the metropolitan area, where Jews comprise a much smaller proportion of the population than they do in the community, Lakeville Jews come into contact with more Gentiles than they would if they worked locally. On the other hand, locally employed Gentiles come into contact with more Jews than they would if they worked in the metropolitan area.

These integrating tendencies are much more marked among Jewish respondents. More than two out of three Jews in all occupational categories except that of the self-employed professional work in an environment that is dominated by Gentiles. (The exception is due largely to the fact that many self-employed Jewish professionals, especially doctors, serve either a mixed clientele in the local community, or a primarily Jewish one in the city.)

It is no less evident that Jews do not occupy a commanding position in the economic environment of the Gentile respondents, except for the self-employed businessmen, many of whom are in business in Lakeville. Otherwise only a small minority of Gentiles find themselves in heavily Jewish environments, while for the overwhelming majority, Jews comprise at most a small proportion of their contacts. In the case of a small percentage of the salaried business and professional people (17 and 11 per cent respectively), and of one out of three of the manual or service workers, Jews are completely absent from their workday world.

THE PERVASIVENESS OF MARKET RELATIONSHIPS

The vocational activity which brings more Lakeville Jews and Gentiles into contact with members of the other faith is the exchange of products and services. In most instances the Lakeville Jew or Gentile is occupied in selling rather than buying goods or services. This is most marked, of course, among the self-employed in both groups (see Table 10–2). Among the independent professionals, for example, a Gentile doctor may treat a Jewish patient, or a Jewish lawyer take a case for a Gentile client.

Self-employed businessmen primarily sell products, though the level at which these transactions take place often differs significantly between the Jews and Gentiles. That is, among the latter these transactions are likely to occur at the retail level, because many of the Gentiles are merchants or small businessmen who sell goods to Jewish consumers. Many of the Jews, on the other hand, are manufacturers or wholesalers,

TABLE 10–2 VOCATIONAL RELATIONSHIPS BETWEEN JEWS
AND GENTILES

In what connection do you come into contact with Gentiles in your work?	Jewish men who have any contact with Gentiles during the workday				
	Self-employed*		Works for others		
	Professional	Business	Professional	Business	Manual or Service
Market relation	100%	100%	90%	98%	—
Peer relation†	88%	82%	90%	94%	—
Subordinate or supervisory relation	67% (42)	88% (73)	87% (31)	79% (53)	—

In what connection do you come into contact with Jews in your work?	Gentile men who have any contact with Jews during the workday				
	Self-employed*		Works for others		
	Professional	Business	Professional	Business	Manual or Service
Market relation	100%	100%	80%	95%	63%
Peer relation†	67%	53%	68%	68%	44%
Subordinate or supervisory relation	0% (6)	27% (15)	40% (25)	68% (19)	13% (16)

* We have included in the category of *self-employed* all those who said that they were sole owners or in a partnership. Otherwise, the general occupational categories that we have adopted correspond in major respects to those employed by the U.S. Bureau of the Census. We have, however, combined the Managers, Officials and Proprietors category with that of Clerical and Sales Workers under the general rubric of *business;* and also the Craftsmen, Operatives, Service Workers and Laborers categories under the rubric of *manual or service worker.*
† Included in this category are those who are colleagues, co-workers, and/or competitors.

whose transactions with Gentiles take place at an intermediate stage of production and exchange.

Market relationships between Jews and Gentiles are almost as pervasive among the salaried employees of business establishments. Here, too, transactions are likely to be conducted at some intermediate stage of production and exchange. Relatively few Jews in this category work in retailing goods, and these are likely to be buyers, not sellers, of goods for their establishments; more Jews work as salesmen, or in some instances as merchandising agents for wholesale or manufacturing firms that make non-durable goods. Many Gentiles are employed in similar sales capacities, but none for either retail or wholesale firms; most do their selling or buying for manufacturing, transportation, and utility companies. Gentiles in salaried business positions are also more likely than their Jewish counterparts to occupy high executive or managerial positions.[2]

Market relationships with Gentiles are somewhat more frequently reported by the salaried Jewish professionals—nine out of ten—than by their Gentile counterparts. Some Gentile manual or service workers have no need for market relationships either with Gentiles or with Jews.

PEER AND HIERARCHICAL RELATIONSHIPS

Next to market relationships, the most extensive kind of Jewish-Gentile association is that between occupational or organizational peers. The salaried Jews, most of whom work for firms with many Gentile employees, are much more likely to have such relationships than are the self-employed Jewish businessmen or any of the Gentiles. Among the self-employed, peer relationships take place primarily within the occupations themselves. Here too, the Jewish professional or business-man of Lakeville is more likely to encounter more Gentile colleagues or businessmen than is his Gentile counterpart to encounter Jewish colleagues.

The least pervasive associations that Lakeville Gentiles and Jews have with members of the other faith are the hierarchical ones, with the exception of the self-employed Jewish businessmen and professionals, who often have at least one Gentile employee in their firms as manual or clerical workers. The self-employed Gentiles do not tend to employ Jews, whether because fewer Jews are available for these subordinate jobs or because Jewish employees are excluded from such firms as a matter of policy.

Among the Lakeville Gentiles and Jews who are employed in salaried professional or business roles, hierarchical relationships with persons of the other faith are found fairly often, usually with the Lakeville resident in the higher position. Such relationships, however, are virtually absent

---

[2] This would account for the fact that only among salaried business employees does the median income of the Lakeville Gentile exceed that for the Lakeville Jew.

among those Lakeville Gentiles who are employed as manual or service workers.

Social Contacts and Vocational Relationships

As seen in Table 10–3, at least eight out of ten Jewish respondents in each occupational category socialize with one or more Gentiles whom they have met through work, whether this work environment is predominantly Jewish or Gentile.

Among the Gentile respondents, however, socializing with Jews is much more variable, depending upon the type of occupation and upon the composition of the work environment. Only among the self-employed professionals is there a general tendency to socialize with Jews irrespective of the numbers of Jews they meet.

THE PATTERNING OF SOCIAL CONTACTS

Among self-employed Gentile businessmen and employed manual or service workers, there is relatively little incidence of socializing with Jews. This is particularly true of businessmen whose major economic relationship with Jews is that of selling goods and services for consumption and not for further sale. Only one out of three of the Gentile respondents who own retail establishments or small contracting businesses engages in any social relations with Jewish customers. And none of the manual or service workers who make, sell, or service commodities for Jewish customers reports any social relations with them.

Much the same pattern is found among many of the Jewish businessmen who own relatively small retail establishments that serve customers of the other faith. Only those Jewish respondents who own fairly large retail establishments are likely to entertain, or be entertained by, a Gentile with whom they have a business relationship (eight out of nine in this category do so). In general, then, if the basic relationship between Jew and Gentile is that of seller to consumer, it remains essentially an impersonal, contractual one which fails to generate any felt need or desire to associate outside of the context of the marketplace. As a result, their relationship fails to develop any significant social character and distinctiveness.

The same restrictions do not operate where the basic relationship is that of buyer and seller at an intermediate stage of production and

TABLE 10–3 INTERGROUP SOCIALIZING AND THE WORK ENVIRONMENT BY OCCUPATION

Jewish socializing with Gentiles in

Jewish men

	Self-employed		Works for others		
	Professional	Business	Professional	Business	Manual or Service
Predominantly Gentile* work environment	81% (32)	89% (64)	88% (26)	92% (47)	—
Predominantly Jewish† work environment	80% (10)	100% (8)	(80%) (5)	100% (6)	—

Gentile socializing with Jews in

Gentile men

	Self-employed		Works for others		
	Professional	Business	Professional	Business	Manual or Service
Predominantly Jewish* work environment	(100%) (2)	50% (10)	67% (6)	83% (6)	(25%) (4)
Predominantly Gentile† work environment	(100%) (4)	(0%) (5)	37% (19)	46% (13)	8% (12)

* These categories include those who say that half or more of the people with whom they come into contact during the course of the day are persons of the other faith.
† Those whose work environment does not include any person of the other faith are excluded from these categories.

exchange. At this level three out of four Gentile manufacturers report that they have socialized with a Jewish wholesaler or retailer of their products, and an even higher percentage of similarly situated Jews say that they have social contacts with some Gentile customer.

Salaried businessmen who are involved in buying or selling at the market level show much the same frequency of quasi-social intercourse, though again it is more limited among Gentiles, except for those working in a Jewish milieu or else those directly involved in market relations with Jews. Thus, all five of the latter report social contacts with Jews, in contrast to only one out of five of those whose primary relationship with Jews is that of co-worker, and in contrast to none of those whose primary relationship is subordinate or supervisory.

Self-employed professionals among our respondents report that market relationships, such as those with clients and patients, are as likely to produce social contacts with persons of the other faith as are relationships with colleagues. This is true whether the professional sees mostly Jews or Gentiles in his daily work.

Among the salaried professionals, client and colleague relationships are also equally productive of social contacts where these professionals work mainly with persons of the other faith—a situation which is much more common among our Jewish respondents. Where they work mainly with persons of their faith, however, the colleague relationship appears to be the more productive of social contact. Two of the three Gentile respondents whose only association with Jews is that of colleague have socialized with them, in contrast to somewhat over one out of five for whom Jews were primarily clients.

Among our Jewish respondents the only profession that deviates significantly from the above is the salaried accountant. None of four who are engaged in this occupation has anything to do socially with a Gentile colleague or client, irrespective of his work environment. This is not the case, however, among the self-employed accountants, three out of five of whom report that their relationship with a Gentile client is likely to eventuate in some form of socializing.

THE INSTRUMENTAL FUNCTION
OF SOCIAL ACTIVITIES

Of course, the fact that Jews and Gentiles entertain each other as part of their professional or business transactions need not of itself signify any real change in the character of their relationship. In other words, it may merely indicate that their lunch and dinner dates, theater parties, and so forth are entered into as a routine, pragmatic way of doing business or consulting with each other. Indeed, the content of most of the socializing that occurs is apparently of this order, according to a more or less consistent 60 to 80 per cent of the respondents in our respective occupational categories.

This motive for socializing is most obvious in the market relationships at the intermediate stage of production and exchange, where we have seen that socializing is most prevalent. In the world of the business executive and the expense account, entertaining and being entertained have become so thoroughly bound up with the process of selling that it is often taken for granted that important customers, whether Gentile or Jew, will be wined and dined or otherwise courted. "I do a lot of entertaining," says a manufacturer's representative. "I take customers out to lunches and dinners because it's part of my job of selling."[3] Another Jewish respondent remarks in a similar vein, "I'm a broker on the stock market and the world is my oyster, and I *have* to entertain by taking people to dinner and even to the theater." According to our Jewish respondents, such socializing is nothing more than following the rules of the game in order to cultivate or retain a customer or to improve relations with a supplier. Whether he happens to be a Jew or Gentile seems to make little difference. As the representative for a transportation firm puts the matter: "It's our policy to entertain all people." Or, on the other hand, a plant manager notes that "the non-Jews with whom I deal are suppliers, and they show their appreciation by taking me to dinner or to lunch."

Likewise, Jewish and Gentile colleagues often socialize in the course of work or of the activities of their professional organizations. Thus Jewish and Gentile professionals may meet in a more relaxed or informal setting than the office to discuss a case. According to a Jewish orthodontist, "Sometimes we get together just on the spur of the moment. Once it happened because we wanted to talk over a case, so we used the lunch hour." A self-employed lawyer reports that "I will meet Gentiles with whom I'm friendly at a bar or at coffee breaks, for purely business reasons and to promote good relations." Or

[3] The quotes in this chapter were obtained from the interviews with Jewish respondents, inasmuch as they were the only ones who were probed concerning the types of social activities that they had engaged in with Gentiles in pursuing their livelihood. But the fact that the comments of the Jewish respondents bear directly on their relationship to Gentiles indicates that the latter also share their orientation toward market and professional relations.

again, Jewish and Gentile employees of a firm may have lunch together as part of their work relations. A research associate in an advertising agency speaks of lunching with his Gentile colleagues: "Most of the time the conversation deals with problems germane to work." Other respondents mention the quasi-social meetings that are used as "extensions of conferences or sales meetings" within an organization, or the more festive occasions used to promote morale and foster personal ties, such as office parties, golf outings, banquets, and so forth.

From a Vocational to a Social Relationship

Given these widespread practices of using social settings to facilitate the exchange of goods, services, or information, it thus becomes apparent why the data in Chapter 8 showed that there is little necessary relation between the interfaith orientation of our respondents and the probability of their socializing in the course of their daily vocational lives.

The increasing occupational and economic interdependence of modern society, as well as the decline of overt or tacit religious discrimination and segregation in many vocations and industries, now enable Jew and Gentile to meet and relate as a matter of course. However, such relations need not and often do not develop much personal content. First of all, the self-interested motivation behind the routine socializing they do together is quite apparent to both parties. A moderately successful dress manufacturer candidly admits, "I entertain buyers and others who can do me some good in business," or, as stated more generally by a partner in a chemical firm, "All this [entertaining] is done with a business motive." Similarly, the recipient of business hospitality is not less aware of its pragmatic and impersonal nature. A manufacturer of photographic equipment succinctly defines such intercourse as "a social gesture designed to result in personal gain," and the owner of a large retail firm remarks that it is taken for granted that no matter how tactful or convivial the entertainment may be, there is always "something in back of it: namely, a business reason."

As a result of this mutual awareness, neither party expects much in the way of genuine companionship to develop from this socializing, particularly since there is inevitably an element of ambiguity or hypocrisy in the more overt forms of friendliness, so that such gestures are often distrusted. In general, the exploitative, competitive, and cynical atmosphere of the marketplace is not the most favorable climate for nourishing sincere friendships. On the other hand, each party feels that it is to his advantage to behave as amicably as possible. "As far as Gentile customers are concerned," says the owner of a plumbing supply house, "who can afford to be less friendly to them?" which pretty well sums up opinion on both sides.

Though these amenities of the marketplace are all expressions of the profit motive, there is, of course, a range in the modes of behavior that condition such relations. At the very least, they engender some concern for the sensibilities of the other party, particularly if he belongs to another faith, and so may help to undo prejudice and defensiveness on both sides. A clothing manufacturer who is much involved with Gentiles remarks that "I don't like to step on anyone's toes if I can help it. These people are my customers or my employees, so naturally I want to get along well with them. I couldn't let there be any difference in my treatment of them." Or again, as a successful liquor distributor puts it, "Sometimes you go out of your way more with a non-Jewish than with a Jewish customer. But they all require service."

Otherwise, the religious difference between parties is often regarded as irrelevant, and they meet as individuals whom mutual self-interest has brought together and whose sense of tact and tactics requires some degree of friendly exchange before or after the point of "getting down to business." A typical lunch is described by a metals manufacturer in these words:

> Yes, most of the social things I have to do with Gentile business clients are for business purposes. We have lunch together, but we don't only discuss business. We talk about athletics, general events; these days it's the space race. In other words, we have a light and airy conversation as well.

In some cases, however, the affability common to such relations may disclose mutual interests, values, and attitudes that come to serve as the basis for a new dimension of the relationship that transcends its commercial basis. At the very least, the socializing of the marketplace fosters in both parties some awareness of each other as persons instead of merely as representatives of an ethnic group. Similarly, the tact needed to conduct these relations, as well as encouraging tolerance and objectivity, may blossom into a more personal form of consideration. A respondent reports one such incident which obviously made a deep impression on him: "When I was ill in the hospital, a Gentile customer sent me a card and telephoned later to inquire about me. None of my

Jewish customers did that. I think that they knew that I was sick, but they didn't want to bother."

These possibilities are perhaps even more common in the relations between professional colleagues. Here the profit motive, with its aggressive and manipulative tendencies, is usually less operative. The basis of social intercourse involves a sharing rather than a trading association, whether in splitting up a work load, providing advice or information, or cooperating in other ways with each other. The outgrowth of these instrumental peer contacts may be an enhanced respect for each other's competence, or a more marked awareness of their mutual commitment to their profession, or a mutual sense of gratitude and trust—all of which have been put through the fire of work crises or daily routines and thereby provide excellent possibilities for more personal ties to develop. As with Jewish businessmen, the professionals who live in Lakeville find such relations with Gentiles quite common in their daily vocational activities: sufficiently so, at any rate, that nine out of ten respondents from both the business and the professional groups say that their best opportunity to come into friendly contact with Gentiles is in their work.

The transformation of these instrumental relations into more personal ones appears to follow a common pattern. As their purpose begins to alter, so does the scene and mode of intercourse. Dining and drinking together, the main gestures of the marketplace, decline in frequency, and other more comradely and individual activities, such as going to the theater or movies, playing golf or bridge together, or attending sports events or social affairs, increase in significance. So, too, does the inclusion of wives in the relationship: almost three out of ten of our Jewish female respondents report that their most friendly contacts with Gentiles stem from their husbands' business friends.

The turning point from an economic to a social association with some personal content is frequently marked by invitations to one's home. To be sure, the economic or professional motive may still be part of the relationship, but if the hospitality of a private residence is tendered, the gesture apparently signifies that the economic interest is no longer the primary one. As the owner of an advertising agency puts it: "I choose whom I want to be with. I don't believe that there have been more than three clients who have been invited to my home—ever. I don't believe in it unless I like the person." Even a less restrictive attitude, such as that of a chemist, points to much the same free choice: "I've had Gentile visitors in my home. These are generally business associates whom I thought I'd enjoy having in my home. They evidently felt the same way."

As the mode of intercourse becomes more disinterested and sociable, so does the valuation of the other party. The profitability or usefulness of the relation is superseded by emphasis on personability, respect, and trust. A young engineer, for example, explains his relations with an associate in these terms: "This Gentile is just a hell of a nice guy. I'd give him my very last dime." Similarly, a wealthy industrialist observes:

> This Gentile is very sincere. That's the quality that draws me to him. He's also honest and objective about himself and others. He doesn't pretend to be what he isn't. He has convictions about seeing that people get their just rights and he's tolerant of people who disagree with him and he is a warm-hearted guy.

By the same token, their mutual vocational interests often continue to reinforce the relationship. As a retailer of art supplies describes his friendship with a business acquaintance, "The things I do with this Gentile are not for business purposes, we just want to be with each other. But it's true we'll discuss business as part of what we do together."

In many instances, then, the initial motive of self-interest assumes an ancillary function, and the social trappings that were initially viewed as a means to an end come to be transformed into a personal tie of some depth and meaning between a Gentile and a Jew.

11

THE VOLUNTARY
ASSOCIATION AND
SOCIAL CONTACT

Another distinctive aspect of modern society that profoundly affects relationships between Jews and Gentiles in Lakeville is its voluntary organizations. In the course of implementing common interests and values and dealing with common problems, they naturally bring together people who may have been strangers to each other and provide a framework and a rationale for their getting to know each other.

Overall, nine out of ten Jews and three out of four Gentiles belong to non-sectarian voluntary groups. Most often these are organizations centered about neighborhood, community, or occupational activities, or related to institutions such as schools, hospitals, or libraries. In other words, they are organizations that serve an "instrumental function," or in another formulation, a "social influence" one.[1] To a lesser extent,

[1] C. Wayne Gordon and Nicholas Babchuk in their article, "A Typology of Voluntary Associations," *American Sociological Review*, XXIV (1959), 22–29, classify such groups as PTA's, neighborhood improvement associations, the League of Women Voters, and the like as *instrumental groups*, which they define as groups whose "major function and orientation are related to activities which take place outside the organization [and which] seek to maintain a condition or to bring

Jews and Gentiles in Lakeville also belong to social, recreational, and cultural groups which satisfy the more private interests and needs of its members and whose function has thereby been defined as "expressive."[2]

Within these different associations the active members can hardly avoid coming into contact with each other. Moreover, in the course of meetings, committee work, and fund-raising drives, opportunities occur, much as they do in professional and occupational relationships, for more specific and close contacts in which personalities are revealed, new reactions form, and personal connections are engendered. For Jewish women, more than 57 per cent say that their voluntary organizations afford the best opportunity to develop friendly contact with persons of the other faith. This is less true of most Jewish men in Lakeville; as we have seen in Chapter 10, they tend to find these contacts in their vocational lives.

The development of friendly contacts occurs with significant frequency and fullness in some organizations. In others, however, relationships tend to remain relatively impersonal and rarely go beyond the requirements of the organizational roles. In this chapter we shall try to identify those affiliations that foster or inhibit the chances that Jews and Gentiles will come into closer touch with each other and to explore the processes that are at work in each case. We hope thereby to shed some light on how organizational ties between Jew and Gentile can and do become transformed into personal relationships based on realistic perceptions and positive feelings.

The Friendliest Associations

In the course of studying voluntary organizations, Alvin Boskoff has found that sociability is a prime feature of "expressive" groups, even of

---

about change which transcends its immediate membership." As they acknowledge, their definition corresponds to that employed by Arnold M. Rose, *Theory and Method in the Social Sciences* (Minneapolis: The University of Minnesota Press, 1954), p. 52, in defining *social influence* groups. Rose adds that such associations "wish to achieve some condition or change in some limited segment of the society as a whole."

2 Both of these definitions distinguish "instrumental" groups from those the respective authors call "expressive," which, in the words of Gordon and Babchuk, "perform a function primarily for the individual participants through activities confined and self-contained within the organization itself. More specifically, they provide the opportunity for carrying on activities such as recreation, of direct interest to the participants or help to provide satisfaction of personal fellowship" (p. 27).

those which involve specific activities, such as garden clubs, hobby groups, and book clubs; indeed, their putative purpose is often subordinate to that of socializing itself:

> Many expressive associations seem upon closer examination by outsiders to pursue their stated interests in a somewhat haphazard way. This leads to the suspicion that these associations are more important as facilitators of social interaction, of expression, and even of sociability than for the content of expression and interaction. Where this suspicion is well-founded, it probably indicates that expressive associations are essentially supplements to one's stock of primary group experiences—perhaps even substitutes for inadequate or frustrating primary group relations.[3]

Following Boskoff, we would assume that their mutual expressive associations would foster greater friendliness between Jew and Gentile members than do the "instrumental" associations, such as the PTA, neighborhood improvement groups, and occupational organizations which are designed for the purpose of "acting" together rather than "being" together.

This assumption finds considerable support, as we shall see, in organizational relationships among persons of the same faith. But it does not apply equally to relationships between Jews and Gentiles, as is suggested by the fact that the groups in which Jewish and Gentile respondents report that they have found their most friendly contacts with people of the other faith are usually not the "expressive" ones. Rather, they are youth groups, such as the PTA and Girl Scouts; groups that deal with neighborhood and community problems, such as neighborhood improvement associations and the League of Women Voters; and business and professional organizations (see Table 11–1).

The only exceptions appear to be Jewish men, whose second most friendly non-sectarian affiliations are the "cultural" ones. However, this exception merely proves the rule, once we take into account the fact that six out of ten of these respondents are referring to groups in which they hold office and whose major function is to promote the welfare of some established cultural institution rather than to provide cultural activities for its members: the board of the "friends" of the local library, the committee to organize Great Books discussion groups in the community, or affiliations with an opera company, art museum, and concert series. In general, then, the cultural groups that they select are similar in function to the "instrumental" groups.

[3] Alvin Boskoff, *The Sociology of Urban Regions* (New York: Appleton-Century-Crofts, 1962), p. 174.

TABLE 11-1 FRIENDLIEST VOLUNTARY ASSOCIATION
BY RELIGION AND SEX

The two types of organizations that are most frequently mentioned by respondents as providing friendliest contacts with persons of other faith				
		Gentile respondents		
	Women	Per Cent*	Men†	Per Cent
1.	Youth-serving	56% (32)	Neighborhood and community	39% (23)
2.	Neighborhood and community	48% (21)	Youth-serving	35% (26)
		Jewish respondents		
	Women	Per Cent	Men	Per Cent
1.	Youth-serving	61% (126)	Business and professional	61% (119)
2.	Neighborhood and community	36% (94)	Cultural	37% (27)

* Percentages are based on those who belong to a given organization and also have at least one other affiliation.

† The third most frequently selected group among Gentile men is the business and professional organization.

Why, then, do such groups foster friendlier relations between Jews and Gentiles than do those that have a more overtly sociable purpose? We asked our respondents what they thought accounted for it. Granting the limitations of subjectivity inherent in these replies, they do provide us with significant clues that we can explore by means of other data we have collected.

THE AVAILABILITY OF PERSONS
OF THE OTHER FAITH

Approximately one out of six Gentiles and one out of twelve Jewish respondents explain that they find more friendly contacts in one of the three major types of instrumental groups they belong to simply because they find more persons of the other faith in these groups. This point seems to be borne out by estimates from our Jewish respondents which reveal that they are exposed to proportionately more Gentiles in their instrumental groups than in any others (see Table 11–2).[4]

TABLE 11–2 GROUPS RANKED ACCORDING TO GENTILENESS OF MEMBERSHIP

Rank order of groups designated as having the highest proportion of Gentiles	Per Cent of Jewish Respondents*
1. Business and professional	62% (133)
2. Neighborhood-community	43% (159)
3. Youth-serving	40% (215)
4. Cultural	34% (77)
5. Social-recreational	31% (140)
6. Health-welfare	29% (59)

* These figures refer to per cent of those belonging to a group who say that it has more Gentile members than do any of their other affiliations.

Our data also show that for Jewish respondents a high correlation exists between the groups that have the most Gentiles and those that are found to be friendliest. This is true whether the group is of the expressive or instrumental type (see Table 11–3).

TABLE 11–3 FRIENDLINESS OF GROUPS BY GENTILENESS OF MEMBERSHIP

Per cent who designate the following groups as providing friendliest contacts with Gentiles	*Jewish respondents* report that group*	
	Has More Gentiles Than Any Other Affiliation	Does Not Have More Gentiles Than Any Other Affiliation
1. Business and Professional	67% (83)	36% (50)
2. Youth-serving	63% (86)	33% (129)
3. Cultural	50% (26)	24% (51)
4. Neighborhood-community	46% (68)	22% (91)
5. Health-welfare	35% (17)	14% (42)
6. Social-recreational	35% (43)	9% (97)

* Only those who have two or more affiliations are included in this table.

[4] We do not have similar data for Gentile respondents. In all likelihood, however, we would have found much the same pattern: namely, more Jews are encountered in the youth and neighborhood community groups than in the cultural, social, recreational, and health-welfare groups. Only in the occupational associations would we probably have found few Jews, because these associations are often predominantly Gentile.

Table 11–3, however, also shows us that the differences in inter-group friendliness among the various groups do not in general disappear even if we take into account the availability of Gentiles. In other words, the youth and occupational associations are still the most frequently named affiliation, while the social-recreational and health-welfare groups are the least frequently named. Only the differences between the cultural and the neighborhood-community groups tend to disappear. Thus we can conclude that numbers alone do not produce the greater intergroup friendliness which is experienced in the youth, occupational, and community groups.

MUTUAL INTERESTS AND PROBLEMS

Approximately one out of two attribute this experience of friendliness to the distinctive interests, problems, and values that motivate the members of these organizations. Moreover, this common basis of affiliation and activity usually bears directly on important life circumstances such as child-rearing, home ownership, or vocation and livelihood, or on significant political or social values that these organizations actively implement. The result is a sharing of similar basic experience that helps to diminish the awareness of group differences and fosters a cooperative and friendly atmosphere.

Thus, a Jewish woman explains her choice of the PTA as providing "a greater sense of friendliness . . . because we all have children who may even be in the same room and in the same grade at school. Therefore we have common interests that sort of bind us together." "We're all young mothers," says another Jewish woman, "and we have our children in common." A Gentile teacher focuses directly upon the functional ties that develop among members: "We're friendly in the PTA because we are all working for the same things—school, children, and facilities." This community of interests and activities based upon an important role and function, whether as parent or teacher, is also evident in the explanations offered as to why neighborhood associations help to promote good intergroup relations. As one member puts it, "I feel a greater sense of friendliness in our neighborhood association because we have common interests as neighbors and homeowners so that makes it like a small community." Or again, "We're all working toward a common goal," says the wife of an architect. "We want to keep our land values up and our neighborhood safe for our children." In another neighborhood association, according to a Jewish manufacturer who recently moved to Lakeville, "People are so friendly because we all live here. We help each other push out stalled cars, we mow each other's lawns—we all, in other words, try to have a better lawn, a cleaner house, and cleaner kids."

Those who choose their professional, business, or trade associations as the scene of their friendliest relations with members of the other faith reiterate much the same point. A Jewish psychiatrist feels "a greater sense of friendliness in the Psychiatric Association because we have a common profession, common cultural background, and common professional interests." A Gentile respondent who grew up in Lakeville similarly explains: "We're all artists interested in graphics or something like that." "We are all practicing medicine," says a Gentile surgeon, "which gives us a singleness of purpose. We have patients in common. We are interested in the welfare of the patients and in the medical standards of hospitals and of our profession." Members of other instrumental groups such as the League of Women Voters similarly explain, "We are all so friendly because we have a common purpose. We want to improve the government, to make people more aware of it—and we work together."

In short, the personal relevance of what is shared and done together in these groups provides a basis for personal intercourse, even though the specific activities do not extend to more deeply personal and private spheres of social interests and needs. Indeed, some of our respondents suggest that the friendliness of such groups comes about because of, rather than in spite of, the lack of more personal social connections that are found in other types of organizations. As a Jewish dentist puts it:

> What makes the Lions' Club so friendly is that the common goals, common interests we share are not personal. Everybody's together to help others as well as himself. In country clubs, however, people join merely for personal enjoyment, and such friendliness between Jew and Gentile cannot and does not exist.

In other words, Jews and Gentiles are more easily drawn together by the common interests that are implemented by the Girl Scouts, the Chamber of Commerce, or the Library Committee because their private social life is pursued elsewhere and does not impinge upon or frustrate the process by which cordial working relations between Jews and Gentiles can develop into genuinely friendly ones. This in turn helps to illuminate why the "expressive" groups, which often make a stronger claim on personal sociability, do not promote friendly relations with the same degree of frequency and may instead inhibit and undermine their development.

THE INHIBITING EFFECT OF CLIQUE AND STATUS FACTORS

Let us explore this paradox a bit more fully. According to one of our respondents, group differences and status issues which tend to separate Jews and Gentiles in the community at large are kept out of organizations such as the League of Women Voters by its instrumental orientation:

> The friendliness that I experience in the League of Women Voters I think may be due in part to the fact that we're not trying to work on a social level. The major emphasis is on study and government, and this tends to minimize social and religious differences.

In other words, a relationship between a Jew and a Gentile in one of these associations does not have to compete with existing networks of close friendship that each has established in his social life, networks which usually comprise members of a person's own faith. Moreover, were social interests more directly and centrally involved in these organizational relationships, both Jews and Gentiles—though more likely the latter—would become more concerned about the status implications of the relationship and would probably begin to apply more rigorous restrictions in choosing the people with whom they were to associate and socialize. In either case, the net result is to inhibit the development of sociable relations between Jews and Gentiles.

If this reasoning is sound, then we can understand better why even those relatively few private clubs which are not restricted have contributed so little to bringing Jewish and Gentile members together. We know from studies of such clubs as well as from spontaneous remarks of our respondents that membership is, as E. Digby Baltzell puts it, "by ballot."[5] Thus, an individual is not free to join because he wants to, as with a PTA or a neighborhood improvement association, or because he meets objective and impersonal qualifications, as with professional associations. He must be sponsored by one or more members and receive the approval of the membership as a whole. The successful candidate, of course, is usually the one who conforms to the standards of ethnic back-

[5] *Philadelphia Gentlemen* (New York: The Free Press of Glencoe, 1958), p. 335.

ground, status, and manners that accord with the social traditions of the club. Moreover, the candidate who already plays an active role in the social circles associated with club members is more likely to be taken in. As Baltzell has shown, the intertwining of family, class, business, and friendship ties within these clubs underlies their formal structure, while the social clubs, in turn, play an essential role in maintaining the coherence of the group and in furthering its social and economic interests. The net result is that the membership in such groups, in Lakeville as elsewhere, tends to be extremely homogeneous in terms of class and ethnic background, and those who come from distinctly different backgrounds are likely to find it very difficult, if not impossible, to gain admittance.

On occasion, though, a particularly influential or otherwise acceptable outsider is taken into these clubs. In Lakeville there are some fourteen Jews who list membership in social organizations that are otherwise more or less restricted to Gentiles. One might assume that such factors as the acceptability of these Jews, the opportunity to fraternize with Gentiles, along with their presumably strong drive to relate to Gentiles that brings them into such groups in the first place, would all conspire to produce strong ties of friendship. We find, however, that only two out of the fourteen Jewish respondents consider these groups to be their friendliest affiliations.

One reason why is suggested by the following Gentile who belongs to the Lakeville Women's Club, an organization which one out of four Gentile respondents who belong to it regards as her friendliest affiliation. The respondent reports on the self-conscious concern with "acceptability" in such groups:

> Well, you know up here we don't allow them [Jews] into our [social] organizations. I should say not; they're not generally socially acceptable. As a result we screen very carefully. However, we do have several in the Women's Club.

Thus, it would appear that status and clique considerations so permeate these groups that even the "acceptable Jews" continue to encounter them because they are, after all, still Jews, and because they have not become members of the established social network of which the club is only a part. Or, as Baltzell has found, "The assimilation of powerful outsiders within the halls of the Philadelphia Club does not always please all members, especially those who revere traditions."[6]

[6] *Ibid.*, p. 349.

Group and status factors may also explain why Jewish respondents infrequently select relatively small expressive groups—such as reading, sports, card-playing, and so forth—as their most sociable affiliation with Gentiles, even though these groups have other than a social purpose. We have already followed Alvin Boskoff[7] in noting that their putative expressive function is subordinate to their social one. As a Gentile respondent puts it: "This book club is really a social group which comes to meetings and listens to book reviews."

Such groups also tend to attract and to accept members with similar social backgrounds, and though they are not as deliberately restricted as the Women's Club, they still show a highly skewed ethnic membership in which the dominant members are likely to be part of a network of social ties that extend beyond the group itself. Thus, it appears that the group characteristics and interests that make the informal expressive groups significant affiliations for people of the same faith create barriers between members of different faiths.

Where these barriers are bypassed, it is, in part, by means of close associations between Jews and Gentiles outside the organization or because of their over-riding interest in a specialized activity that holds the group together. Thus, more Jews select such groups than they do the more general social and women's clubs as their friendliest affiliation. A Jewish architect observes, "What makes my bridge group so friendly is that personality and religion don't seem to matter at all. It's just your bridge." Or again, a young Jewish housewife: "What makes the Theater Guild so very friendly is that there is a sort of intangible feeling of brotherhood. We all have a definite goal and similar interests." This suggests that if the putative activity of many of these groups were implemented more seriously and were separated from class and caste factors, their Jewish and Gentile members would develop more friendly relationships.

In any event, this happens more often in the quasi-public cultural, sports, and recreational clubs. These organizations are structured in a relatively formal way and are open to anyone who expresses an interest in membership and who meets minimal membership requirements. As a result, there is more of a mixture of Jews and Gentiles than is ordinarily found in the smaller informal groups. A Jewish woman who relishes the cultural life of Lakeville reports that:

> In the Art League we try to promote appreciation of art, and the variety of people that we get appeals to me. We have every type of person from

7 *Op. cit.*

Warner observes of the upper class in his study, *Democracy in Jonesville:*

> They [members of the upper class] perform charitable activities by contributing to needy individuals and institutions. The ability to make charitable contributions is evidence of their wealth, and at the same time it points to their own superior status as compared to the less fortunate people who receive their charity. By performing these activities, which are not only necessary but also honorable and noble, the superiority of the upper class becomes manifest to the whole community.[8]

Moreover, according to David L. Sills, voluntary health associations in particular "tend to develop informal patterns of recruitment" due to the "lack of guidance from the organization or the absence of institutionalized patterns."[9] Thus, Sills finds that approximately three out of five volunteers were brought into the National Foundation for Infantile Paralysis through friendship with other volunteers. As a result, such organizations tend to attract a relatively homogeneous membership, who have prior ties. This fact, along with the status emphasis that is commonly found in welfare and charity work, helps to explain why the atmosphere of the Lakeville organizations is not particularly conducive to friendly relations between Jews and Gentiles.

The one notable exception we find is among the respondents connected with the auxiliaries of Lakeville Hospital. Six out of the ten Jews and four out of the eleven Gentiles who work as volunteers for the hospital report their group to be the friendliest association with members of the other faith. The reason offered is almost invariably that of the instrumental relations between Jewish and Gentile volunteers. A Gentile woman who has lived in Lakeville for thirty-five years and objects to the influx of Jews considers the Hospital Gift Service her most friendly affiliation with them "because we're all working for the same goal, making money for the Hospital. We all do work together so beautifully; no friction at all." Much the same response comes from a Jewish member of the Gift Service, who speaks of "our ability to work together on projects of mutual interest for the community good." Another Jewish respondent suggests that these cordial relations were not initially taken for granted, and that they stemmed directly from the growth of work relations between Jewish and Gentile volunteers:

[8] New York: Harper & Row, 1949, p. 134.
[9] *The Volunteers* (New York: The Free Press of Glencoe, 1957), p. 114.

When we first started the occupational therapy program, we [Jews] were on probation. But the further we go, the more we're accepted. At the council meeting we decided to see what it was doing, and we found that it was creating a very positive reaction for Jews. They [Gentiles] are proud of what we're doing.

The psychological significance to Jews of these cooperative relations is apparent in many of the responses. First of all, these relations help to dissolve feelings of defensiveness, diffidence, or estrangement in being with Gentiles. "In the League of Women Voters," as a Jewish newcomer puts it, "Gentiles don't make you conscious of differences. We work well together. There is no 'cliquiness' to separate Jew from non-Jew." A Jewish sales manager speaks of the feeling of "togetherness" in his business group: "You just don't get the feeling of being an outsider because you are a Jew in this largely non-Jewish group." Instead, our respondents report that they come to be judged as individuals and that their value is reckoned in terms of their performance. As one lawyer remarks, "In the Bar Association I feel that I am considered and treated as a normal human being, as if there were no differences between us in religion or otherwise." A businessman speaks similarly of the Chamber of Commerce: "If they find out you are an honest and straightforward person, there is no problem of being accepted. They become just as friendly as if you were a non-Jew." A clinical psychologist relates that the friendliness of Gentiles in his professional association is demonstrated "by my being singled out for special assignments in spite of the fact that I am Jewish. In general they look upon me as a person and not as a Jew."

A significant number of our Gentile respondents—approximately 25 per cent—agree with our Jewish ones in attributing the friendliness fostered by their non-sectarian organizations to "good working relations" or to "feelings of acceptance" between members of the two faiths. There is, however, a quite different emphasis in their respective descriptions of the process. Rather than speaking of their own efforts to work with and to be accepted by their Jewish associates, they as well as other Gentile respondents typically dwell on the capabilities and attractiveness of the Jews which have made *them* acceptable. Thus the wife of a school principal explains: "There is greater friendliness in the PTA because Jews are such good workers. They are so friendly and cooperative." Or again, a leader in the local Little League: "There is such friendliness in the Little League Scouts because of the willingness of the Jew to make the organization a success." "Jews are the intellectuals in the League of Women Voters," says a sophisticated career woman. "In my professional research association, Jews have very interesting ideas," says an electrical engineer. "No one really knows the possibilities of this kind of research, and [Jews] aren't as stuffy as some."

It is worth noting that a small number of Jewish respondents attribute the friendliness of Gentiles in their organization to the latter's personal qualities. However, they are much less inclined to speak of Gentile abilities and virtues that improve the quality or effectiveness of the organization than of their lack of religious prejudice. A typical example of this difference is provided by a highly cultivated Jewish woman: "What makes my relations with Gentiles in the League of Women Voters so friendly is that they are open-minded and liberal people, and there is no stress on religion."

SOCIAL INTERACTION WITHIN THE ORGANIZATION

Besides committee meetings, special projects, and other work relationships, instrumental groups also provide social occasions designed to bring their members into closer rapport and to strengthen their identification with the organization. The League of Women Voters, for example, holds teas, the PTA's have informal social hours after their formal meetings, and neighborhood associations often sponsor dances and block parties. These semi-social occasions serve an important purpose for Jewish and Gentile members by creating opportunities for more personal relations. So does the impromptu socializing that may precede or follow meetings or come at breaks in the proceedings, and so forth.

Through these channels the feelings of friendliness and of mutual interest that have developed between Jews and Gentiles in their organizational roles can begin to be expressed in less structured settings that enable them to encounter and relate to each other as individuals rather than merely as functionaries of the organization. In characterizing these modes of relations, respondents report particularly hearty greetings, animated conversations, usually centering around the group's function, and going out together for coffee or a drink.

Such extensions of their organizational ties, however, need not signify much in the way of friendliness. Eating and drinking together, for example, are principal ways of expressing friendliness, regardless of the level of comradeship. Talking or working well together are mentioned more frequently in those organizations where a less friendly atmosphere is experienced. More significant than the mode of intercourse is the spirit in which it is conducted. Where relations remain only moderately friendly, this spirit is likely to remain self-consciously polite and superficial. As a young woman married to a university professor puts it, "I'd say that my relations in the PTA with the Gentiles are somewhat friendly. They're quite cordial and civil and we chat about teachers and children, but much of it is on a superficial level." "I think Gentiles all want to get along with us in the PTA, so they're cordial," says another young housewife who prefers to socialize with other Jews. "We talk about our children. They smile at me and acknowledge my presence." "It's really not too chummy in the Cub Scouts," reports a businessman who recently moved to Lakeville. "However, the atmosphere is pleasant, and we're readily accepted as newcomers, and there are no cliques there."

Other Jewish respondents who report "very friendly" relations with Gentiles in their instrumental groups speak of much the same modes of intercourse but characterize them as being more warmly and spontaneously tendered. Thus, according to a very successful lawyer who has lived in Lakeville for almost twenty years, "In the Bar Association, I feel a much warmer welcome. Why, some of the [Gentile] members will go out of their way to extend greetings to me. They'll even come over to my table more frequently than I'll go over to theirs." "I just feel a greater friendliness in the PTA," says a young advertising executive. "Why, someone may walk over from the other end of the gymnasium to shake my hand and to kibitz with me." Another advertising man speaks of the "relaxed, amiable conversations in the Scouts. We kid back and forth and it's just a very relaxed kind of companionship." And a member of the League of Women Voters singles out the annual excursions to the state conventions: "These are loads of fun. It's like college bull sessions except for the drinks in the room, but defenses are down at these sessions."

THE EXPRESSIVE GROUP

For those respondents whose friendliest relations with Gentiles come from an "expressive" group, the modes and tone of their contacts are somewhat different. While "good working relations" are among the most common expression of friendliness in the instrumental groups, friendliness between Jews and Gentiles in the expressive groups stems less from performing organizational roles than from participating in the group activity, such as play reading, playing cards, or golf, as the case may be. Further, the spirit of friendliness encountered in the instrumental groups tends to be more often that of "feeling accepted," a fact which points again to the importance of the organizational experience itself in giving the Lakeville Jew a sense of being accepted as an individual and as a functioning member of the group. In the non-sectarian expressive groups, however, feeling accepted is more likely to be taken for granted as a basis for membership rather than seen as a state subsequently experienced within the group. "Warmth" of relations is the term much more frequently used to characterize the kind of friendliness that emerges in these relations. This latter difference is significant, for it indicates that those Jewish respondents who have been able to penetrate the group and status barriers of the expressive groups find much fuller acceptance and companionship with Gentiles than they are likely to find in the instrumental groups (see Table 11–4).

TABLE 11–4 EXPRESSIONS AND DEGREE OF FRIENDLINESS BY TYPE OF GROUP

Per cent who say that a chief way in which friendliness is expressed in organization is through the following	*Degree of friendliness experienced in friendliest affiliations**			
	Very friendly		Moderately friendly	
	Friendliest affiliation of Jewish respondents			
	Instrumental	Expressive	Instrumental	Expressive
Behavior†				
Working well together	36%	7%	34%	14%
Playing together	14%	27%	15%	21%
	(110)	(15)	(73)	(14)
Feeling tones‡				
Warmth	40%	67%	20%	36%
Feeling of acceptance	31%	11%	27%	18%
	(75)	(18)	(44)	(11)

* Only those who belong to two or more non-sectarian organizations are included in this table. In addition, we have excluded the category "somewhat friendly," because only two persons who selected an expressive group as their friendliest affiliation fall into this category.
† Percentages are based on all those in a given category who mentioned one or more acts.
‡ Percentages are based on all those in a given category who mentioned one or more feeling tones.

From an Organizational to a Social Relationship

Our findings for Jewish respondents indicate that until a relatively high level of friendliness is reached, relations between Jew and Gentile are more likely to be confined almost exclusively to the organization itself (see Table 11–5).

TABLE 11–5 INTERFAITH SOCIALIZING BY TYPE OF GROUP AND ITS LEVEL OF FRIENDLINESS

Per cent of Jewish respondents who socialize with Gentiles among those whose friendliest affiliation is	*Level of friendliness*		
	Very Friendly	Moderately Friendly	Somewhat Friendly
An expressive group	80% (15)	50% (14)	*
An instrumental group	57% (110)	37% (73)	21% (24)

* Only two cases fall into this category, and one of these respondents says that socializing is a major expression of friendliness.

Clear-cut as the findings are in this table, they do not show whether these extra-organizational relationships have been initiated or merely reinforced by the organizational experience. As we have already suggested, one of the distinctive characteristics of the expressive group is the likelihood of prior social ties with fellow members. Indeed, our data reveal that one out of five Jewish respondents and one out of ten Gentile respondents whose friendliest group is an expressive one mention these prior friendships as one of the reasons for so designating it, while almost none of those who choose an instrumental group offers this reason.[10]

Our concern in this section, however, is with those social relationships which have been initiated—rather than reinforced—by voluntary organizations. With respect to the development of these contacts, we find much the same pattern as that reported in Table 11–5 namely, the more

[10] In view of this, it is conceivable that the degree of friendliness that is reported may be primarily due to these prior ties and not to anything that is independently experienced within the organization. Our data show, however, that this is not the case; for those who mention prior ties as the reason for selecting an affiliation as their friendliest do not experience any greater friendliness in that organization than do those who base their selection on other reasons more clearly related to the organizational experience itself.

friendly a given organization, the more likely it is that a Jewish respondent will have gone out with a Gentile member. In terms of these contacts initiated by organizational membership, the expressive groups again contain the greatest potential for stronger social ties (see Table 11–6).

TABLE 11–6 Social Contacts between Jew and Gentile by Type of Group and Its Friendliness

Per cent who report social relations with Gentiles whom they met through	How friendly would you say are your contacts with Gentiles in your most friendly affiliation?		
	Very Friendly	Moderately Friendly	Somewhat Friendly
An expressive group	95% (22)	63% (16)	*
An instrumental group	73% (121)	54% (89)	46% (26)

* Includes only two cases.

Furthermore, the friendlier the Jewish respondent's contacts in an organization, particularly in an expressive one, the more likely it is that this socializing will be independent of the organizational activities as such. Thus, some seven out of ten respondents whose organizational relations with Gentiles are "very friendly"—in contrast to only one out of three whose relations are "somewhat friendly"—report that the basis of their socializing has shifted from group interests to personal ones. As a commercial artist explains, "What we do together now has very little to do with the organization. We like each other enough to visit each other, and there we engage in friendly social conversation."

This socializing usually takes the form of dining out, attending the theater or movies, and going to dances and social affairs, and if the relationship becomes friendly enough, of formally entertaining each other in their homes. At this juncture, though, it makes little statistical difference whether the relationship has emerged from an expressive or an instrumental organization. In this manner an organization relationship becomes transformed into a social relationship. Once it begins to take on personal significance, it gains its own direction and momentum from being sustained by the individuals themselves. Thus a longtime Jewish resident reports, "Some of us in the Country Club Association have become friends. We see each other and entertain each other in our homes." Similarly, a newcomer relates that "we show our friendliness in the Wildwood Neighborhood Association by being relaxed and natural as people. We visit back and forth."

Occasionally, organizational relationships may even develop into the closest ties that a Jew or Gentile have with each other (see Table 11–7). However, our data show that this happens less frequently than might be expected, particularly among women. Though the voluntary association offers more of them the best opportunity for friendly relations with persons of the other faith, it initiates the friendliest of these relationships less often than work or neighborhood situations.

TABLE 11–7 SOURCE OF FRIENDLIEST INTERFAITH RELATIONSHIP BY RELIGION AND SEX

Place where respondent first met best friend of other faith	Jewish respondents		Gentile respondents	
	Men	Women	Men*	Women
In an organization	5%	10%	13%	17%
At work	57	24	39	18
In neighborhood	15	32	32	51
At school	14	13	5	6
Elsewhere	9	21†	11	8
	100%	100%	100%	100%
	(178)	(180)	(81)	(100)

* The minor differences between this and Table 10–1 are due to the inclusion in this table of men who are not employed full time.
† One out of ten Jewish women replied "in their homes." No other female or male matched this figure.

This paradox may be partially explained by the relative recency of the organizational relationships. Both the Jews and Gentiles are likely to have known the friends made through these organizations for a shorter period of time than friends made at work or in school (see Table 11–8).

Our data also allow us to infer that many of our respondents did not begin to participate in voluntary associations until they became adults, and did not participate in non-sectarian ones until their recent experience in Lakeville. Thus many of the respondents would already have established their closest friendships with persons of the other faith before they even became involved with voluntary associations in Lakeville.

TABLE 11–8 DURATION OF INTERFAITH FRIENDSHIP
BY SOURCE AND RELIGION

Median length of time that best friend of other faith has been known:	*Where did you first meet best friend of other faith?*			
	At Work	In Educational Institution	In Some Organization	In Neighborhood
By Jewish respondents	10.9 years	16.6 years	5.8 years	5.6 years
By Gentile respondents	10.6 years	20.5 years	5.9 years	6.1 years

These considerations, of course, do not explain the matter fully, for we find that the more frequent friendliest relationships that were initiated in the neighborhood are as recent. This suggests that certain limitations on friendliness may be built into the character of the organizations and their relations to the social environment. Despite their potential for social intercourse, the expressive groups presumably do not usually foster the closest relationship between Jew and Gentile because of the background and status barriers to which we have previously alluded. Moreover, those who consider an expressive group to be their friendliest affiliation may already have been part of a social clique containing the closest friend of the other faith before joining the organization. As for the instrumental group, the reason that it seldom fosters the closest personal relations between Jew and Gentile is presumably its direct connection with the two environments, work and neighborhood, that are the major sources of these relations. In other words, the interests and concerns that bring Jew and Gentile together in these organizations are also bound up with these environments. The reason the neighborhood and the job context operate more effectively in strengthening intergroup friendships is that they provide more varied and frequent opportunities to get to know each other.

It would seem that the principal intergroup function of Lakeville's voluntary groups is to provide the opportunity for cooperative, realistic, and friendly relationships with *many* persons of the other faith. This requires a type of manifold organizational structure to bring them together and put them into active relations with each other. By doing so, the voluntary associations play a significant role in acclimating Jews and Gentiles to each other in the community, in undoing habits of prejudiced and stereotyped thinking, and in providing, through the experience of working or playing together, a new and more stable basis for individual relations between the two faiths.

12

THE NEIGHBORHOOD
AND SOCIAL CONTACT

It is evident from the last chapter that the neighborhoods of Lakeville are a favorable environment for the development of
close relationships between Jews and Gentiles. We might have expected
this from the facts that members of both faiths are likely to live near
each other, and that "neighboring" in the suburbs, as sociologists have
long pointed out, is a much more accepted and significant form of social
behavior than is true of urban environments. The suburban life style
makes it likely that neighbors will frequently meet and chat, and in time
socialize and become friendly. Such a process is typical between
neighbors with a more or less common background, but where group
differences intervene (as so frequently happens these days in Lakeville),
whether or not more than perfunctory neighborliness will develop depends upon a number of complex factors. In this chapter we shall try
to locate and explain those neighborhood conditions that apparently
foster meaningful social relations between Lakeville's Jews and Gentiles,
and we shall try once again to illuminate the process of their development. Our data also enable us to compare and contrast these relations
with those that exist among neighbors of the same faith under similar
conditions.

Neighborly Relations

In Lakeville, 97 per cent of the Jews and 82 per cent of the Gentiles live in neighborhoods[1] where one or more members of the other faith resides. Whether the area is heavily mixed or not, Jews and Gentiles will begin to meet each other on the street, in yards, in stores, and so forth, and in time will recognize each other as neighbors. Thus almost nine out of ten of our respondents who live in these neighborhoods know members of the other faith well enough to identify them as such. Moreover, even in the neighborhood situations where only a few Jews or Gentiles live, seven out of ten of our respondents have established a conversational relationship with at least one neighbor of the other faith. Such conversations usually turn upon small talk, care of their homes, or neighborhood and community problems.

Socializing with Neighbors

Neighborliness in the suburbs, however, means much more than an occasional chat over the backyard fence. Along with borrowing things, sharing rides, caring for each other's children and other forms of co-operation and assistance, neighborliness also means becoming friendly and socializing with each other.

DAYTIME SOCIALIZING

In fact, for many women socializing is an important daytime activity. This is particularly true of women who are less than thirty years of age. Among our Jewish respondents, two out of three young women, in contrast to less than one out of ten of those fifty years of age or older, spend three or more hours per week during the day in activities with neighbors.

What they do is likely to be of a casual nature, such as drinking coffee together (45 per cent), visiting in each other's homes (24 per cent), child tending (56 per cent), or shopping together (17 per cent). But whether or not they do so with a neighbor who is of a different faith is closely related to how many such neighbors there are in their neighborhood. The more Gentile neighbors a Jewish woman has, the more likely

---

[1] For the definition of neighborhood, see footnote 1 in Chapter 7.

she is to socialize with at least one of them during the day (see Table 12–1). On the other hand, with the exception of those who are in overwhelmingly Gentile neighborhoods, Jewish women are almost as likely to socialize with a Jewish neighbor irrespective of how few or many there are in the neighborhood. That is to say, in most neighborhoods Jewish women socialize primarily with their Jewish neighbors.

TABLE 12–1 DAYTIME SOCIALIZING OF JEWISH WOMEN BY ETHNIC COMPOSITION OF NEIGHBORHOOD*

Per cent of Jewish women who spend considerable time socializing during the day	Per cent of respondent's neighbors who are Gentile				
	1–20%	21–40%	41–59%	60–79%	80–99%
With one or more Gentile neighbors	29%	47%	69%	85%	90%
With one or more Jewish neighbors	97%	98%	100%	89%	70%
	(31)	(49)	(32)	(27)	(10)
Average per cent of Jews among neighbors with whom Jewish women socialize	92%	86%	79%	56%	32%

* The percentage classes that are reported here and in other tables in this chapter exclude the 0 and 100 per cent figures—neighborhood situations in which none or all of the respondent's neighbors are Jewish or Gentile. In addition, the lower limits of the two classes beyond the mid-category have been slightly modified so that they read 60 per cent and 80 per cent instead of 61 per cent and 81 per cent respectively. This preserves the symmetry of classes on either side of the middle category and makes it possible to compare the behavior of our Jewish and Gentile respondents in similar neighborhood situations. For example, a 1–20% Gentile neighborhood corresponds to an 80–99% Jewish one.

EVENING SOCIALIZING

Among our respondents, socializing with neighbors in the evening assumes significantly different aspects. It is less restricted to the younger women; it also typically involves the men, and becomes part of the social life of the married couple. As such, it tends to lose the more informal, spontaneous character of daytime socializing and to become a more planned and structured activity, such as a dinner party, a bridge game, or a social affair, concert, or other entertainment attended in each other's company.

As Table 12–2 indicates, Jewish women are even less likely to spend considerable time socializing with a Gentile neighbor during the evening than they are during the day. Even in the most Gentile neighborhood, almost half of all neighbors with whom Jewish women socialize in the evening are Jewish.

TABLE 12–2 EVENING SOCIALIZING OF JEWISH WOMEN BY NEIGHBORHOOD

Per cent of Jewish women who spend considerable time socializing during the evening:	Per cent of respondent's neighbors who are Gentile				
	1–20%	21–40%	41–59%	60–79%	80–99%
With one or more Gentile neighbors	19%	34%	44%	68%	71%
With one or more Jewish neighbors	100% (37)	98% (61)	100% (39)	92% (25)	79% (14)
Average per cent of Jews among neighbors with whom Jewish women socialize	93%	90%	83%	69%	45%

In other words, when Lakeville Jews socialize as couples, they are much more likely to spend time with other Jews in the neighborhood, a fact that seems to be quite independent of the number of Gentiles who are available (see Table 12–3). The same observation was made by Herbert J. Gans in his study of Park Forest, a suburban community outside of Chicago:

> In the daytime Park Forest was inhabited by housewives and the ever present children, and the Jewish women participated in the social life of the courts in which they lived. They interrupted their household duties to chat and "visit with" a neighbor over a morning cup of coffee, or while watching the children in the afternoon. . . . In these non-intimate, quasi-occupational relationships, which in many ways resembled their husbands' relationships at the office, ethnic distinctions were minimized.
>
> In the evening and weekend social relationships of couples, however, the Jewish husband and wife turned primarily to other Jews.[2]

[2] Herbert J. Gans, "The Origin and Growth of a Jewish Community in the Suburbs: A Study of the Jews of Park Forest," *The Jews: Social Patterns of an American Group,* ed. Marshall Sklare (New York: The Free Press of Glencoe, 1958), p. 226.

TABLE 12-3   EVENING SOCIALIZING OF JEWS BY SEX
AND NEIGHBORHOOD

Per cent of Jews who have socialized* with a Gentile neighbor in the evening	Per cent of respondent's neighbors who are Gentile		
	1–40%	41–59%	60–99%
Men	30%	53%	77%
	(79)	(43)	(35)
Women	28%	49%	74%
	(99)	(39)	(39)
Per cent who have socialized* with a Jewish neighbor			
Men	97%	100%	85%
	(81)	(43)	(34)
Women	100%	100%	87%
	(97)	(39)	(40)

* This item differs from that reported in Table 12–2; it refers to any Jewish or Gentile neighbor with whom respondent has socialized, and not merely those with whom respondent has socialized a great deal.

The probability of socializing with Gentile neighbors, however, depends largely on how many Gentiles live in the neighborhood: only those Jewish respondents who live in heavily Gentile neighborhoods report almost as many evening and weekend contacts with Gentiles as with Jews. (The figures are actually the same in the 90 per cent Gentile neighborhood.)

In certain respects our Gentile respondents follow this pattern. The only exception is in balanced neighborhoods, where Gentile women—though not men—tend to socialize less with Jewish neighbors than do Gentile women who live in neighborhoods with fewer Jews. This exception disappears in the neighborhoods where Jews are in the majority: such is the neighborhood situation that is most conducive for Gentiles to evening socializing across group lines (see Table 12–4).

Evening and weekend socializing among Gentiles also is related to the makeup of the neighborhood. Where they comprise the majority, they are more likely to spend time with members of their own faith; and even where they are in the minority, they are still as likely to associate with Gentile as with Jewish neighbors.[3]

[3] Our data also indicate that in heavily Jewish neighborhoods—80 per cent or more—socializing with either Gentile or Jewish neighbors shows a marked decline among Gentile respondents who are fifty years of age or older. Many of them

TABLE 12-4 EVENING SOCIALIZING OF GENTILES
BY SEX AND NEIGHBORHOOD

Per cent of Gentiles who have socialized with a Jewish neighbor in the evening	Per cent of respondent's neighbors who are Jewish		
	1–40%	41–59%	60–99%
Men	45%	54%	71%
	(55)	(13)	(17)
Women	43%	28%	66%
	(58)	(18)	(29)
Per cent of Gentiles who have socialized with a Gentile neighbor in the evening*			
Men	96%	60%	63%
	(25)	(5)	(8)
Women	81%	73%	67%
	(32)	(11)	(15)

* The question pertaining to socializing with Gentile neighbor was asked of only half our Gentile respondents.

In general, then, respondents of both religious groups tend to select their neighborhood companions from within the group, except where the existence of a preponderant majority of the other group tends to equalize their choice. Moreover, as we shall see later in the chapter, the levels of intimacy which we have gauged in neighborhood relations are significantly higher between Gentile and Gentile or Jew and Jew than those between Jew and Gentile. Finally, it will also become evident that a higher level of intimacy is typically required before Jews and Gentiles begin to socialize with each other on an evening or weekend basis than is required by members of the same religious group.

The Gentile Neighborhood: A More Favorable Environment

The relatively restrictive attitude of Jews and Gentiles to socializing with neighbors of the other faith on more than a casual basis, as well as the higher threshold of intimacy that is required for it to take place, is apparently breached only in certain neighborhoods where the Jew

have apparently withdrawn from neighborhood social life. The younger Gentiles who live in these neighborhoods, on the other hand, are the most likely of all Gentiles to socialize with a Jewish neighbor (84 per cent).

or Gentile is in a distinct minority. He thereby finds himself—or may, indeed, have deliberately chosen to live—in a different cultural milieu than he has probably been accustomed to, with a broad range of Jews or Gentiles, as the case may be, to choose from in establishing friendly relations across group lines. The force of numbers, however, does not operate equally in bringing Jews and Gentiles together. As can be seen in Table 12–5, the Gentiles who are in the majority in their neighborhood are more likely to socialize with Jews than Jews who are in the majority tend to socialize with Gentiles. By the same token, Jews more frequently socialize with Gentiles in Gentile neighborhoods than Gentiles do in Jewish ones.

TABLE 12–5 INTERGROUP SOCIALIZING AMONG NEIGHBORS BY RELIGION AND NEIGHBORHOOD

| | Proportion of neighbors who are Jewish or Gentile* | | | | |
| | Jewish neighbors comprise | | | Gentile neighbors comprise | |
	Preponderant Majority	Majority	Relatively Equal Number of Both	Majority	Preponderant Majority
Per cent of Jewish respondents who have socialized† with a Gentile neighbor	16% (63)	37% (115)	51% (82)	73% (52)	82% (22)
Per cent of Gentile respondents who have socialized with a Jewish neighbor	55% (11)	71% (35)	39% (31)	48% (54)	41% (59)

* The percentage classes that correspond to each of the categories are 80–99% for those neighborhoods in which Jew or Gentile comprise the *preponderant majority* of the respondent's neighbors; 60–79% for those in which either comprise the *majority;* and 41–59% for those in which there is a relatively equal number of *both Jewish and Gentile neighbors.*
† Henceforth, unless otherwise indicated, socializing refers to evening or weekend socializing.

The differences between the two environments can be seen even more sharply if we translate the percentages that are reported in Table 12–5 into the number in each group who presumably live in that neighborhood:[4] that is, how many of every 100 people who live in each environ-

4 We are assuming for the present that the percentage classes refer to neighborhoods and not merely to neighbors.

ment are likely to have social contacts that cross religious group lines? Our computations show that in preponderantly Jewish neighborhoods (averaging 90 per cent), a total of 20 of every 100 persons—14 of the 90 Jews and 6 of the 10 Gentiles—are likely to socialize with neighbors of the other faith. This contrasts sharply with the figure for preponderantly Gentile neighborhoods, which equals 45—37 of 90 Gentiles and 8 of 10 Jews. These differences remain manifest in neighborhoods where the proportions average 70–30. In fact, neighborhoods with a moderate Gentile majority contain the highest number (56 out of 100) of Jews and Gentiles who maintain social contacts with each other. In Jewish neighborhoods with a comparable majority, the figure is 47 out of 100 Jews and Gentiles, and in neighborhoods where Jews and Gentiles are relatively equal in numbers, the total is 46.

THE VOLUNTARY ASSOCIATION AND NEIGHBORHOOD SOCIALIZING

This contrast in the relation between environment and intergroup social relations is produced by a number of factors. Apparently one of the more important is the role of the voluntary organizations in bringing neighbors together in environments where Gentiles comprise the majority. The reason for this is less a matter of deliberate policies of integration than of the patterns of Jewish and Gentile memberships in these organizations.

The process can be best seen by focusing on two types of organizations, the PTA and the neighborhood improvement association, which draw their members from a local area and which, as we saw in Chapter 11, are among the most successful in bringing Jew and Gentile into meaningful and friendly association.

As Table 12–6 shows, however, Jews and Gentiles do not belong equally to these organizations. In the case of the PTA, many more Jews than Gentiles are members, no matter what the composition of their neighborhood may be. In the neighborhood improvement associations, this difference is much less marked. It is worth noting that these organizations are somewhat more attractive to both Jews and Gentiles who are in a minority in their respective neighborhoods.

The significance of these patterns of recruitment is readily apparent once we take into account the character of the various neighborhoods. For example, where Jews comprise a majority, their attraction to the PTA makes the local association even more Jewish than the neighbor-

TABLE 12–6 Membership in PTA and Neighborhood Groups by Religion and Neighborhood

	Proportion of neighbors who are Jewish or Gentile:		
	60–99% Jewish	41–59% Jewish or Gentile	60–99% Gentile
Per cent who belong to the PTA			
Jewish respondents	52% (211)	44% (95)	54% (101)
Gentile respondents	15% (46)	16% (31)	15% (115)
Per cent who belong to neighborhood associations			
Jewish respondents	19% (211)	24% (95)	26% (101)
Gentile respondents	22% (46)	10% (31)	15% (115)

hood. If so, the Jewish members have even less opportunity to meet Gentiles there, which reduces the effectiveness of the association in fostering intergroup relations. Thus, as Table 12–7 shows, only three out of ten of those who belong to the PTA have social relations with their Gentile neighbors—a figure that is only 3 per cent higher than that for Jews who belong neither to the PTA nor to a neighborhood association.

TABLE 12–7 Interfaith Socializing by Religion, Group Membership, and Neighborhood

Per cent who have socialized with a neighbor of the other faith and	*Respondents who live in neighborhoods where their own faith is in the*			
	Majority		Minority	
	Jews	Gentiles	Jews	Gentiles
Who belong to a neighborhood association	46% (37)	71% (17)	85% (20)	80% (10)
Who belong to the PTA	30% (100)	69% (16)	78% (46)	71% (7)
Who belong to neither	27% (63)	35% (82)	68% (25)	65% (31)

On the other hand, Gentiles who live amid a Jewish majority have an even greater opportunity to come into contact with Jews in the PTA than in the neighborhood, and almost seven out of ten of those who are members socialize with a Jewish neighbor. Whether this is due to the agency of the PTA or merely to the operation of the factor of the greater number of Jews is hard to say, since Gentiles who do not belong to the PTA socialize with Jews only slightly less.

The neighborhood improvement association appears to have a much more pronounced effect in fostering Jewish-Gentile relations in dominantly Jewish neighborhoods. Its greater popularity with Gentiles tends to partly offset the plurality of Jews, so that the organization is somewhat less Jewish than the neighborhood. This apparently increases opportunities for Jewish and Gentile neighbors to associate and develop social ties, though since approximately only one out of five respondents belongs to neighborhood associations, their influence is limited.

As we might expect, a markedly different pattern emerges in Gentile neighborhoods, where the proclivity of Jews to belong to both organizations compensates in large measure for the preponderance of Gentiles. The effect on Gentile respondents is particularly pronounced: while only one out of three who belong to neither organization socializes with Jews, seven out of ten of those who belong to these organizations do so. Jewish members of the PTA or the neighborhood association in these areas also tend to socialize in greater numbers with Gentiles than those who are not members.

AGE DIFFERENTIALS AND SOCIALIZING

One reason why there are so many Jews in the PTA is that they form an appreciably younger group whose children are more likely to be of school age. Age differences also contribute more directly to the neighborhood differentials we have been examining, for they considerably reduce the probability of social contact between Jew and Gentile in predominantly Jewish neighborhoods. Indeed, both Jews and Gentiles who do not socialize with each other in these Jewish neighborhoods often give the age disparity as the most salient explanation. As a young housewife puts it, "Well, the non-Jews in this neighborhood are much older, and we do not share any interests with them." Or more succinctly, in the words of another young woman who has recently moved to Lakeville, "Most of the Gentiles could be my mother. They're that old." A more specific reason that is commonly offered is the lack of school-age children among Gentile neighbors. A woman who is very active in children's and cultural organizations remarks, "Well, there's more of an actual mutual interest with Jews because of the age of our children. I meet them at school functions. I don't see the non-Jews. They're so much older."

"It might be the age difference and it might be religion," says a new-comer who moves easily in a Gentile environment. "I imagine if they had children the same age as mine, we might be friendly."

Gentile respondents offer much the same explanation. "I'm more friendly with Gentiles because of the age difference," says the elderly wife of a publisher. "They're as old as I am, whereas the Jews are interested in their small children." As with Jewish respondents, religious differences seem to play only an ancillary role: "Well, I think you have more things in common with Gentile neighbors," says a middle-aged architect. "We do in particular, because we go to the same church and are more or less of the same age."

However, the age differential between Jew and Gentile is actually no greater in these neighborhoods where Jews are the majority than it is elsewhere. What may make it seem so to our respondents is that so many Jews are present in these neighborhoods that their general youth-fulness is emphasized, particularly since Gentiles have fewer young people among them than they would if their age distribution were similar to that of the Jews.

Both factors, however, do more than support an illusion; they also influence the actual opportunities of Jew and Gentile to meet someone of their own age group. Fewer younger Gentiles are available than their Jewish peers would find if the age differentials did not exist or the population proportions were more equal: only three out of ten younger Jews report that they socialize with Gentile neighbors. The younger Gentiles in these neighborhoods find no dearth of Jewish peers, and their level of social contact is as high as that of the Jews who live in domi-nantly Gentile neighborhoods: in both groups of respondents, three out of four socialize with a neighbor of the other faith. In Gentile neigh-borhoods, on the other hand, the population proportions serve to offset somewhat the differences in age, and there younger Gentiles are more likely to find Jewish peers with whom to socialize: three out of five do so.

Among the older age group, however, the force of age differentials and numbers no longer favors the Gentile who wishes to associate with Jews but instead operates to his disadvantage, whether he is part of the majority or the minority in a given neighborhood. Where the older Gentile is in the majority, he finds fewer older Jews available than the older Jew finds Gentiles where he is in the majority. All these reasons help to explain why most Gentiles over fifty have less contact with Jewish neighbors than their Jewish peers have with Gentiles. The Jewish peers, in fact, are almost as active socially in this area as the younger Jews.

Indeed, were there proportionately as many Gentiles in the older age group as there are Jews in the younger age group, then the age differentials would contribute little to the differences in socializing between the neighborhoods, inasmuch as the older Gentiles in Gentile neighborhoods would have as limited an opportunity for intergroup contacts with peers as do younger Jews in Jewish neighborhoods. However, since a majority of Gentiles are in the younger age group, neighborhood socializing reflects the pattern of the younger more than that of the older age groups.

NUMERICAL PREDOMINANCE AND PSYCHOLOGICAL FIT

Significant as the factors of age and neighborhood organizational preference may be in affording greater opportunity for Jew and Gentile to meet and get to know each other in the more Gentile neighborhoods, whether they actually do so depends in large measure on how favorably disposed they are to associating with members of the other group.

This disposition has been summarized in an index of general orientation toward the other faith. For the Jewish respondent, this index consists of two major components: the sub-index of integration-mindedness that was developed in Chapter 7; and the replies to the question, "In general, do you find that you are less comfortable with Gentiles than you are with Jews?" both of which, as was seen in Chapter 8, are highly predictive of social behavior with Gentiles. The "highs" in the general index are defined as those with a score value of 6 or more on the sub-index *and* with the equivalent of a "no" answer to the specific question. The "moderates" have *one* but not both elements that characterize the highs. And the "lows" have neither; in other words, their score is 0 to 5 in the sub-index, and their answer is "yes" to the question.

For the Gentile respondents, the index of general orientation toward Jews consists of three major components, which were examined in Chapter 9. First there is the question, "If it were up to you, what per cent of the people living in this neighborhood would you like to be Jews?" Replies to this were scored on the basis of how likely a person who held a given view was to socialize with Jews. Accordingly, those who responded "half or more" were given the score of 3, those who said "some Jews but not as many as half" were scored 2, those who said "don't care" were scored 1, and those who said that they didn't want any Jews living with them were scored 0.

Secondly, there is a specific index of anti-Jewish imagery from reactions to six statements, most of which described Jews in a relatively negative manner. Those who agreed with three such statements or answered in a way that reflected an unfavorable attitude toward Jews were deemed as having "high anti-Jewish imagery" and were subsequently given a score of 0 in the index of general orientation. The rest were judged to have "low anti-Jewish imagery" and were given a score of 1.

In addition to negative images, we also scored for positive ones, using a battery of fifteen items. Those who considered at least three out of five of the traits by which they distinguished Jews as desirable were defined as having a "highly positive image" of the Jew and accordingly given a score of 1 in the general index. The rest were considered to have a less positive image of the Jew and were given a score of 0.

Thus our index of general orientation includes three kinds of data: (1) the extent to which Gentiles are willing to accept Jews as neighbors, (2) the extent to which they perceive Jews as an undesirable collective type, and (3) the extent to which they perceive them as a desirable collective type. On the basis of our scoring procedures, the maximum favorable score that can be achieved by a person is 5; the maximum negative one is 0. Few respondents, however, score at either extreme (only 7 per cent are in the 5 category and only 11 per cent in the 0 category). As a result, we decided to increase the number of cases to be treated at these and at other points on the index by collapsing the six-point index into three major categories: (a) those who are deemed "highly" favorable toward the Jews (score values 4 and 5), (b) those who are "moderately" favorable (score values 2 and 3), and (c) those who are "low" favorable (score values 0 and 1).

We note immediately that those who are most favorable toward relations with members of the other group are likely to be in the statistical minority in their neighborhood (see Table 12–8).

Consequently, no matter which group dominates a neighborhood, the relative distribution of respondents who are highly oriented toward relations with the other faith tends to be the same in one as in another. What does distinguish the Gentile from the Jewish neighborhood is the extent to which this psychological orientation is actually expressed in

TABLE 12–8 SCORE ON INDEX OF GENERAL ORIENTATION BY RELIGION AND NEIGHBORHOOD

Per cent who score high on index of general orientation toward other faith	Proportion of neighbors who are Jewish or Gentile		
	Majority Is Jewish	Relatively Equal Numbers of Both	Majority Is Gentile
Jews	13% (211)	19% (95)	35% (101)
Gentiles	41% (44)	27% (30)	14% (111)

behavior. So significant are these behavioral differences that less than half as many Jews in a Jewish neighborhood who have a high score (33 per cent) associate socially with a Gentile neighbor as do Gentiles in a Gentile neighborhood (75 per cent). As Table 12–9 shows, only those who score lowest on the index are as unlikely in the one neighborhood as in the other to report social contacts with a neighbor of the other faith.

TABLE 12–9 INTERFAITH SOCIALIZING BY RELIGION, GENERAL ORIENTATION, AND NEIGHBORHOOD

Per cent who have socialized with neighbor of the other faith, and whose score on index of general orientation toward other faith is	*Respondents who live in neighborhoods where their own faith is in the*			
	Majority		Minority	
	Jews	Gentiles	Jews	Gentiles
High	33% (24)	75% (15)	79% (29)	83% (18)
Moderate	31% (88)	46% (65)	81% (26)	61% (18)
Low	26% (66)	21% (29)	63% (19)	50% (8)

Among those respondents who are in the minority in the two neighborhoods, there is virtually no difference in the social behavior of those who are the most favorably disposed toward the other faith. Whether they are part of a Gentile or a Jewish minority, at least eight out of ten socialize with neighbors of the other faith. Among those with a moderate positive orientation, however, differences between the neighborhoods are quite marked. Those who belong to a Jewish minority in their neighborhood still produce as high a percentage of social contact with Gentiles as do those with a highly favorable orientation. Among the Gentile minority in a Jewish neighborhood, however, a very sharp reduction in intergroup socializing occurs among Gentiles who are less favorably disposed toward the Jew. Despite the different patterning of majority and minority behavior in the two neighborhoods, it remains evident that at most levels of the index a given orientation is more likely to be translated into social relations in a Gentile than in a Jewish neighborhood.

What accounts for this persistent distinction in neighborhoods? In part, of course, it stems from the previously mentioned numerical advantages to be found where Gentiles predominate. However, other factors need to be taken into account, chiefly the distinctive differences between the psychological orientations of Jews and Gentiles toward intergroup relations.

As we have already observed elsewhere, a positive orientation among Jews reflects a strong attraction to the larger community, which in its mores remains dominantly Gentile, and a firm conviction that they have the right and responsibility to participate in and be accepted by it. This desire for acceptance combines with the insecure self-image of the Jew in relation to Christians that remains as part of the post-immigrant mentality and, perhaps more deeply, as part of the Jews' long experience in the West as a persecuted minority. The result is that the neighborhood which best reflects the Jewish condition in Lakeville is the one in which the Jew is in a relatively subordinate and marginal position.

This hierarchical view of social reality also underlies the Lakeville Gentile's orientation toward Jews, since his status in America, as well as his inherited attitude as a Christian toward Jews, typically enables him to assume, consciously or not, that he holds the dominant position and that *his* approval of the Jew is the main issue in their relations. Accordingly, the relevant attitude of the Gentile is that of his willingness to have Jews in his neighborhood, his judgment of a Jew's behavior in measuring up to his own standards, and his perception and evaluation of Jewish differences. Thus a positive orientation among Gentiles presumes a distinct willingness to accept Jews but little need or desire to first be accepted by them.

Therefore the neighborhood in Lakeville whose ethnic setting best fits the typical psychological orientations of both Jews and Gentiles is the one in which the latter comprise the majority. For along with their numerical dominance, Gentiles in these neighborhoods are also likely to control its clubs and organizations and to set its prevailing social tone by virtue of the fact that at least one out of three of them is a longtime resident.[5] All of which means that the Lakeville Jew who lives mainly among Gentiles finds that his desire to be part of the general community leads him naturally and frequently into situations where he must come to terms with his neighbors. So it is not surprising that even those Jewish respondents who are only moderately integration-minded are likely to have social relations with Gentiles that go beyond casual neighboring. The Gentile's response to a Jewish neighbor, under these conditions, corresponds very closely to his disposition toward Jews. Thus, three out of four Gentiles who score high on our general index report that they go out with or entertain one or more of their Jewish neighbors, in contrast to only one out of five Gentiles who does so among those who are least favorably disposed toward Jews.

In those neighborhoods where Jews comprise the majority, a more complex relationship emerges between psychological orientations and social environment. First of all, the Jewish dominance is of recent origin, for in such neighborhoods the proportion of longtime Gentile residents is much greater than that of longtime Jewish ones. Moreover, it remains merely a numerical dominance. The continued influence of the Gentile ethos is suggested by the fact that Gentiles continue to hold proportionately more positions of leadership in the PTA and in the neighborhood associations than Jews do (see Table 12–10).

Even as a minority, then, the Gentiles' psychological orientation which assumes their control of the social environment is not seriously affected, and their relations with Jewish neighbors continue to correspond to their general attitudes toward Jews. Among the Jewish majority, on the other hand, the gap between psychological orientation and social situation apparently has an inhibiting effect on their intergroup relations. This is particularly marked among those who score high on our index of general orientation. Although this group includes the Jews who are

[5] Gentile predominance can, of course, cut the other way as well. Thus in neighborhoods where Gentiles comprise a majority of 60 to 79 per cent, 27 per cent of the Jewish and 52 per cent of the Gentile respondents who do not socialize with the other group offer the fact of Gentile predominance as the major reason. Both claim that the Gentiles, having lived so much longer in the neighborhood, have developed a network of relations which has not been opened to the Jewish newcomers. As a result, Jewish respondents say, they have confined their neighborhood relations to their own faith.

On the other hand, more interfaith socializing occurs in these neighborhoods than any others. What best serves to breach the barriers of a settled Gentile ethos has been the existence of other social and organizational alternatives such as the PTA and neighborhood associations, which the above respondents have failed to make use of or take into account.

TABLE 12–10   Office Holding in Selected Groups
by Religion and Neighborhood

Per cent who hold office in	Proportion of neighbors who are Jewish or Gentile	
	Majority Is Jewish	Majority Is Gentile
PTA		
Among Gentile respondents	29% (7)	24% (17)
Among Jewish respondents	8% (109)	5% (42)
Neighborhood improvement association		
Among Gentile respondents	20% (10)	41% (17)
Among Jewish respondents	15% (40)	8% (26)

most disposed to integrate with Gentiles, they do not establish social relations with Gentile neighbors as frequently as do the most tolerant Gentiles when they are in the majority.

If we pursue this rather surprising finding, it appears to stem from a revealing distinction within our general index. First, it is necessary to separate the two major components: the one bearing on the Jewish respondent's value orientation toward the Gentile world (or what we have called his degree of integration-mindedness) and the other bearing on his personal reaction in relating to Gentiles. As we would expect, those who are highly integration-minded participate somewhat more frequently in neighborhood affairs. For example, 60 per cent belong to the PTA and 26 per cent to neighborhood associations—roughly ten percentage points higher in each case than the statistics for the less integration-minded.

Despite their evident interest in these quasi-public activities, however, many of the same respondents show no comparable desire to become involved with individual Gentiles in personal relations. Only if we distinguish between those who score "very high"[6] and those who score "high" do we find any distinctive tendency—among the former— to socialize with Gentiles—the respective percentages being 50 and 32 per cent. In other words, a respondent in a Jewish neighborhood must be thoroughly committed to integration—generally to the point of

[6] This category includes those with a score value of 8 or more on the index of integration-mindedness; the remaining "highs" are those with score value of 6 or 7.

having a Christmas tree in his home—before he is likely to become socially involved with his Gentile neighbors. Often, too, such relations are dependent upon his relative security in handling them. Those respondents who are uncomfortable in socializing with Gentiles are almost as likely as their less integration-minded co-religionists in the neighborhood to avoid personal contacts and to confine themselves to membership in non-sectarian organizations.

Thus, it appears that the Jew who is in the majority in a neighborhood has two distinct options for becoming "integrated" into the neighborhood. He can confine his interest to membership in such organizations as the PTA and neighborhood groups where Jews are in the majority and which do not require serious social relations with Gentile neighbors. This is obviously the most popular alternative. Only a small number of respondents take up the second option of seeking out and socializing with Gentile neighbors.

The Significance of Neighborhood Relations

It remains to gauge the content of the social relations that develop between Jewish and Gentile neighbors. To what extent do they engage the two parties as individuals? Do they afford a realistic perception of the other, as well as the play of feelings of warmth and intimacy? Since neighborly relations are often centered upon conversation, one way of estimating their quality is to examine the kinds and frequency of topics that are discussed. Accordingly, we developed a set of analytic categories of conversational topics ranging from "small talk" to "intimate marital difficulties" that can be used to characterize the levels of intercourse between Jewish and Gentile neighbors.[7]

As seen in Table 12–11, relatively few Jews and Gentiles reach the upper levels of intimacy. In only one out of five such relationships are personal matters such as financial problems ever discussed, and only a

[7] So uniform were the responses to these items that we were able to develop in each case a six-point cumulative scale, using Guttman's scaling technique, in which each point on the scale not only indicates the *number* but also the *kinds* of items that have been selected. Thus, if a respondent were to say that he discusses two of the topics with a neighbor, the specific items that he would usually check are "small talk" and "controversial political issues." Or, if he were to say that he discusses four, the type that he would almost invariably fail to check is "intimate marital difficulties."

The scale types and their score values are shown below. In each case we have

TABLE 12–11 LEVEL OF CONVERSATION WITH FRIENDLIEST NEIGHBOR BY RELIGION

Per cent whose high-est level of discussion on scale of conver-sational topics is	*Friendliest neighbor with whom conversation was held is*			
	Of different faith		*Of same faith*	
	Jewish Respondents	Gentile Respondents	Jewish Respondents	Gentile Respondents
Intimate marital difficulties	3%	2%	17%	12%
Personal prob-lems*	20	18	42	33
Controversial po-litical issues	13	9	13	14
Small talk	50	51	26	34
None of above	14	20	2	7
	100%	100%	100%	100%
	(407)	(192)	(407)	(192)
Average score value on scale of conver-sational topics	1.62	1.43	2.89	2.42

* This category includes financial problems and/or other personal problems and worries.

small fraction of these share the most intimate matters such as marital difficulties.

On the average, the friendliest relationship between neighbors of different faiths tends to rest upon the exchange of small talk and at most political or other controversial views. As such, these topics suggest a relatively limited acquaintance with each other's character and private

---

italicized that item which represents the highest level of conversation reached by a respondent of that scale type.

Categories	Scale types					
	5	4	3	2	1	0
A. Intimate marital difficulties	*A*					
B. Financial problems and worries	B	*B*				
C. Other personal problems and worries	C	C	*C*			
D. Controversial political issues	D	D	D	*D*		
E. Small talk (or call each other by first names)	E	E	E	E	*E*	

life and fairly guarded manners, particularly in contrast to the content of friendship with neighbors of the same faith.[8] What helps perpetuate their more limited character is the fact that neighborly relations between Jews and Gentiles have to attain an even higher level of intimacy than do those with persons of the same faith for socializing to occur. In intra-faith relationships, for example, small talk provides a significant enough basis for getting together socially, but in interfaith relationships, social-izing becomes general only at the level of exchanging controversial views (see Table 12–12).

TABLE 12–12 SOCIALIZING WITH NEIGHBORS BY RELIGION AND LEVEL OF CONVERSATION

Per cent of Jewish respondents who have socialized	Highest level attained with friendliest neighbor of given faith on scale of conversational topics			
	Intimate	Personal	Contro-versial	Small Talk
With a Gentile neighbor	75% (12)	70% (76)	61% (44)	37% (168)
With a Jewish neighbor	98% (61)	99% (160)	98% (50)	86% (71)
Per cent of Gentile respondents who have socialized				
With a Jewish neighbor	80% (5)	77% (34)	74% (19)	47% (101)
With a Gentile neighbor	88% (17)	86% (35)	91% (35)	63% (41)

The probability that Jew or Gentile will attain this level of friendliness with some neighbor of the other faith increases with the number of persons of the other faith living in the neighborhood. But even in neighborhoods dominated by the other faith, these relationships do not, on the average, develop the friendliness of the intrafaith relationship, for whether few or many persons of the other faith are available, Jew and

[8] In the next chapter we shall examine what happens when the most neighborly relationship becomes the friendliest relationship that develops between Jew and Gentile.

Gentile are likely to seek out someone of their own faith to socialize with, and in the process they tend to build a relatively personal relationship (see Table 12–13).

TABLE 12–13   SCORES ON SCALE OF CONVERSATIONAL TOPICS BY RELIGION AND NEIGHBORHOOD

Mean score values attained on scale of conversational topics by Jewish respondents in their relationships	Percentage of neighbors who are Gentile		
	1–40%	41–59%	60–99%
With friendliest Gentile neighbor	1.48	1.61	1.90
With friendliest Jewish neighbor	2.89	3.03	2.77
Mean score values attained on scale of conversational topics by Gentile respondents in their relationships	Percentage of neighbors who are Jewish		
	1–40%	41–59%	60–99%
With friendliest Jewish neighbor	1.33	1.26	1.80
With friendliest Gentile neighbor	2.51	2.16	2.35

13

THE LIMITS
OF FRIENDLINESS

If we put together the vocational, organizational, and neighborhood contacts between Jews and Gentiles that we have been studying, it is evident that the opportunities for relations between members of the two faiths in contemporary Lakeville are frequent and ubiquitous. Indeed, only a handful of our respondents—15 per cent of the Gentiles and 4 per cent of the Jews—report that they have no "real relationship" with any person of the other faith.

Most of these relationships, as we found, do not go beyond casual acquaintance—that is to say, beyond the social contexts in which they arise. Others may develop within these contexts into fairly stable associations, as between colleagues, neighbors, or members of organizations, or eventually blossom into a full friendship. In concluding our study of Jewish–Gentile relations in Lakeville, we shall try to limn the character of the more meaningful ties that have developed between Jews and Gentiles. How much emotional substance and personal meaning are present in the friendliest of these relationships? How often does it match in intimacy the friendliest relationship with a member of one's own faith? In other words, just where in the scale of relations that an individual cultivates do Jewish–Gentile friendships in Lakeville tend to be located?

Intragroup and Interfaith Friendships: A Contrast in Intimacy

Obviously even the most friendly relationships between Jews and Gentiles vary in content, purpose, and strength from one to the next. It is evident, however, that generally speaking, few of them surpass or even equal the level of intimacy that our respondents have achieved in their closest friendship with a member of their own faith. Only 9 per cent of our Jewish respondents and 8 per cent of our Gentile ones say that they are closer to a friend of the other faith, while an additional 14 and 10 per cent respectively report that they are equally close to both.

THEIR DIFFERENT TIME SPANS

Our respondents offer various reasons for this difference in intimacy. One of the more common and salient ones—given by somewhat more than half the respondents—is that they have known their best intra-faith friend a good deal longer. Our statistics bear out this fact: the median time span of the intrafaith friendship is fifteen years for Jewish respondents and eighteen years for Gentile ones: the corresponding figures for the interfaith friendship are ten years and eight years respectively. What this usually means is that many of the intrafaith friend-ships were formed in the crucial years of growing up together, while the interfaith ones were more frequently initiated when both parties were adults. A department store executive with an "egalitarian" point of view remarks: "I've known my Gentile friend for eighteen years and we've grown up together. Any eighteen-year acquaintance is better than a three-year one." "Naturally I'm closer to my Jewish friend whom I've known all my life," says the wife of a manufacturer who comes from an integrated background. "The Gentile one I've become friendly with be-cause she lives next door. I'd met her a great deal, but we hadn't known each other all that time." More specifically, respondents point to the strengthening effects of "continuing memories and experiences" of "com-mon friends and acquaintances," of the need to cope "with the same circumstances of life," such as making their way out of an ethnocentric background into the general society, or facing the mutual difficulties of setting up careers and marriages.

Important as such a history doubtless is in accounting for the stronger ties between friends of the same faith, it is not a sufficient explanation. If it were, then we would expect that in the relatively few cases where an interfaith friendship is of equal or greater duration, there would be a corresponding probability of intimacy. That this is not the case is suggested by Table 13–1, which shows that these respondents are still more likely to feel closer to their intrafaith friend. In quantitative terms, only among those Gentiles who have known their Jewish friend nine or more years longer than their Gentile friend do the majority feel closer to the former. Among Jews with a corresponding history, somewhat less than half select their Gentile friend; however, there is a noticeable increase in the probability of greater intimacy as the time span of the relationship increases.

TABLE 13–1 THE CLOSEST FRIEND BY RELIGION AND LENGTH OF RELATIONSHIP

Per cent who say that they feel as close or closer to friend of other faith than to friend of same faith	*In comparison to friend of same faith, respondent has known friend of other faith*				
	9 or More Years Less	1–9 Years Less	Same Length of Time	1–9 Years Longer	9 or More Years Longer
Jewish Respondents	17% (96)	19% (126)	26% (85)	33% (62)	47% (30)
Gentile Respondents	10% (63)	25% (61)	17% (46)	20% (20)	57% (14)

SOCIAL REINFORCEMENT

It is evident that time plays an important part in strengthening and deepening the ties between friends of the same faith, but that other factors are also involved. One of them is the greater support that intrafaith friendships receive from family and social relationships. A Jewish businessman who feels strongly that he should not discriminate between Jews and Gentiles in his factory or neighborhood still maintains a circle of close friends who are all Jewish. As he explains, "One of the things I share with my Jewish friends is that our wives have common interests. This is most important." Many other respondents seem to agree. "I am closer to my Jewish friends for the obvious reason," says a young housewife who remains critical of many of her Jewish neighbors. "Not only that we've known each other longer, but that we can see each other as couples. Our husbands have been friends for years." As a result, there are various interlocking bonds between the families that enlarge the friendship and make it more meaningful. A well-to-do woman who sees a good deal of Gentiles explains, "My Jewish friend and I share almost everything. Our husbands are in business together, our children are of the same age, most of our social life is similar." Or again, as another respondent phrases it, "There's this mutual love and affection between our wives and children that my Jewish friend and I also share." These multiple bonds appear to be significantly less common in interfaith friendships, whether because of the relative recency of the relationship or for other reasons that we shall take up later. In any event, as a Jewish designer who works mostly with Gentiles observes, after speaking of the close family ties she has with her Jewish friend, "Such is not the case with my Gentile friend's family. This serves to limit the relationship between this friend and me."

Furthermore, friends of the same faith are also more likely to belong to the same organizations and to move in the same social circles. Respondents frequently point to their mutual affiliations in a local church or temple, a country club or American Legion post, a gardening society or a bridge circle—and often to a combination of them. As a result, "We're together more," says a lay leader of a local church. "Our paths cross more often." Or as a well-to-do sales executive who grew up in Lakeville describes it, "My Gentile friend and I have in common our recreation, school, and church activities and the fact that we belong to groups to which our Gentile friends also belong. Thus we see our Jewish friends less often in group activities." In other words, a friend of the same faith is much more likely to be part of a natural ongoing social environment that keeps both parties in touch with each other and reinforces many of their mutual interests as well as their ties of background, status, and so forth. A Gentile merchandiser who keeps his frequent contacts with Jews confined to business puts it this way: "I'm closer to my Gentile friend because he's a person I know and spend time with. Again, it's not the fault of religion, it's the circle we move in."

Without this ramifying network of mutual affiliations, Jewish and Gentile friends see each other less often, and since they must implement the relationships more or less by themselves, they may not be able to maintain sufficient proximity and familiarity to keep the friendship close. Speaking of the "closer bond" with her Jewish friend, a longtime Jewish resident observes, "I've drifted apart from my Gentile friend, in part because we're not in the same social swim." This lack of "real social bonds," as a sophisticated Jewish woman observes, often leads to a much more individualized type of relationship which may have its own personal grounds for intimacy but lacks more immediate incentives and reinforcements. Thus another Jewish respondent says, "I'm closer to the Jewish friend because of more frequent contact and because I share this friend with my husband. The Gentile friend is just my friend." And the Gentile wife of a cabinetmaker remarks, "Our friendship is not as with my Jewish friend, which is just a friendliness between us girls." One quantitative sign of this difference is that while only 20 per cent of our Jewish respondents say that they usually entertain their best Jewish friend by themselves or outside their homes, we find that 53 per cent do so with their best Gentile friend.

THE SHARING OF INTERESTS AND VALUES

The more extensive and intimate social basis of intrafaith friendship is paralleled by the differences that Jewish respondents report in the interests that they share with their respective best friends. "Similar interests" is frequently reported to be the main tie in both types of friendship—58 per cent refer to it in explaining their friendship with a member of their own faith, and 64 per cent in explaining their friendship with a member of the other faith. However, there is a sharp distinction between the kinds of interests that are shared. As Table 13–2 indicates,

TABLE 13–2 INTERESTS SHARED BY JEWISH RESPONDENTS WITH CLOSEST FRIEND OF EACH FAITH

Among Jewish respondents who say that they share interests with friend	*Person with whom interests are shared*	
	Closest Friend Is Jewish	Closest Friend Is Gentile
Per cent who select following		
House and family	35%	37%
Work	17%	37%
Cultural interests	29%	19%
Recreational interests	43%	20%
	(248)	(257)

a Jew and Gentile commonly share the interests of home and work, while friends of the same faith show a greater tendency to share cultural and recreational interests.

Two examples should suffice to point up this difference. The first respondent is a chemist who has recently moved to Lakeville and is living among Jews for the first time in his life:

> I see my Gentile friend much more often. We have more things in common. We love to bowl and to do the same things. Our interests are alike; just playing pinochle, going out to lunch. We get along so well.

The second is a Jewish department store executive whose vocational associations are mainly with Gentiles while his social ones are mainly with Jews:

> I know my Jewish friend much longer. I have much more in common with him. We like the same things, activities like golf, other sports, bridge, listening to music. He plays and I sing. I could never get as close to the Gentile friend. The Gentile's cordial. I know him as well as any Gentile. Our interests are in things dealing with the neighborhood and in playing bridge together. We also have house problems which we share because we both bought a house from the same builder.

The broader spectrum of mutual interests between friends of the same faith also corresponds to a similarity of tastes, viewpoints, and values which is found to be much more prevalent in these friendships. As a prosperous Jewish businessman observes:

> My Jewish friend and I have pretty much the same political views and outlooks. It's a liberal point of view. . . . Both of us see our work in the same perspective. We consider it important, but don't let it dominate our lives. Children and family are also important, as is the kind of education we want for our children.

Or again, a highly trained Jewish career woman remarks:

> I share lots of things with my Jewish friends. We're interested in books. We like the same kind of jokes, movies. We feel about organized religion the same way. We tend to feel the same about politics and we don't like people with false fronts or women in mink coats—symbolically speaking, that is.

And a Gentile high school principal typically remarks of his Gentile friend: "Our ideas are very much alike, and we're drawn to each other because of this and because of our philosophy of life and what we consider the things to enjoy."

Similar beliefs and attitudes may also play a significant role in inter-faith friendships. There is a marked tendency, though, for this sharing to be confined to a particular area of thought, such as politics, morality, or religion. Thus 44 per cent of those who say they share their values with a friend of the other faith are referring to some such specific field of agreement, while the 73 per cent who make the same observation about their friendship with a co-religionist are referring to the type of general agreement in ideas and values described in the quotations above. This more comprehensive matching of personal predisposition is in keeping with the broader bases of social ties and personal interests we have noted. Together they go a long way toward explaining the greater warmth, intimacy, and trust that most of our respondents find in relationships with friends of their own faith.

THE PSYCHOLOGICAL BARRIERS

So far we have been dealing mainly with positive factors that foster a greater degree of intimacy between Jewish or Gentile friends. It is also well to note the major inhibiting factor in Jewish–Gentile friend-ships, which is the abiding awareness of the historical tensions between the two faiths. As we have observed earlier, particularly in Chapter 8, Jewish respondents are especially sensitive to this tension. Though they may consider a Gentile friend to be quite unlike the "typical" Gentile, only a tried and true relationship is capable of dissolving their under-lying doubts and anxieties. In other words, Jews continue to worry that even friendly Gentiles harbor ethnic stereotypes, and they tend to remain uncertain about how this friend really regards their Jewishness. "I'm almost afraid," says a well-to-do second-generation housewife who remains closely attached to Judaism and the Jewish community. "I think it's in the back of the Gentile's mind that he thinks of the Jew–Gentile difference. I think if anything happens to break up the relationship, it will be because they think of you as a Jew, and so it may end as a conflict between Jew and Gentile and not as a conflict between persons." Another housewife who is much less closely identified with the Jewish community reveals similar apprehensions: "This Gentile friend of mine is very friendly, but she has had unfortunate experiences with Jews. I don't say she's anti-Semitic, but I'm afraid of a definite opinion regard-ing Jews." Or, more generally, a successful contractor who deliberately confines his relations with Gentiles to business contacts sums up his distrust in this way: "I don't allow myself to get too friendly with Gentiles. I don't want to get hurt."

Even if a Jew has no overt fears of prejudice and consequent defensiveness, the mere sense of cultural difference may inhibit the possibilities of a growing attachment between him and a Gentile. Explaining why there is a distance between him and a Gentile friend, a well-educated businessman who has lived in Lakeville for almost two decades remarks, "I suppose there is this unconscious barrier of difference in our religions that makes me feel closer to my Jewish friend than to my Gentile one." Or, in the words of a scholarly actuary: "When you're with Gentile people, you may enjoy them, but there is always some kind of wall. You meet a Jewish person and it's like Old Home Week." "She's a fine, warm person," says a longtime resident of her best Gentile friend. "But I never was as friendly or as close to [her], probably because, to be honest, she's a Gentile." And of course, in obvious contrast to the barriers of suspicion and inhibitions that still mark Jewish relations with Gentiles, there is the free-flowing kindred feeling between close Jewish friends. Even a corporation lawyer who remarks that he does not "feel ill at ease with Gentiles" immediately goes on to say, "I'm closer to my Jewish friend, in part because he's Jewish. There is a greater sense of comfort, of feeling at ease with him." This allows for more natural, spontaneous behavior. As a Lakeville resident of thirty years observes, "With my Jewish friend I can be more myself and not be afraid that she'll be offended." A newcomer says, "I never have to be on guard with my Jewish friend. I can share my innermost thoughts and problems." And at its very best, the favoring psychological climate of an intrafaith friendship may produce the intimacy of "complete understanding" that a successful young publisher speaks of—as "a way of life, a form of integrity and honesty between us." Indeed, Jews and Gentiles frequently refer to their best friend of the same faith as being like a "sister" or "brother." As one Jewish respondent says, "It's like being a family without the tension."

Intragroup Neighborliness: A Standard for Assessing Interfaith Friendships

In sum, most Jews and Gentiles in Lakeville report that their closest relationship outside their faith still does not approach the scope and depth, the compelling sense of vitality and intimacy that they share with their best friend of their own faith.[1] All of which is not to say that friendships between Jew and Gentile remain casual and perfunctory. Using our standard of topics of conversation to measure the intimacy of a relationship, we find that most of these friendships transcend the level of small talk and polite exchange of greetings of a neighborly relationship between members of different faiths. Indeed, they much resemble in content a good relationship between neighbors of the same faith (see Table 13–3).

TABLE 13–3   LEVEL OF CONVERSATION WITH CLOSEST FRIEND AND NEIGHBOR OF EACH FAITH BY RELIGION

Highest level attained on scale of conversational topics

Jewish respondents	*Person with whom topics are discussed*			
	Best Friend Who Is of Same Faith	Closest Friend of Other Faith	Friendliest Neighbor* of Same Faith	Friendliest Neighbor* of Other Faith
Intimate marital difficulties	48%	19%	18%	3%
Other personal and financial problems	48	49	41	20
Controversial political topics	1	16	12	14
Small talk	3	15	27	51
None of above	—	1	2	12
	100%	100%	100%	100%
	(306)	(306)	(302)	(271)
AVERAGE SCORE VALUE	4.24	3.22	2.87	1.64

Gentile Respondents				
Intimate marital difficulties	28%	7%	13%	0%
Other personal and financial problems	48	33	33	10
Controversial political topics	10	23	12	10
Small talk	14	30	37	61
None of above	—	7	5	19
	100%	100%	100%	100%
	(164)	(164)	(151)	(82)
AVERAGE SCORE VALUE	3.51	2.26	2.45	1.15

* In Tables 13–3 and 13–4 this category excludes those who are also considered the closest friend of the same or other faith.

[1] Unless otherwise specified, we shall be dealing in this section with the bulk of the respondents, whose best friend is of their faith.

As the table indicates, such friendships often develop sufficient rapport so that controversial political matters and even personal concerns such as financial difficulties are discussed, much as they are with a particularly friendly neighbor. If we also test for such topics as Jewish–Gentile relations, anti-Semitism, and child rearing—which were not included in our scale of conversational topics—we still find that the two kinds of relationships show much the same percentages among respondents of both faiths (see Table 13–4).

TABLE 13–4 Selected Topics Discussed with Closest Friend and Neighbor of Each Faith by Religion

	Person with whom topics are discussed			
	Best Friend Who Is of Same Faith	Closest Friend of Other Faith	Friendliest Neighbor of Same Faith	Friendliest Neighbor of Other Faith
Per cent of Jewish respondents who discuss the following				
Jewish–Gentile relations*	78%	58%	50%	19%
Anti-Semitism*	71%	38%	42%	9%
Child rearing	91%	71%	73%	46%
	(306)	(306)	(302)	(271)
Per cent of Gentile respondents who discuss the following				
Child rearing	68%	51%	55%	35%
	(164)	(164)	(151)	(82)

* These items were not asked of Gentile respondents.

Similarly, the average score values on our scale of conversational topics for the two relationships resemble each other more than the scores for any of the other relationships reported in Table 13–3. In effect, neither score is as high as that for the relationship with the best friend of the same faith, nor as low as that for the relationship with the friendliest neighbor of the other faith.

However, despite their similar score values, we find that in fact only about one-third of our respondents whose best friend is of the same faith (30 per cent of the Jews and 37 per cent of the Gentiles) establish the same level of conversation with their friendliest neighbor of their own faith as they do with the closest friend of the other faith. The rest are more intimate with one or the other. More Jewish respondents appear to confide in the friend and more Gentiles in the neighbor, though these are only minor variations.

Thus the relatively similar average values for the two relationships mask the fact that they do not provide a common basis of rapport for most individuals. In preferring one relationship to the other, the respondent tends to discuss matters of personal concern in the one, and controversial political topics or small talk in the other.

To attain or to exceed the same degree of intimacy between neighbors of the same faith, relationships between a Jew and a Gentile must go beyond the confines of neighborliness itself and take on other dimensions of friendliness. Thus we find that the most neighborly relation between a Jew and a Gentile that is not their friendliest relation with a member of the other faith tends to be of a relatively casual nature (see Table 13–5).

TABLE 13–5 INTIMACY AND INTERFAITH FRIENDSHIP AND NEIGHBORLY RELATIONS BY RELIGION

	Jewish respondents whose		
Per cent whose conversation with designated Gentile is	Friendliest Neighbor Is *Not* Friendliest Gentile	Friendliest Neighbor Is Friendliest Gentile	Friendliest Gentile Was Met Initially in a Neighborhood
More personal than	9%	26%	49% *
As personal as	31	21	25
Less personal than	60	53	26
that with friendliest Jewish neighbor	100%	100%	100%
	(413)	(19)	(65)
	Gentile respondents whose		
Per cent whose conversation with designated Jew is	Friendliest Neighbor Is *Not* Friendliest Jew	Friendliest Neighbor Is Friendliest Jew	Friendliest Jew Was Met Initially in a Neighborhood
More personal than	4%	14%	51% *
As personal as	35	40	23
Less personal than	61	46	26
that with friendliest Gentile neighbor	100%	100%	100%
	(193)	(57)	(35)

* This figure also includes those who said that they are closer to friend of other faith than to friend of same faith, or that they are equally close to both.

On the other hand, if this neighborly relation is the friendliest one, then it is more likely to approximate or to exceed the level of intimacy found between neighbors of the same faith. And only as the relationship develops a sufficiently personal and distinctive character so that it is pursued for its own sake once the parties are no longer neighbors is there a marked tendency to transcend the neighborly standards.

At first glance it might appear that the development of this degree of friendliness between a Jew and a Gentile is primarily a function of time. That is, if the friend of the other faith is no longer a neighbor, then the relationship will probably have been of longer duration than one in which the friend is still a neighbor. This possibility, however, is not borne out by our data. We find that among those relationships that are at most nine years old (not enough cases go beyond this duration to yield significant conclusions), the relationships which are no longer part of the neighborhood context are much more likely to go beyond the level of intimacy between neighbors of the same faith than are those interfaith relationships which still remain confined to the neighborhood.

In other words, no matter how friendly neighborly relationships are between Jews and Gentiles, they still tend to rank significantly lower in intimacy than neighborly relations between Jews or Gentiles. Thus they follow the same pattern, and presumably for much the same reasons, that we found in analyzing the two kinds of closest friendship. And only as relationships between Jewish and Gentile neighbors develop an intrinsic purpose and value which no longer need to be supported by neighborly contact are they likely to become significantly intimate.

Similarly, we find that the friendliest interfaith relationships which originate in voluntary organizations are also unlikely to exceed the intrafaith neighborly standard. Since many of these relationships have been formed during the respondent's residence in Lakeville, they therefore operate within the general neighborhood norms of intimacy which prevent them from matching relationships with members of one's own faith. Only those that have originated at work appear to exceed the neighborhood standard significantly.

But if a relationship between Jew and Gentile does exceed the neighborly standard for an intrafaith relationship, it is evident that its content and character may become that of close friendship. For we find that most of those respondents who have achieved this level of intimacy consider the relationship itself as not only the friendliest that they have developed with a member of the other faith, but indeed one of the

TABLE 13-6 THE INTERFAITH FRIENDSHIP AS A CLOSE RELATIONSHIP BY RELIGION

	Conversation with friendliest person of other faith is		
	Less Personal Than	As Personal As	More Personal Than
Per cent who include person of other faith among their close friends*	that with friendliest neighbor of same faith		
Jewish Respondents	42%	43%	70%
	(85)	(92)	(221)
Gentile Respondents	25%	32%	57%
	(59)	(60)	(85)

* We asked both Jewish and Gentile respondents the following question: "Are there any persons in your collection of [really close] friends who were born [of the other faith]?"

Although the person subsequently identified as the best friend of the other faith in the interview was not explicitly mentioned in this question, it seems reasonable to suppose that he would be one of those who would be included as a close friend if the respondent answered "yes" to the above question.

friendliest that they have developed with Jew or Gentile (see Table 13–6).

Our findings, then, indicate that the most neighborly, rather than the most friendly, relationship which Jews and Gentiles develop with someone of their own faith is a more pertinent standard for assessing the friendliest relationship that develops between Jew and Gentile. The comparability of the two relationships may well stem from the likelihood that both arise and operate within a more limited social environment than does the relationship with the best friend of one's own faith. As a result, the choice of friend of the other faith or neighbor of the same faith seems typically to grow out of and be limited to a specific context rather than to constitute an expression of a long-standing and ramifying intimacy. As one Gentile respondent puts it in explaining the stronger ties that he has with his Gentile friend:

> I feel closer to my Gentile friend for about thirty-five million reasons. Most are probably self-evident, but in general I would say that this Gentile is a friend of choice; the Jew, a friend of proximity. True, I see this Jew every day; we go to lunch and such things, but basically it's a friendship of convenience rather than one of choice.

V | CONCLUSION

14

THE OVERVIEW

In the preceding chapters we have attempted to study the relations between Jews and Gentiles in an established, traditionally Protestant community where Jews now form a significant part of the social environment, so that the modes of thought, feeling, and behavior with which members of the two faiths confront each other are conditioned by their daily circumstances of life as well as by their individual backgrounds and group ties. To do justice to these complex and changing relations, we have employed a comprehensive approach that relates the perceptions and responses of Jews to Gentiles, and vice versa, to various aspects of this social environment. Through it all, however, we have tried to keep two basic questions directly in view: *First,* what are the main sources of conflict and comity between Jews and Gentiles in Lakeville? *Secondly,* what are the chief forces and situations in the lives of individual Jews and Gentiles that bring them together, and how frequent and significant are these contacts?

Probably the single most important factor in Jewish–Gentile relations in Lakeville has been the recent influx of Jewish residents. This has shifted as well as expanded the population base, affected the traditional character of the community, and introduced immediate problems of municipal growth. Consequently it has placed the Jewish newcomer in a particularly vulnerable position. He is the main scapegoat of the residents who disapprove of the cultural and political changes in Lakeville as well as of those who simply disapprove of Jews. The common image of the newcomers has been that of an aggressive and ethnocentric band of Jews who have only recently achieved the status which they seek to display and to confirm by living in Lakeville. Thus they are accused of trying to wield their newly obtained wealth to acquire social and even political power in the community. At the same time they are accused of clannishness, of lacking dignity and taste, of not knowing how to use their money, and of exaggerating its importance in their own lives and in their relations with others.

This image does not accurately represent the kind of Jew who has moved into Lakeville in recent years, since he is likely to be better educated and acculturated and to possess much more modest circumstances and status drives than the image implies; but it does serve important functions for different segments of the Gentile community. Those who appear to feel most threatened by the influx are longtime residents of moderate and low income. They worry that the traditions of Lakeville as a Christian community will be undermined, that the Jews will become politically potent in contrast to their own sense of powerlessness, and that the free-spending newcomers will continue to raise taxes, force up standards of living, and create new norms of status and conduct. Such complaints by this group of Gentiles take on a particular urgency because of their beliefs that their children are being exposed to the precocious *nouveau riche* behavior of the newcomers' children and will seek to emulate it. Thus the influence of the Jews will undermine the habits of modesty, frugality, and sobriety that they have sought to inculcate in their children. The main sphere of this danger is the local high school, since teen-agers are felt to be the most susceptible to the deviant manners and values of their peers. The wealthier old-guard Lakeville residents who have not followed many of their peers in moving out of the community are also disturbed by the waning of the genteel traditions of Lakeville which they attribute to the influence of new "Jewish" money and manners.

If the only Jews in Lakeville were newcomers and if all the newcomers were Jews, it seems likely that these concerns would increase the tensions between Jew and Gentile and result in a more openly expressed antagonism than we have observed. What modifies this situation is that some newcomers are Gentiles, who tend to look more favorably on the changes in the community and more favorably on the Jews as an enlightened, energetic, and civic-minded agents of progress in Lakeville.

The potential sharpness of the group conflict has also been modified by the presence of the longtime Jewish residents, who are viewed as an acceptable, even exemplary, group by their Gentile counterparts. Their image is that of a solidly established social and economic elite which has developed a style of life that is modest, tasteful, and proper. By virtue of his roots in the community and his adaptation to its prevailing mores and manners, the longtime Jewish resident is perceived to be a model of tact and deference who is willing to play a responsible role in the community without seeking to undermine its Christian traditions.

Thus there are three fairly distinct images of the Lakeville Jew, two of which are definitely positive in content. This diversity, however, is of small comfort to the Jewish newcomer, who is aware of the distaste, enmity, and invidious comparisons that he has evoked. He feels that he is being attacked from all sides, that his contribution to the community is not being given its due weight, and that his sensibilities are not being respected. Despite the justness of this reaction, which much of our data confirms, it is also apparent that the Jewish newcomer benefits from the fact that he has moved into a community where a small group of Jews was firmly established prior to his arrival. Thus he need not be a pioneer in making a place for himself in Lakeville. There are pathways of adjustment and acculturation that he can follow in adapting his behavior and values to the norms of the community and in aligning his identity as a Jew with his new situation as a mobile, middle-class suburbanite. That many of the Jewish newcomers are strongly motivated to follow these paths toward greater acceptance is suggested by their own life style as well as by their strong desire to dissociate themselves from behavior patterns which could be construed as aggressive, indecorous, clannish, or defensive.

Style of Life: Similarities and Differences

One of the major pathways of acculturation that Lakeville Jews— both newcomers and old-timers—have taken is clearly revealed in their leisure interests and activities. They have been particularly attracted to a model of leisure that reflects Lakeville's history as a summer colony of an elite Gentile group. Their favorite sport is golf; they are widely committed to the performing arts and are among the most avid supporters of Lakeville's own cultural traditions; and one of their favorite pastimes is playing bridge. So widely diffused are these preferences and interests among Jews that even those of moderate and low income, particularly among the women, have adopted them. Only the activities of men in the low-income bracket depart significantly from this model.

Among the Gentiles, however, this elite model tends to be confined to those of high income. And even in this stratum, the men show a marked attraction to another traditional model of leisure: that which reflects Lakeville's past as a home-centered small town in which a person, usually of relatively modest means, spends his leisure time in tinkering around the house and garden or in hunting and fishing.

Just as Jews and Gentiles differ in their attraction to the leisure traditions of Lakeville, so do they differ in the range of activities in which they become involved: Gentiles tend to specialize in their activities and Jews tend to generalize them. In other words, the average Gentile is intensively involved in a relatively few hobbies, games, or groups, while the average Jew extends his participation over a greater variety of them. For example, Jews typically participate in more sports and play more of the different games of cards than do Gentiles. This is due, in part, to the desire of the Jews to participate in a sport or card game (such as golf or bridge) that is characteristic of the community norms as well as in one more or less indigenous to their own background (such as handball and gin rummy). We have found a similar pattern in their organizational affiliations. The average Jew has many more affiliations than the average Gentile, though he does not devote appreciably more time to working in them. Thus, while youth-serving and health-welfare organizations are popular among both Jewish and Gentile women, only the former are likely to belong to both concurrently; the Gentile woman tends to move from one to the other in a sequence that follows her family cycle. Similarly, Jewish men are much more likely to belong to both occupational and fraternal groups than are Gentile men.

Finally, in keeping with these generalized and specialized patterns, we have observed that Jews are more likely than Gentiles to engage in activities regardless of whether they are personally interested in them. This is true of their participation in sports or in cultural activities such as concert going. Similarly, Jews are more likely than Gentiles to belong to organizations that they do not participate in.

Why these seemingly consistent ethnic differences in the use of leisure recur is open to speculation. In part, they may be less a function of uniquely Jewish or Gentile group differences as such than of the composition of the two subcommunities. As we have already noted, the Jews of Lakeville are much more homogeneous than the Gentiles in age, income, and education. Given these similarities, we would expect greater consensus among Jews in their tastes and interests. In addition, many of them are relatively new to the community and are anxious to belong to it, which provides a further incentive for them to conform to the elite leisure mode even though they may not have a personal interest in its activities. Inversely, the Gentiles who are established at one strata or another in the community experience less pressure to adapt to the elite model and are therefore more likely to do what they want to with their leisure time rather than what they perceive will gain them acceptance. All of which suggests that the distinctive orientation of the Jews, as well as their socio-economic composition, contributes to their patterns of leisure use. As we have further observed, Lakeville Jews in their twofold desire for integration on the one hand, and for maintaining group ties and interests on the other, are likely to involve themselves in both sectarian and non-sectarian activities and associations. Thus for this reason also they tend to distribute their affiliations over a broader range than Gentiles do. Though they may be unable to participate fully in more than a few of these groups, their membership in the others allows them to be identified with the two communities.

In sum, the extensiveness of the Jews' activities suggests that they are attracted more by certain extrinsic functions which these activities serve than by the activities themselves. Thus playing golf and bridge, for example, are likely to be viewed as a good way of getting together with people and of establishing one's claim to a desirable status in the community.

Climate of Opinion and Mutual Acceptance

Despite the many underlying differences and difficulties that mark Jewish–Gentile relations in Lakeville, overt group conflict is quite rare, and the general social atmosphere is usually characterized by tranquility and tolerance. In part this is due to the passing of sufficient time for the initial impact of the population change to have spent itself, and for the municipal measures adopted to accommodate it to take effect. Also, in the intervening years the more bitterly hostile residents, particularly among the elite, have moved out of the community. At the same time, their need and desire to adapt to the prevailing social norms of the community and to participate in its daily life have made the Jewish newcomers more sophisticated in Lakeville terms; their presence has become less visible and objectionable. Some five years after the main influx, Jews and Gentiles in Lakeville today share many of the same interests in their homes, neighborhoods, schools, leisure activities, and so forth. Such common interests make the remaining differences between them less manifest and contribute to the tranquil surface of Lakeville society.

This process of "settling in" has also been abetted by the prevailing value systems of the Jewish and Gentile communities. Among Jews the basis of these values is clearly their strong desire for integration. Accordingly, few of them are willing to restrict their commitments and associations to their co-religionists and to the Jewish community. They are motivated to gear their behavior to Gentile standards, and though some of the newcomers may be willing to provoke group conflict in a matter such as Christmas celebrations in the schools, the general tendency is to avoid giving offense in the interests of being accepted.

Lakeville's Gentiles, of course, are in a different social position. Because of their dominance in the community and in the general society, they have little motivation to win the favor of the Jews. Consequently, their behavior is determined by how willing they are to accept Jews. In Lakeville, four out of five Gentiles say they are willing to live among Jews, though the degree and grounds of their tolerance vary in several respects. Some 23 per cent would prefer to have only a minority of Jews: the figure they give averages just over 20 per cent of the neighborhood population. A smaller group would allow at least as many Jews as Gentiles. The rest, the substantial minority of 43 per cent, say they "don't care" how many Jews live in their neighborhood. By using our findings on the extent to which Jews, as a group, are perceived to be different from Gentiles, on the positive or negative evaluation of these differences, and on the number of Jews who are believed to exhibit these traits, we were able to classify the variety of Gentile attitudes into four general categories: the "exclusionist," the "exemptionist," the "pluralist," and the "egalitarian."

The Contexts and Limits of Friendliness

Much of the interfaith tolerance in Lakeville is of the passive "live and let live" variety. It is unlikely, then, that Jewish–Gentile relations would develop much personal content without the community institutions and the individual pursuits that bring members of the two faiths together in some meaningful way. In the course of their daily lives Jews and Gentiles frequently find themselves in some sort of functional relationship where it is to their mutual advantage to work together amicably. Such functional relationships do more than cause Jew and Gentile to meet; they also provide a continuing context for them to get to know each other, to become friendly, and possibly to develop the strong ties of friendship. What is more, the separation of these functional relations from the more private spheres of life allows Jew and Gentile to participate in them without the usual inhibitions of class and ethnic factors.

Thus the necessity of making a living involves most Lakeville men in some economic or work relationship with people of the other faith. Such relationships often entail some social entertainment to promote business transactions or to improve cooperation within a work group or firm. Since these quasi-social arrangements have become widespread in the business and professional world, there is abundant opportunity for Jewish and Gentile men to get together in social situations.

In such situations each party understands that the motive of self-interest has brought them together, and therefore each takes in stride whatever socializing that ensues as part of the rules and requirements of the economic game. But in the course of their transactions they may get to know a bit more about each other and to like each other as individuals, so that the original relationship is transformed into personal friendship.

Indeed, the business and professional world is one of the most fertile grounds for our Jewish and Gentile respondents to cultivate significant interfaith relationships. Another is the organizations within Lakeville. Those organizations that provide most opportunities for Jews and Gentiles to come into friendly and meaningful contact are the youth-serving, neighborhood-community, and vocational groups—in other words, those designed to serve an "instrumental" rather than an "expressive" function.

The friendliness of the instrumental organizations derives from the personal relevance of the community of interests and needs that Jew and Gentile share. These extend beyond the organization itself and reflect the fact that many of Lakeville's Jews and Gentiles perform similar social roles and face similar problems in child rearing, home ownership, and their professional lives. In addition, the instrumental groups designed to serve these common interests and needs do not

impinge upon the more private spheres of life. Thus relationships between Jew and Gentile in these associations do not compete directly with
existing networks of friendship and do not involve status factors, both
of which often inhibit Jews and Gentiles from relating to each other.

For our purposes, one of the significant features of these instrumental
associations is that they provide a variety of opportunities for members
to work together in small groups where they are joined by a specific
common purpose and where the potential for personal contact and
cooperative spirit is high. Thus committee work and the like provide
settings where both parties can approach and work with each other as
individuals and not merely as members of a group.

Once a basis of mutual acceptance and friendliness is derived from
such contacts, it is unlikely that the relationship will be confined to these
settings and functions. Instead it will usually take on more personal
overtones and give rise to activities such as entertaining at home, sharing
outside social engagements, and following other leisure activities that
enable the relationship to develop a character of its own and to be
sustained by the individuals themselves.

The third major ground of Jewish–Gentile contact in Lakeville is the
neighborhood, and we have found that the neighborhood which best
serves this purpose is the one where Gentiles remain in the majority.
This finding is explained partly by the influence of certain demographic
factors and group affiliations that affect the relative frequency and
suitability of interfaith contacts. In a Gentile neighborhood, for example,
the tendency of Jews to belong to the PTA makes more of them available in this organization than in the neighborhood itself and thereby
enhances the effectiveness of the organization in bringing Jews and
Gentiles together. In a Jewish neighborhood the PTA is less effective
in this respect, because the selective recruitment to the organization
makes it even more Jewish than the neighborhood is and reduces the
possibility of Gentile participation. In addition, the age differences
between Jews and Gentiles, which are relatively uniform in the various
neighborhoods, create the probability that more of the younger Jews
will find Gentile peers in a Gentile neighborhood rather than a Jewish
one. Finally, we have observed that the neighborhood in which the
Gentile occupies the majority status and the Jew the minority one more
naturally fits the psychological orientation of each group toward the
other, and thereby facilitates social intercourse.

So pervasive are the opportunities in Lakeville for Jews and Gentiles
to come into contact with each other and to cultivate practical, coopera-

tive relationships that the great majority of them report they have developed an identifiable friendship with at least one person of the other faith. In measuring the character and quality of this relationship, we found that it rarely matches in warmth, intimacy, interest, spontaneity, and trust the friendliest relationship that respondents have developed with someone of their own faith. Still, the best interfaith relationships are not casual or chance acquaintanceships, but have considerable personal content and significance. The level of intimacy they achieve tends to resemble that of the relations Gentiles and Jews develop with the friendliest neighbor of their own faith. However, few respondents who have both such relationships establish the same level of personal commitment in both; that is, they are more confiding and engaged with their friend than their neighbor, or vice versa. This finding indicates that the two relationships may be functional substitutes for each other.

To attain or to exceed the maximal standard set by neighborly intrafaith relations, friendships between Jews and Gentiles must go beyond the neighborhood context where they may have originated and must be pursued in and for themselves. The same requirement seems to be true of friendships that may have originated in voluntary associations within the community. Only those that have emerged from the context of work appear to be capable of transcending the neighborly standard whether they are pursued at work or elsewhere. Should a friendship between a Jew and a Gentile exceed the level of the neighborly, it often continues to grow until it is cherished by our respondents as one of the most meaningful relationships they possess, with Jew or Gentile alike.

The Aura of Unreality

In the final analysis, though, despite the significant contacts between Jews and Gentiles and the benign atmosphere that prevails in Lakeville, an air of uncertainty and fantasy still characterizes their relations. In part, this results from the fact that their relationships rarely go beyond acquaintanceship to acquire the warmth and mutual trust of close friendships. As a result, few Jews and Gentiles appear to be in a position to gauge the feelings of the other with any accuracy, and thus they consult their own underlying anxiety or complacency, as the case may be.

Contributing even more significantly to this air of unreality is the very basis on which the Jew is accepted. He is judged as an individual and is accepted *if* he conforms to the standards set by a Gentile-dominated tradition. The orientation is essentially egalitarian in nature, and the goal is the assimilation of the Jew into the traditional mold of the community. The overall outlook is optimistic, for it is expected that in time even the Jewish newcomer will rid himself of his abrasive behavior and become fully acceptable.

But all Jews do not want to be cast into this mold; what this optimistic theory of acculturation and adaptation fails to confront is the Jewishness of the Jew. Most Gentiles in Lakeville are not concerned with the deeper meaning of Jewishness; they appear to treat it as just another barrier to the incorporation of the Jew into the community. In this they are joined by some Jews, particularly among the oldtimers. However, to the majority of Jews in Lakeville the problem of being a Jew is not confined to that of integration into the community or the development of amicable relations between Jew and Gentile. While deeply favoring intergroup amity, they are also involved in a different and perhaps even more perplexing enterprise: that of working out their identity as Jews and developing a viable pattern of Jewish living. This desire for a religio-ethnic subcommunity which is simultaneously "Jewish" as well as compatible with and integrated into the larger structure of Lakeville and American society is as much a fact of life in present day Lakeville as is its Gentile past. This desire is analyzed in Volume I.

Despite the recent changes in Lakeville, most Gentiles and some Jews continue to press for uniformity with and conformity to an older version of the community. In effect, they refuse to legitimate the genuine diversity that already seems to characterize Lakeville. But until they do, or at least come to terms with it more effectively than they have, there will remain an air of fantasy and an undercurrent of unresolved tension between Jew and Gentile in the community.

INDEX